THE THAKSINIZATION OF THAILAND

T0351475

Nordic Institute of Asian Studies
STUDIES IN CONTEMPORARY ASIAN HISTORY
Series Editor: Robert Cribb, Australian National University

INDONESIAN POLITICS IN CRISIS
The Long Fall of Suharto 1996–98
Stefan Eklöf

THE INDONESIAN MILTARY AFTER THE NEW ORDER
Sukardi Rinakit

POWER AND POLITICAL CULTURE IN SUHARTO'S INDONESIA
The Indonesian Democratic Party (PDI) and Decline of the
New Order 1986–98
Stefan Eklöf

THE THAKSINIZATION OF THAILAND
Duncan McCargo and Ukrist Pathmanand

THAKSIN – THE BUSINESS OF POLITICS IN THAILAND
Pasuk Phongpaichit and Chris Baker

PIRATES IN PARADISE
A Modern History of Southeast Asia's Maritime Marauders
Stefan Eklöf

DEMOCRACY AND NATIONAL IDENTITY IN THAILAND
Michael Kelly Connors

Of related interest and available from NIAS Press

CIVIL SOCIETY AND DEMOCRATIZATION
Social Movements in Northeast Thailand
Somchai Phatharathananunth

WOMEN AND POLITICS IN THAILAND
Continuity and Change
Kazuki Iwanaga (ed.)

SAYING THE UNSAYABLE
Monarchy and Democracy in Thailand
Søren Ivarsson and Lotte Isager (eds)

THE
THAKSINIZATION
OF THAILAND

Duncan McCargo and
Ukrist Pathmanand

 niaSPRESS

First published in 2005
Reprinted in 2007 and 2010
by NIAS Press
NIAS – Nordic Institute of Asian Studies
Leifsgade 33, DK–2300 Copenhagen S, Denmark
tel: (+45) 3532 9501 • fax: (+45) 3532 9549
E–mail: books@nias.ku.dk • Website: www.niaspress.dk

© Duncan McCargo and Ukrist Pathmanand 2005

British Library Cataloguing in Publication Data
McCargo, Duncan
  The Thaksinization of Thailand. - (Studies in contemporary
  Asian history ; 4)
  1.Thailand - Politics and government - 1988- 2.Thailand -
  Economic conditions - 1986-
  I.Title II.Pathmanand, Ukrist
  320.9'593'09051

ISBN 978-87-91114-45-8 (cloth)
ISBN 978-87-91114-46-5 (paper)

Typesetting by Translations ved LJ
Printed in the United Kingdom
by Marston Digital

Contents

Charts

Tables

Preface and Acknowledgements

THIS BOOK REPRESENTS A MODEST ATTEMPT to review a number of important issues raised by the premiership of Thaksin Shinawatra. It makes no claim to be a comprehensive overview of Thaksin, nor is it a political biography. Rather, we focus on five key areas relevant to Thaksin's rise: the telecommunications business, Thai Rak Thai as a political party, the repoliticization of the military, Thaksin's use of language and media and his creation of new political economy networks. Ukrist was the primary author of chapters 2, 4 and 6, and McCargo of chapters 1, 3 and 5.

Ukrist Pathmanand would like to thank his research assistants, Benjamas Yodpanya and Rappeport Thanamai. He is very grateful for the support of the Centre for Southeast Asian Studies (CSEAS) at Kyoto University, where he was a visiting research scholar from February to July 2004. Under the excellent directorship of Professor Koji Tanaka, CSEAS provided Ukrist with the time and space to work on this manuscript.

Duncan McCargo would like to thank Chunyao Yi for her research assistance and indexing, and Chris Baker, Michael Connors, Shawn W. Crispin, Michael H. Nelson, Naruemon Thabchumpon and Sombat Chantornvong for their helpful advice. Thanks also to Larry Diamond for encouraging him to work on Thaksin.

We are both very grateful for the support of Gerald Jackson at NIAS, who encouraged us to pursue a book project which started from a chance conversation at ICAS 3 in Singapore. None of those thanked here are in any way responsible for the tone or content of the book. All the mistakes are ours.

Leeds and Bangkok
October 2004

CHAPTER 1

Introduction: Who is Thaksin Shinawatra?

'He likes to be called Police Lt. Col. Thaksin Shinawatra', one senior official said on condition of anonymity. 'He went to a police academy, not the most liberal setting. If you picture him with a police uniform, that is basically the inner man'.[1]

ON HIS FIRST DAY AS PRIME MINISTER, Thaksin Shinawatra ate a simple lunch with representatives of the Forum of the Poor – a grassroots organization whose protests on a range of environmental and livelihood issues had dogged the term of his Democrat predecessor, Chuan Leekpai. His actions immediately following the 6 January 2001 electoral landslide were rather different: he took a day off to drive around Bangkok in his Porsche, popping into a branch of Starbucks. The contrast between these two faces of Thailand's new leader nicely illustrated the contradictions epitomized by the Thaksin phenomenon. On the one hand, Thaksin was a representative of the nouveau riche Sino-Thai business elite, given to the flaunting of wealth and conspicuous consumption. Yet his choreographed and scripted first day in office reflected his populist agenda, his courting of special interests and his strong desire to distance himself from the image of bureaucratic inflexibility and high-minded disdain that had characterized the 1997–2000 Chuan government. Just who Thaksin is remains a difficult question to answer, given his multi-faceted political identity. Understanding where he came from involves first briefly reviewing developments in Thai politics prior to 2001.

Thailand has long been characterized by competing tendencies towards democracy and authoritarianism. Such tendencies were evident from the manner in which the absolute monarchy was brought to an end in 1932: Thailand (then Siam) experienced a transition to constitutional rule which was initiated by a small group of elite actors, some of a liberal orientation, but many possessed of an authoritarian orientation that reflected their military backgrounds. For the next 41 years, Thailand alternated between short periods of parliamentary rule and longer spells of military rule.[2] The armed forces, especially the army, became intensely politicized and staged numerous destabilizing coups d'état. Rivalries between the army, the navy, the police and the civilian bureaucracy were often virulent and corrosive. Following the onset of the Cold War, Thailand's armed services received substantial support from the United States, which increasingly looked upon the country as an important bulwark to prevent the spread of communism in Southeast Asia. Until the 1960s, Thailand's competing forces could operate relatively unchecked by any higher authority. However, by the 1960s the monarchy was gaining increasing extra-constitutional authority. This was evidenced by the King's pivotal role in the violent events of 14 October 1973, which culminated in the collapse of a military dictatorship following pressure from the nascent student movement and other emerging social forces.

The resulting period of parliamentary rule was short-lived, giving way to a rightist backlash and the bloody crushing of the student movements on 6 October 1976. Nevertheless, there could be no simple and lasting reversion to military domination of the political order, and from 1977 onwards Thailand embarked on a process of gradual political liberalization. By the 1980s, parliamentary democracy of a sort had been re-established, in which an unelected ex-military premier functioned with the backing of an elected parliament, heading a cabinet that mixed technocrats and politicians. Thailand was widely believed to be 'gradually moving toward full membership of the new and larger comity of liberal democratic nations'.[3] This optimism was undermined by the military coup of February 1991, which demonstrated residual military ambitions to dominate the political order. In the wake of the putsch came a popular uprising that ended with the fatal shooting of dozens of unarmed civilians (May 1992), two new constitutions (1991 and 1997) and five general elections (March 1992, September 1992, July 1995, November 1996, and January 2001). The 1997 constitution was in many respects the most important – albeit delayed – outcome of the May 1992 violence, a thoroughgoing attempt to reform the Thai political situation in a liberal direction.[4] As the first general election held under the auspices of that constitution, which also introduced a new electoral system overseen by an independent election commission, the January 2001 election was of pivotal significance for Thailand.

These political developments cannot be understood in isolation from wider processes of socio-economic change in Thailand during this period. Thailand was growing economically at a rapid rate from the early 1960s onwards, and was experiencing a transformation from a rural-based agricultural economy to a more modern economy characterized by thriving agribusiness, export-oriented industrial production (typically based on industrial estates concentrated in Bangkok and the five adjoining provinces), and a dynamic service sector fuelled by a highly successful tourist industry. This change had a number of effects. First, many farmers became workers in the industrial and service sectors, leaving their villages either permanently or for much of every year. A new middle class emerged in urban areas, supported by the growth of university and college education. A wealthy Bangkok-based business elite emerged, as did an overlapping elite whose income derived mainly from provincial business. Some of these businesses were perfectly legal, but others including smuggling, people trafficking, illegal logging,[5] gambling, prostitution and even drug-dealing.

These changes had direct impacts on the political system. In the 1930s, 1940s and 1950s, the political order was dominated by government officials (both civilian and military), officials who were mostly ethnically Thai. High status in Thai society was reserved for ethnic Thais who came from well-known families (ideally with some connection to one of the many branches of the polygamous Siamese royalty), and was based on class, educational status and formal position. The Chinese were largely excluded from direct political power: instead, they formed mutually beneficial business arrangements with ethnic Thais. A Thai official or general would put some deals or contracts in the direction of a Chinese collaborator, and would be well rewarded for doing so. But by the 1960s Sino-Thais were eligible to enter the ranks of the military and the civil service in their own right; they were now Thai citizens, and had less obligation to kowtow to ethnically Thai officials. Increasingly, Sino-Thais sought to assume senior government positions themselves.

The opening up of the political order, combined with the economic successes of Thailand during the 1960s, 1970s and 1980s, saw a new generation of Sino-Thai politicians starting to emerge. Many sought to use bases in the provinces to have themselves elected to parliament; others assumed the role of provincial or regional power brokers, who could help determine who became MPs and ministers. By the 1990s, Thailand's prime ministers, for all their differences of class origin and career, were at least partly of Sino-Thai descent, including Anand Panyarachun (former ambassador), Chuan Leekpai (lawyer and professional politician), Banharn Silpa-archa (provincial construction contractor) and Chavalit Yongchaiyudh (former army commander). No longer did the Chinese need to work through Thai patrons and fixers – they could achieve the highest levels of power themselves. However, none of these Sino-Thai prime ministers had come from the big Chinese families that dominated Bangkok's business community; none was a true representative of the country's nouveau riche entrepreneurial class. The only real businessman was Banharn, and he was a representative of the provincial business sector rather than the national-level elite. Thaksin's rise to the post of prime minister demonstrated that a leading Sino-Thai businessman could attain the country's highest office. By 2001, as many as 90 per cent of Thai MPs had some Chinese ancestry.[6] Thaksin's arrival in Government House was a postponed reality, the culmination of processes of socio-economic and political change that had been taking place throughout the 1980s and 1990s. Thaksin was the ultimate outcome of the merger of money and politics that had characterized this 20-year period.

PRECURSORS OF THAKSIN

Thaksin's political rhetoric was a compound of several different elements. On the one hand, he was the billionaire tycoon, one of Thailand's wealthiest citizens. Since he was so rich, the argument went, he was above the petty and not-so-petty corruption that had characterized many other leaders. He pledged to run Thailand according to business principles, thinking and acting in a new way that was quick, decisive and effective. In other words, he would function as Thailand's Chief Executive Officer, or CEO. This rhetoric was highly attractive to many who were dissatisfied with the country's bureaucratic political and administrative culture, and contrasted strongly with the legalistic style of his predecessor, Chuan Leekpai. However, this CEO approach was also replete with authoritarian implications, suggesting that a strong leader was needed who could cut through existing practices and procedures. In certain respects, it resonated with earlier modes of authoritarian political culture in Thailand. Nor was Thaksin only a businessman – he had started his career in the police, attending pre-cadet school along with many now-senior military and police officers. Thaksin was not a normal businessman, but one whose career had been forged through an extended period in an important branch of the Thai state. Perhaps more than any other government agency, the police was characterized by pervasive corruption, low standards and low public esteem.[7]

Thaksin's rhetoric was also bound up in an ambiguous approach to national identity and the wider world. The very name of the Thai Rak Thai (Thais love Thai) Party was rich in overtones of old-fashioned nationalism, designed to capitalize on the popular sense that the Chuan government had capitulated to the demands of international bodies such as the IMF in framing a response to the 1997 economic crisis. Thaksin implied that he would not serve as the poodle of Western interests, and talked frequently of the need for Thailand to develop its own indigenous solutions to a variety of problems, rather than aping models from outside the country. Yet at the same time, Thaksin apparently sought to emulate Dr Mahathir Mohammad of Malaysia, by combining nationalist rhetoric with a strong international role, and positioning himself as a regional leader. His own business activities demonstrated a desire to project beyond Thailand onto the regional stage. Ironically, he also forged a very close relationship with the Bush administration, serving as a regional lieutenant in prosecuting the American-led war on terrorism. As a result, the American administration granted Thailand 'non-NATO ally' status.[8] In other words, Thaksin's approach to the rest of the world was somewhat shizophrenic.

In consequence, it is possible to see a number of figures as precursors of the Thaksin premiership. One such figure is undoubtedly Field Marshal Plaek Phibunsongkhram, who served two important periods in office. Phibun combined intense nationalism (his first period coincided with the rule of Hitler and Mussolini, and he has sometimes been described as a fascist) with a crude aping of Western values and practices: he even ordered all men to wear hats, and instructed husbands and wives to kiss each other good-bye. Only by instilling greater self-discipline could Thais hope to compete on the wider world stage. While Phibun sought to project himself as a regional figure and close ally of Japan, he was also deeply concerned with advancing Thai national interests, which he often saw in terms of irredentist moves to 'reclaim' sections of territory from neighbouring British and French controlled states. Phibun created a cult of personality around himself, benefiting from the weakness of the Chakri dynasty during his terms as prime minister.

Another figure whose career resembles Thaksin's in various respects is Field Marshal Sarit Thanarat, a military dictator who came to power in the late 1950s. Sarit sought to forge a strong sense of national identity through the maxim 'Nation, religion, king', and was preoccupied with forging national discipline through a strict law-and-order regime. He personally intervened to deal with crimes such as arson through on-the-spot extra-judicial killings, gaining a reputation for decisiveness. However, Sarit was also responsible for building up the legitimacy of the monarchy as a central platform of the anti-communist struggle, and thereby created a long-term shift in the balance of power within Thailand. He was a key ally of the

American military in the ideological struggle against communism in Southeast Asia.

Thaksin is the first police officer to have become prime minister of Thailand. The policeman who came closest was General Phao Sriyanon, a ruthless political operator who vied for power with Sarit in the 1950s, playing off various branches of the US military and intelligence services against those controlled by his rivals in the Army. Thai police officers have long craved the return of a strong figure able to restore the collective pride of the police following its successful marginalization by the Army during the Sarit period. In some respects, Thaksin may be seen as Phao's long-awaited successor. Yet the fact that Thaksin came to power as a civilian makes his strongman propensities all the more disturbing.

THAKSIN'S BACKGROUND

Thaksin Shinawatra was born in 1949 to a well-to-do Sino-Thai family from the northern city of Chiang Mai.[9] His ancestors started off as tax farmers, later becoming silk traders and producers before diversifying into a range of other business interests. His father was a local politician in Chiang Mai, while his uncle Suraphan was an MP who eventually served as deputy minister of communications.[10] Thaksin began his career in the police force, graduated from the police academy as the top student and earned a doctorate in criminal justice from Sam Houston State University, Texas, in 1979. After marrying Pojaman Damapong, daughter of the powerful Deputy Police Chief Samoer Damapong, Thaksin secured exclusive contracts to supply various government agencies – including the police – with IBM computers. He left the police in 1987 to focus on business interests – involving pagers, mobile phones, telephone directories and Thailand's first satellite – that would make him one of the leading entrepreneurs of Thailand's 1986–97 boom years. As Baker notes, many of Thaksin's earlier business ventures were not particularly profitable; his big successes came later, when he gained his first mobile phone concession in 1990, started his first satellite project in 1991 and subsequently saw a staggering rise in the value of shares in his companies.[11] All his businesses began with government licenses or concessions.

Instead of forming alliances with bureaucrats (including military and police officers) like a typical Sino-Thai entrepreneur, Thaksin took the unusual step of joining the bureaucracy himself. The police suffer from serious image problems in Thailand because of pervasive corruption. In the perception of most Thais, for a boy from a good family to join a civilian branch of the civil service could imply a willingness to gain prestige and job security, while working on behalf of the country for a low salary. Joining the army might imply a quest for status and, traditionally, political power or influence. Joining the police, however, is generally seen as reflecting a simple desire to make money. Thaksin himself acknowledged that he never envisaged a lifelong career in the police: he saw it as a stepping stone to greater things.[12] In order to advance himself further, he needed to move beyond bureaucratic connections and gain clout with politicians. Ultimately, seeing that competitors such as Telecom Asia (part of the vast CP group) were better connected to the political world than his own companies, Thaksin decided to enter politics in his own right. In view of his considerable wealth, he was courted by various political parties in the early 1990s, including the Democrat Party, New Aspiration and Palang Dharma.

Thaksin's first move was to hook up with the Palang Dharma Party, briefly serving as foreign minister in 1994–95. This ministry lay within the quota controlled by the party's founder and Chamlong Srimuang.[13] Palang Dharma was at this point a middle-ranking party with 47 MPs. The party had benefited from Chamlong's image as a populist figure, who opposed corruption and led the anti-Suchinda protests that had culminated in the violent showdown of May 1992. In effect, it was the best political 'brand' in Thailand, a party with a very positive public image, especially in Bangkok. Since September 1992, Palang Dharma had been the junior partner in a coalition government led by Chuan Leekpai of the Democrats. Criticism of his role in May 1992 meant that

Chamlong himself was no longer in the running for the premiership. He was therefore anxious to hand the leadership of the party over to a credible figure, who could use it as vehicle to make a strong showing in the next general election. In effect, Chamlong invited Thaksin to take over a ready-made party. Thaksin's term as foreign minister was a kind of trial run prior to his formally assuming the leadership of the party. However, his spell as foreign minister was marred by controversy: he was widely criticized for spending his own money to improve Ministry facilities (buying new radio equipment for embassies, for example), and became embroiled in a controversy over whether his 'monopolistic' business assets rendered him constitutionally ineligible to serve in the cabinet. He therefore resigned after only 100 days.

When Chuan Leekpai was obliged to dissolve the parliament in May 1995, following a bruising no-confidence debate and the resignation of Palang Dharma from the coalition, Thaksin assumed the leadership of the party. He was a key figure in brokering the emergence of the seven-party coalition that took office in July under the premiership of Banharn Silpa-archa. The fact that this coalition was announced on the very night of the election clearly indicated that plans had been laid well in advance. Thaksin became a deputy prime minister, an ambiguous position in the Thai political hierarchy, typically assigned to senior figures who are not sufficiently well-placed to head a major ministry. This reflected the poor performance of Palang Dharma in the election, down from 47 seats to 23. Thaksin, given a brief to solve Bangkok's notorious traffic problems, suggested that he could achieve this in just six months. He apparently believed that a computerized system to control the city's traffic lights – which are notoriously operated manually by traffic police, using far longer timings than international norms – could transform the situation. Unsurprisingly, however, Bangkok traffic failed to improve, and his earlier pledges were quietly forgotten. Thaksin was criticized by Bangkokians for having used their support to help create and then sustain the inept Banharn administration.[14] In the November 1996 election Palang Dharma was reduced to only a single seat. Thaksin left the scene, apparently unfazed at having personally wrecked a medium-sized political party in just over a year.

Undeterred by the damage to his reputation produced by his failed alliance with Banharn, Thaksin agreed to become a deputy premier for a second time in August 1997, immediately after the July currency crisis that precipitated the Asian financial crash.[15] The government of Chavalit Yongchaiyudh had been seriously undermined by the crash, and was desperately seeking to regain credibility. As part of his fight for political survival, Chavalit enlisted Thaksin to join his cabinet. Unsurprisingly, this proved a futile move: faced with domestic opposition and with a complete collapse of international confidence, Chavalit was forced to step aside only a couple of months later.

Thaksin's three forays into the world of politics during the mid-1990s were characterized by certain recurrent features. First, he was only too willing to use his wealth and connections as a fast track to high office: only once did he actually stand for election to parliament, in 1995. Second, his moves smacked of opportunism. Third, he acted at the behest of others, or in ways that seemed to serve the political ends of second-rate prime ministers. Fourth, he acted in ways that alienated actual or potential supporters, testifying to an overconfidence and a disdain for the views of the voting public. In his defence, it may be argued that he was acting from a position of relative weakness: as a political outsider, he was forced to rely on what more established politicians (Chamlong, Banharn, Chavalit) had to offer him. Since his function in each case was to enhance the standing and legitimacy of a problematic coalition through lending his name to a senior post, he had little to gain and everything to lose from these actions. Thaksin clearly learned from these episodes that he needed to shape his political career on his own terms, rather than subordinating his own position to the needs of others. Following Chavalit's ouster, there were no other obvious future premiers waiting in the wings: there was no obvious alternative to the sharp-tongued Chuan Leekpai, personally incorruptible, remarkably intelligent, but lacking in vision and permanently beholden to his financiers and lieutenants. Thaksin was now in a position to seek the premiership for himself, rather than playing a secondary political role. For a CEO used to having most matters his own way, the country's top job was dramatically more appealing than a senior cabinet role.

Thaksin's bid to become prime minister was based on a new political vehicle, the Thai Rak Thai (Thais love Thai) Party. The launch of the party coincided with a new mode of political optimism following the passage of the 1997 constitution, which included a range of liberal reforms. Public dissatisfaction with the quality of Thai politicians and of the political system had produced growing demands for reform in the wake of May 1992. There was public unease about the symbiotic relationship between business people (including the rising provincial business class) and politicians, which often ensured that constituency MPs were little more than the stooges of local and national business elites. Political parties were much-criticized as factionalized alliances of interest groups, divorced from the concerns of the electorate. Practices such as candidate-buying (encouraging electable politicians to switch parties by using financial inducements), vote-buying and the corruption of government officials made the electoral process wide open to manipulation and abuse.[16] Vote-buying and electoral fraud appeared to have increased considerably from the mid-1980s onwards, and the scale of illegal practices in the 1995 and 1996 general elections exceeded all previous levels.

At the same time, voters were becoming increasingly dissatisfied with money-based electoral politics, pervasive corruption, 'low quality' politicians (many elected politicians were simply construction contractors – in some cases, they were actually quite prominent criminals) and the way 'policies' were subordinated to business interests. The 1990s saw increasingly vocal demands for reform of the political system. Reform, however, meant different things to different people.[17] For some, it was about boosting technocratic competence; for others, it really meant cleaning up electoral politics; and for others, it meant strengthening rights and increasing popular participation. Ultimately, the reform campaign was steered by a small coalition of elite actors from various quarters, working through a drafting body that included representatives from all 76 provinces. The result was a series of messy compromises, many opposed by elected politicians and senior bureaucrats. Michael Connors was not alone in arguing that the new constitution showed the extent to which 'liberalism became an emergent force challenging the anarchic and hierarchical pluralism of money politics'.[18]

Important reforms included the creation of a powerful Election Commission, empowered to oversee voting and order re-runs of flawed contests, and the establishment of several other new, independent bodies. These included a National Counter Corruption Commission, a Constitutional Court, an Administrative Court and a National Human Rights Commission. New laws limited the ability of MPs to switch parties (switches had to be made at least 90 days before an election, making last-minute horse-trading impossible). A central plank of the reforms was their division of elected representatives into three categories. Senators, who had previously been appointed and frequently inactive, were to be elected on a non-political basis, serving as 'wise elders' who could monitor the lower house and check its power. Meanwhile, the lower house would be divided into two categories: 400 constituency MPs and 100 party-list MPs. Only party-list MPs could become ministers; the idea was that these MPs would be drawn from the better-educated, technocratic classes, allowing 'good' people to enter parliament without sullying their hands with constituency politics. Constituency MPs were to be a lower category of parliamentarians, concerned primarily with representative functions. These changes were designed to engineer the political process, placing politicians into boxes that would delimit their capacity for action.

In practice, however, it quickly became clear that politicians were well able to foil the intentions of the constitution drafters, finding ways of subverting attempts to classify them, of intervening in supposedly apolitical bodies designed to police them and using the new electoral procedures to bring endless challenges to election results. Both the 2000 senate elections and the 2001 lower house elections were characterized by large numbers of complaints to the Election Commission and numerous re-runs of elections. Some senate elections were actually re-run seven times, and results were challenged in over 300 of the 400 lower house constituencies in 2001. Such developments merely served further to alienate the electorate and undermine the credibility of the whole electoral process. If the pre-1997 system made it too difficult to challenge electoral outcomes, the post-1997 system made challenging results an easy and cost-free process.

Thaksin's arrival on the scene with his new party seemed initially to chime in with some of the aspirations of the reform movement. Because Article 110 of the 1997 constitution made it illegal for any MP to own a company holding a state concession, Thaksin transferred the bulk of his assets to his wife and children. Technically speaking, he no longer owned Shin Corp. Thai Rak Thai sought to define itself as a technocratic party, a party led by a successful entrepreneur who wanted to bring the same levels of professionalism to politics as he had brought to his private sector activities. Thaksin was surrounded by an impressive group of advisors and associates. His slogan, 'Think new, act new', resonated with a reformist emphasis on the need for considerable changes in ideas and ways of working. His party claimed a more programmatic set of policies, presenting the electorate with a clear-cut manifesto for change. Superficially at least, Thai Rak Thai proved highly successful in promoting its message, which was well received by the media and by many commentators. In the wake of the Asian crisis, the Chuan administration stood accused of slavish conformity to the demands of the World Bank and the IMF; Chuan's critics argued that Thailand had 'lost face' in the eyes of the region and the wider world. Thai Rak Thai offered to redeem Thailand's national pride, restoring to the country the image (and self-image) of a successful and independent nation. Some had compared the crisis to the 1767 sacking of Ayutthaya by the Burmese – the greatest humiliation in Thai history – and suggested that nineteenth-century kings had successfully fended off Western colonialists, only for Thailand to be subject to de facto colonization a hundred years later. As one of Thailand's most successful entrepreneurs, Thaksin argued that he was uniquely positioned to lead the country through a process of renewal.

What kind of renewal was Thaksin concerned with? It quickly became apparent that he was not interested in the 'reformist' renewal symbolized by the 1997 constitution. Underlying the reform movement of the 1990s was a set of core assumptions: money should be separated from politics; good and competent people should be able to participate in the political process; popular participation in politics and civil society should be boosted; and new institutions and new rules of the game were needed to control political actors and prevent abuses of power. Thai Rak Thai arguably stood for an opposite set of ideas. Wealthy entrepreneurs, the most successful element of Thai society, should play the leading role in running the country. Other actors in the political process should be subordinated to a 'vision', an overall business plan devised by a CEO leadership. Popular participation was limited to a 'consumption' mode: voters and citizens would be the end users of products developed by a technocratic and entrepreneurial elite. Dynamic leadership should not be hemmed in by institutions or regulations, which should be subordinated to the will of the executive. Ironically, this mode of politics had many features in common with earlier kinds of political order in Thailand, which had centralized power in the hands of bureaucrats and military officers. This time, however, the centralization was entirely around the office of an elected prime minister.

The 6 January 2001 elections completely reshaped the political landscape in Thailand: on 9 February 2001, 339 of the 500 MPs in the new lower house voted for Thaksin to become prime minister. This was an unprecedented parliamentary majority. Small and medium sized parties were largely wiped out and only five parties – Thai Rak Thai, the Democrats, New Aspiration, Chart Thai and Chart Pattana – reached the threshold (5 per cent of the popular vote) to gain any of the 100 party-list seats. Thai Rak Thai subsequently absorbed New Aspiration and by March 2002 Thaksin presided over a grand coalition with Chart Thai and Chart Pattana, opposed only by the Democrats. In one respect, the designs of the constitution drafters had borne fruit: the new system made the position of small parties virtually untenable, so concentrating power in the hands of a limited number of larger parties.

Another aspect of the constitutional reforms had a direct impact upon Thaksin himself, doubtless causing him to regret his brief entanglement with the Chavalit government of 1997. The National Counter Corruption Commission had accused him of failing to properly declare his assets at the time he served as deputy prime minister, and passed the case on to the Constitutional Court. The case was somewhat technical, since there was no allegation of actual corruption, and it had no bearing on his time as prime minister from February 2001 onwards. Nevertheless, it spoke volumes concerning Thaksin's attitudes to the post-1997 political reform process. In the face of a possible five-year ban on holding public office, rather than adopting a respectful attitude towards the Constitutional Court, Thaksin mobilized his allies to bring intense pressure to bear on the court and its judges. Prominent supporters argued that Thaksin was the only person fit to serve as prime minister, and circulated mass petitions in support of him. One such important advocate was Prawase Wasi, a leading architect of the political reform movement, who suggested that Thaksin was one of the very few people to understand the problems of the country in all their complexity. The implication was that Thaksin was a sort of 'white knight', a saviour sent to redeem Thailand from its troubles – an argument that reflected popular belief in the capacity of strong, charismatic leadership.[19] These strains of thinking were, of course, diametrically opposed to the argument advanced during the political reform process, when the crafting of institutions and procedures was seen as the solution to structural problems in the politics and society of the country. Special religious ceremonies were held on Thaksin's behalf, including one in Khon Kaen attended by 20,000 people. It was widely argued that there was no other person suitable to serve as prime minister at this crucial juncture in Thailand's history. Thaksin himself was publicly critical of the anticorruption body and the court, suggesting at a provincial rally in December 2000 that his party already had 10 million members, and that the people's power would triumph.[20]

In August 2001, the court announced a confusing 8–7 verdict that effectively cleared Thaksin of the charge. Tellingly, three weeks elapsed between the announcement of the acquittal and the publication of the court's full judgement. Ridden with inconsistencies, the judgement showed that only four judges found Thaksin 'not guilty' on the facts; another four argued that the case was moot, since for various reasons the relevant legislation did not apply to Thaksin at the time of the alleged offence. The verdict of the constitutional court was arguably in accordance with the majority public sentiment in 2001: the idea of Thaksin being disqualified from office on essentially technical grounds was an unwelcome prospect for most Thais. The furore highlighted the extent to which quite draconian penalties had been incorporated into the post-1997 regulatory frameworks, penalties that made convictions difficult to achieve. But most clearly, it illustrated that the optimism surrounding the 1997 constitution was now dissipating. No longer were new institutions the answer to Thailand's political problems; and the incoming administration held them in ill-concealed contempt. Thaksin's approach to the new institutions was to penetrate them, politicize them and to subordinate them to his own will and purposes. Institutions were only as effective and credible as their weakest core members. At best, the verdict was an unsatisfactory muddle; at worst, it was completely flawed. In April 2002, the NCCC suspended four of the judges who had acquitted Thaksin, citing breach of authority. Three of them immediately appealed to the Administrative Court over their suspension. Equally disturbing were the self-centred responses to the case by Thaksin and his allies, which illustrated the extent to which Thailand's political class had failed to embrace the substance of democratic reform. After the verdict, he told reporters that the 11 million votes his party had received gave him a greater legitimacy than these appointive bodies. According to this argument, Thai Rak Thai's landslide election victory trumped all the 1990s reforms, overriding checks and balances to legitimate the administration and give the prime minister a massive mandate, a casting vote on all substantive decisions.

ALTERNATIVE READINGS OF THAKSIN

The Thaksin phenomenon can be seen from a variety of perspectives: Thaksin is either just another businessman turned politician, the first elected leader with a substantive party political platform, a true representative of the super-rich business elite, an authoritarian leader deeply influenced by his police background or a populist who skilfully manipulated rhetoric and symbols to broaden his appeal.

There was nothing new about businessmen entering politics; a good example was Banharn Silpa-archa, prime minister from 1995 to 1996, who made little secret of the interrelationship between his business activities and his political life. Banharn was famously nick-named 'Mr ATM', because of his proclivity for distributing cash incentives to help broker deals and fix parliamentary votes. The money was frequently doled out in the gents lavatories of the parliament building. During a period in opposition, Banharn lamented that he and his party were terribly 'thirsty', deprived of income and resources. For the businessman turned politician, politics was the extension of business by other means. Scholars such as Ockey, Sombat and Pasuk have chronicled the rise of politicians in this mode, who typically have links with illegal provincial business, and may even be considered 'god-fathers'.[21] If we believe that Thaksin's primary purpose in entering politics was to further his business interests by securing concessions and contracts for his own companies and for those of his associates, it is possible to view Thaksin in this light. Thaksin's response to this allegation, echoed constantly by his supporters, is that he is too rich to be corrupt: he has made so much money already that he has no need to indulge in the kind of larcenous politically-facilitated business activity favoured by other businesspeople who have entered politics. Thaksin's amazing wealth is often cited as a kind of shining virtue, rendering him immune from ordinary human temptations.

Where Thaksin does have elements in common with the likes of Banharn is on the question of social class: the traditional Thai idea of a political leader as someone from a good family, or else someone rendered socially legitimate through an honourable career of public service (especially through the military). This class issue was closely related to the question of ethnicity. As a Sino-Thai entrepreneur, Thaksin shared with Banharn some questionable class origins. The older Thai elite, especially people from prominent families with a distinguished history of public service, looked down on Thaksin as an arriviste. It seems clear that a desire to improve their social standing was an important motivation for businessmen turned politicians. But Baker argues that Thaksin's 2001 victory 'immediately rendered obsolete the old Thai politics of alliance between provincial businessmen and bureaucrats'.[22]

In another view, Thaksin is the first Thai politician to be seriously committed to manifesto-based politics. Whereas previously party platforms were not taken at all seriously, Thai Rak Thai's election promises provided the basis of most of Thaksin's major moves during his first year in office. Pledges to provide a moratorium on farmers' debt, to offer a million-baht development fund for every village in Thailand and to introduce a healthcare scheme allowing people to receive medical treatment for a token 30 baht were crucial planks of Thai Rak Thai's election strategy, and help account for their landslide victory. In this respect, it is possible to see Thaksin as a genuinely reformist politician, moving Thai politics away from a set of empty choices between self-interested parties and towards a range of active alternatives from which voters could choose.

A third view recognizes the salience of Thaksin's policy stances, but sees them as an essentially populist approach. In other words, policies designed to capture the imagination of voters are not part of a substantive political design, but crude devices to draw voters to a party. Chris Baker has argued that Thaksin's electoral appeal was based on nationalist rhetoric, an attempt to bring on board rural voters by tapping into a popular sense of resentment against the IMF and the forces of globalization. He suggests that this is significantly different from the old-fashioned nationalist rhetoric of the military, and of older political parties such as the Chart Thai (Thai Nation)

Party, arguing that 'Thaksin's nationalism evokes a community of "Thai people" without fully embracing the vocabulary and symbols of nation and state'.[23] In part, this reflected Thaksin's difficulties in laying claim to nationalist symbols, which had in recent decades been intimately associated with the monarchy. Baker also argues that Thaksin placed less emphasis on the centrality of agriculture than, say, Latin American populists: the primary objective of Thai Rak Thai was to turn farmers into businessmen and entrepreneurs. Thailand's future did not lie in farming, but in raising its economic game. There was a rich irony in a billionaire telecommunications magnate adopting pro-poor populist rhetoric: Thaksin was seeking to offer a way out for the poor, which would allow them to transcend their poverty rather than to celebrate and dignify it.

For Baker, Thaksin is an essentially new phenomenon in Thai politics, an example of large scale domestic capital entering the core of the system. Whereas in previous administrations big capital had some direct representation in the cabinet or in parliament, the core political leadership comprized provincial businesspeople or bureaucrats. In other words, Thaksin was the first major Thai entrepreneur to grow weary of working through middlemen, to be unwilling to pay respect to those he considered his inferiors in terms of an under-standing of wealth generation and the realities of the global economy. This marked a sea change in the Thai political order.

Jim Glassman has argued that Thai Rak Thai and Thaksin are engaged in a substantive project of economic nationalism, albeit an opporunistic nationalism that is not especially coherent or especially strong, and which belongs to a 'post-nationalist' era.[24] He sees this era as one in which 'the powers of states have been increasingly harnessed to the projects of a highly mobile band of internationalized capital-ists, leading to intensified social struggle both within and against both the state and these internationalized capitalists'. In other words, he sees Thaksin as a political phenomenon with implications that go far beyond the Thai case. While this is an interesting argument, there seems little evidence that Thaksin is part of a highly mobile band of internationalized capitalists: all his business ventures are intimately linked to the Thai state. Glassman credits what Kasian Tejapira has termed the 'Octobrists' (former radicals who cut their political teeth in the 1970s) for having a significant influence over the shaping of Thai Rak Thai's populist policies.[25]

We doubt it. This book will spend little time analysing the nature of Thaksin's political thought, since we firmly believe that his invocation of ideas such as nationalism, statism, the social contract or the supposed virtues of SMEs (small and medium enterprises) should not be taken seriously. These concepts are nothing more than linguistic tools. It is our belief that Thaksin is an opportunistic politician, for whom ideas are simply a means to an end. He is not animated by the pursuit of ideas, but by the pursuit of wealth and power. Thaksin's greatest achievement is the creation of a formidable political and economic power network, the mother of all *phuak*.[26]

As time has passed, Thaksin has begun to appear less radical, more conventionally nationalist, and increasingly preoccupied with policies that seem to reflect his business background and interests. Yet the energy of his administration remains formidable and he has generated an extraordinary range of projects and initiatives. There is already ample material available for numerous important books on Thaksin's premiership. In this volume, we have been able to focus on just five key areas: his involvement in the telecommunications industry, his creation of Thai Rak Thai, his relationship with the military, his use of language and media and his involvement in new forms of political economy networks. Each topic is approached slightly differently, but we have been guided by two central questions: what is new about Thaksin's way of operating? and how far has he been successful in 'Thaksinizing' areas of Thailand's economic and political order?

NOTES

1 Daniel Lovering, 'Thailand's tycoon prime minister spares no expense on political empire', Associated Press, 9 June 2003.

2 For the best overview of Thai politics up to the late 1970s, see John L. S. Girling, *Thailand: Society and Politics*, Ithaca NY, Cornell University

Press, 1982. Another invaluable text is Pasuk Phongpaichit and Chris Baker, *Thailand: Economy and Politics*, Singapore, Oxford University Press, 2002.

3   Chai-Anan Samudavanija, 'Educating Thai democracy', *Journal of Democracy*, 1, 1, 1990, p. 115.

4   For accounts and analyses of the political reform process, see Duncan McCargo (ed.), *Reforming Thai Politics*, Copenhagen, Nordic Institute of Asian Studies, 2002.

5   Thailand has had a logging ban since 1988.

6   Pasuk Phongpaichit and Chris Baker, *Thaksin: The Business of Politics in Thailand*, Chiang Mai, Silkworm, 2004, p. 12. This is a murky area: Pasuk and Baker state that estimates range from 60 to 90 per cent, but give no sources.

7   On police corruption, see Pasuk Phongpaichit and Sungsidh Piri-yarangsan, *Corruption and Democracy in Thailand*, Bangkok, Political Economy Centre, Chulalongkorn University, 1994, pp. 99–120. The original book contains some details that were not included in a later edition published by Silkworm, and so is worth seeking out.

8   See N. Ganesan, 'Thaksin and the politics of domestic and regional consolidation', *Contemporary Southeast Asia*, 26, 1, 2004, pp. 36–37.

9   For an excellent discussion of Thaksin's family background, see Pasuk and Baker, *Thaksin*, pp. 25–61.

10 Ukrist Pathmanand, 'The Thaksin Shinawatra Group: a study of the relationship between money and politics in Thailand', *Copenhagen Journal of Asian Studies*, 13, 1998, p. 67.

11 Chris Baker, 'Pluto-populism: Thaksin and popular politics', in Peter Warr (ed.) *Thailand beyond the crisis*, London, Routledge, forth-coming.

12 Pasuk and Baker, *Thaksin*, p. 37.

13 On Chamlong, see Duncan McCargo, *Chamlong Srimuang and the new Thai Politics*, London, Hurst, 1997.

14 Sixteen of Palang Dharma's seats were in Bangkok.

15 On the crisis, see Pasuk Phongpaichit and Chris Baker, *Thailand's Crisis*, Chiang Mai, Silkworm, 2000.

16 For details, see Sombat Chantornvong, *Luektang wikrit: panha lae tang ok* [Elections in Crisis: Problems and Solutions], Bangkok, Kopfai, 1993; William A. Callahan and Duncan McCargo, 'Vote-buying in Thailand's Northeast: the case of the July 1995 general election', *Asian*

Survey, 36, 4, 1996, pp. 376–392; and Surin Maisrikrod and Duncan McCargo, 'Electoral politics: commercialization and exclusion', in Kevin Hewison (ed.) *Political Change in Thailand: Democracy and Participation*, London, Routledge, 1997, pp. 132–148.

17 Duncan McCargo, 'Alternative meanings of political reform in Thailand', *The Copenhagen Journal of Asian Studies*, 13, 1998, pp. 5–30.

18 Michael Connors, 'Framing the "People's Constitution"', in Duncan McCargo (ed.), *Reforming Thai Politics*, Copenhagen, Nordic Institute of Asian Studies, 2002, p. 44.

19 The idea of the largely charmless Thaksin as a 'charismatic' leader is a curious one for international audiences – he is clearly no Sukarno. Nevertheless, the Thai concept of *barami* (often misleadingly translated as 'charisma') also involves popular Buddhist notions of merit accumulated in past lives, and in this area the billionaire scores very highly.

20 Michael H. Nelson, 'Thailand's house elections of 6 January 2001: Thaksin's landslide victory and subsequent narrow escape', in Michael H. Nelson (ed.), *Thailand's New Politics: KPI 2001 Yearbook*, Bangkok, White Lotus, 2002, p. 368.

21 See the chapters by James Ockey, Sombat Chantornvong and Pasuk Phongpaichit in Ruth McVey (ed.), *Money and Power in Provincial Thailand*, Copenhagen, Nordic Institute of Asian Studies.

22 Baker, 'Pluto-populism'.

23 Baker, 'Pluto-populism'.

24 Jim Glassman, 'Economic "nationalism" in a post-nationalist era: the political economy of economic policy in post-crisis Thailand', *Critical Asian Studies*, 36, 1, p. 61.

25 Glassman, 'Economic "nationalism"', pp. 50–51.

26 *Phuak* means clique, group, faction or in-crowd.

CHAPTER 2

Thaksin and the Politics
of Telecommunications

I don't care about politics that much. I have very few political genes in my body. ... I have more management skills than political skills. – *Thaksin Shinawatra,* Far Eastern Economic Review, *16 November 2000*

THAKSIN SHINAWATRA'S INVOLVEMENT in the telecommunications business can be divided into three major phases: the concessions phase (1988–97); the post-crisis phase (1997–2000); and a third phase that began with his assumption of the premiership in February 2001. In each phase, competition in the business was approached differently. During the concession period, Thaksin had to conduct business under highly competitive circumstances and political uncertainties, and with strong reliance on political connections. These conditions were similar to those faced by other telecommunications groups. A major turning point took place at the time of the 1997 Asian economic crisis. The crisis pushed all of Thailand's telecommunication corporations into deficit, with the exception of Thaksin's company, which had smaller debts than any of its rivals. Another turning point was the founding of the Thai Rak Thai Party in July 1998, which started a sequence of events leading to Thaksin's own entry to Government House. Since then, new opportunities in the telecommunications sector have emerged for Thaksin's businesses. Expansion and new investment in both the domestic and regional spheres have brought about new sources of wealth for Thaksin and his family.

THE CONCESSION PHASE, 1988–97

Telecommunications groups are a relatively new business sector in Thailand. While some business groups operating in this field date back to the pre- or post-Second World War period (for example, the International Engineering Group, CP Group and Samart Group), most of these began in other fields and only gradually developed interests in telecoms. This growth was shaped by many related factors, such as the economic and political changes that took place during the late 1980s and the introduction of the Build-Transfer-Operation (BTO) concession system. These factors brought about fierce competition among the players and the search for favourable political connections by telecoms businesses anxious to secure all-important government concessions.

Thaksin Shinawatra, who came from a famous silk merchant family in Chiang Mai, graduated with a doctoral degree in criminology from the United States and was appointed to a position in the Royal Thai Police.[1] Later on, he established a computer representative company selling IBM hardware to a range of government departments, using his position in the bureaucracy as well as his family connections.[2] However, back in 1988, the computer business was not a highly profitable one.[3] Nor were all of Thaksin's business ventures successful. He had previously applied for a loan to invest in the condominium business and was later forced to alter the project into one for serviced apartments.[4] Eventually, this project was aborted due to construction problems.[5]

The turning point for Thaksin was the registration of his first company on the Stock Exchange of Thailand in 1989: Advanced Info Service Public Company Limited (AIS). Subsequently, three other companies run and owned by Thaksin Shinawatra expanded from computer sales into new technology-based services: a phone membership service, wireless phone networks, mobile phone systems and a news exchange service. These grew rapidly to satisfy the need of urban Thais, at a time when the booming Thai economy was among the fastest-growing in the world. In December 1993, Thaksin's Shin Satellite (SATTEL) was the first company in Thailand to launch its own satellite, reflecting a move into broadcasting and mass communications. Thaksin also extended his telecommunications business into Indochina – Vietnam, Laos and Cambodia – and also to the Philippines, Indonesia and India.

Another milestone which brought about increasingly fierce competition among the rival players in telecommunications sector was the changing political circumstances and the introduction of the BTO concession system to the telecommunications business. This system was unique to Thailand, giving concession holders long-term rights to operate monopolistic businesses. The dissolution of parliament and the resignation from politics of General Prem Tinsulanond in 1988 marked the end of Thailand's 'semi-democratic' era, which affected the administration, political balance and the reform of the telecommunications sector in later years. The Thai business sector could no longer deal primarily with bureaucrats and technocrats, but had to negotiate deals with frequently-changing ministers in a series of governments. Between 1991 and 2001, Thailand had no fewer than nine different governments.

Thailand's political system transformed from a semi-democratic to a more democratic regime loosely based on a party system, which experienced a continuous economic growth of 7 to 8 per cent for approximately ten years.[6] High levels of confidence in the economy enabled the private sector to encourage the government to liberalize and also to reform the telecommunications business, which had been traditionally dominated by state enterprises. Attempts to reform and liberalize the telecommunications sector in Thailand began in the late 1980s, during the fifth phase of General Prem's government (1986–88). During that time, Thailand's politics were still overshadowed by the military, and the telecommunications sector was monopolized by bureaucrats in the National Security Council as well as the officials of two crucial state enterprises: the Telephone Organization of Thailand (TOT) and the Communications Authority of Thailand (CAT). These organizations played a leading role in Thailand's telecommunications policy, yet lacked the ability to keep pace with the extraordinary growth in demand. Although Prem's government supported the liberalization of the public sectors, progress slowed down due to objections from the military and from senior officials of both enterprises. Nevertheless, a major breakthrough occurred when the first BTO concession was granted to Pacific Telesis for mobile phone services in 1986. This proved that the BTO concession system could be implemented successfully in Thailand.[7]

During General Chatichai Choonhavan's adminstration (1988–91), support for the liberalization of the telecommunications sector increased. However, reform under the concession system in this period was very different from that under General Prem's government. More participants were involved in planning the policies. Representatives from the old guard – notably, the military and high ranking

Table 2.1: Approvals and modifications of Thai telecom concessions, 1988–2002

Government	Minister of Communications	Events
Chatichai 4 Aug 1988– 23 Feb 1991	Montri Pongpanich	Approval of the three million phone numbers project
Anand 1 2 Mar 1991– 7 Apr 1992	Nukul Prachobmoa	Division of the three million phone numbers contract: two million numbers for Bangkok and environs, and one million for the provinces
Chuan 1 23 Sep 1992– 13 Jul 1995	Winai Sompong Wichit Surapongchai	Allocation of code 01 to TAC - Influenced the expansion of 1.1 million phone numbers project - Extended TAC contract from 15 to 22 years
Banharn 13 Jul 1995– 25 Nov 1996	Sombat Uthaisang (deputy minister but key player)	- An additional 600,000 numbers for TA - 500,000 numbers for TT & T - Approval of PCT for TA and TT&T - Extended AIS contract from 20 to 25 years - Extended TAC contract from 22 to 27 years

Table 2.1: Approvals and modifications of Thai telecom concessions, 1988–2002 *(continued)*

Chavalit 25 Nov 1996– 9 Nov 1997	Direk Chareonpol	- Hastened ongoing processes of TOT and CAT - More explicit plans to transform concession contracts
Chuan 2 9 Nov 1997– 9 Feb 2001	Suthep Theuksuban Wan Muhammad Nor Matha	Approval of the 1900 phone programme
Thaksin 9 Feb 2001– present	Surapong Suebwonglee	- Amending the contract of quota distribution in one-to-call system by decreasing from 25% to 20% (15 May 2001) - Revising the contract with AIS to make the roaming network between GSM 900 system and GSM 1800 (DPC) expenditure deducted before making quota distribution to TOT (1 May 2002)

Sources: Data from Noppanand Wannadhebsakul and first-hand research by the authors.

bureaucrats – lost their decision-making power. Instead, telecommunications business groups and the prime minister's advisors had become the major players in shaping telecommunications policy. Chatichai proposed numerous BTO concessions. The new system was supported by senior officials of TOT and CAT, because it yielded mutual benefits. The executives of both departments were able to maintain their authority over telecommunications services, yet also had access to a new source of income by granting the con-cessions. Private investors, on the other hand, were given the op-portunity to develop a new telecommunications infrastructure in Thailand.

Within a matter of two years, Chatichai's government pushed through no less than 22 telecommunications concessions to the private sector (see Table 2.1). Shin Corp was granted seven concessions – more than any player in the sector – valued at almost 20,000 million baht. These included a mobile phone monopoly granted by TOT without any process of competitive bidding. Paiboon Limpaphayom, who headed TOT during this period, later became the executive vice-chairman of Shin Corp.[8] Thaksin also gained a cable television license, awarded when an old friend and fellow ex-cop, Chalerm Yubamrung, held ministerial responsibility for broadcasting. Jasmine International and Thai Telephone and Telecommunication (TT & T) received five concessions. TT & T was granted only one standard phone concession worth 39,600 million baht. United Communication (UCOM) was granted a 27-year wireless phone concession worth 5,000 million baht. Telecom Asia was granted three concessions, one of which was the standard phone concession in the Bangkok area with the highest value in history, estimated at 97,800 million baht.

After being granted these concessions, these telecommunications corporations registered on the Stock Exchange of Thailand to raise more capital for further expansion as well as building political networks to compete and to protect the benefits from their telecommunication business. The resulting huge injections of stock market capital brought about enormous wealth to these groups, and to a number of politicians and senior military officers who were involved in the granting of concessions. Shinawatra Group, or Shin Corp as it is now known, registered four companies on the stock market: Shinawatra Computer and Communication (1990), Advance Info Service or AIS (1991), International Broadcasting Corporation or IBC (1992) and Shinawatra Satellite or SATTEL (registered in 1994). Other communications companies soon followed suit: Telecom Asia, Samart Group and International Engineering registered in 1993, while TT&T-Jasmine and UCOM registered in 1994. This pivotal launch of the 22 concessions and the registration of these business organizations on the stock market became the foundation that strengthened and empowered the domestic telecommunications companies, paving the way for the birth of the Big Four Telecoms, whose oligopoly has reigned over Thailand's telecommunications sectors to date.[9] The concessions were in effect a double license to print money: they granted the companies concerned huge incomes from the services they could operate, as well as the opportunity to boost company values through flotations on the stock market.

The big four telecoms are corporations which were all granted large-scale concessions from the government. Two of them, TA and TT & T, were granted standard phone concessions, whereas the other two, Shin Corp and UCOM, were granted concessions for wireless phone services.[10] Despite the apparent sharing of benefits contained in the allocation of concessions, a fierce battle took place among the Big Four from 1988 to 1997 for two major related reasons. The first concerned the micro-politics of the concession system itself, and the second was the wider instability of Thai politics at that time. The concession system relied heavily on the personal discretion of the current Minister of Transport and Communications. Even after having been granted their concessions, telecommunications companies continued to negotiate with politicians to enhance their benefits. This ongoing re-negotiation of details posed a constant threat to the interests of rival telecom groups. The instability of Thai politics from 1988 to 1997 caused a number of problems in the telecommunications business: not only did the government change eight times within nine years,[11] but each of these coalition governments comprised numerous parties. Broadly speaking, UCOM was aligned with the Democrats, TT&T with the Democrats and Chart Thai, and Telecom Asia with New Aspiration – but these were fluid alliances rather than fixed positions.

Examples of concession re-negotiations were legion. During Chuan Leekpai's first term in office (1992–95), when Colonel Winai Sompong from the Palang Dharma Party was Minister of Transport and Communications, there was a move to allow UCOM's TAC to use the phone code 01 – the most popular prefix for mobile phone lines. Wingfield notes that in 1993, the Chuan government actually replaced the entire CAT board, which subsequently approved nine major projects with a total value of 8 billion baht.[12]

During Banharn Silpa-archa's government, in 1996, Sombat Uthai-sang, a non-MP deputy minister of Transport and Communications, modified many contracts with telecommunications corporations, such as the extension of 500,000 and 600,000 numbers to TA and TT&T respectively, and granting permission of PCT to TA and TT&T (see Table 2.1). Shortly afterwards, there was a change in the portfolio of the deputy minister to Pinij Charusombat from Seritham. More contract revisions were therefore pushed forward by the groups. Shin Corp extended its contract from 20 to 25 years, and reduced the state contribution from 30–35 per cent to 30 per cent.[13] UCOM extended TAC's concession from 22 to 27 years and reduced the state contribution from 26 per cent to 24 per cent.[14] These changes illustrated the bargaining relationships between telecom groups and individual ministers, bargaining that undermined the integrity of the original decisions on the allocation of concessions. Changes of minister led to both costs and opportunities for telecom companies seeking to protect and expand their concessions.

THAKSIN AS FOREIGN MINISTER, 1994 TO 1995

Thaksin made his first foray into politics when he served as foreign minister under the Palang Dharma quota in the Chuan government from 1994 to 1995. During this early period, Thaksin was afraid of criticism from the public and from rival communications companies, and his term as a minister was overhadowed by debate as to whether such a prominent holder of government concessions had any business serving in the cabinet. Thaksin preferred to use more backhanded methods, supporting Dr Wichit Surapongchai, a former managing director of the Bangkok Bank, to assume the position of Communications Minister. During this period the Communications ministry was under the Palang Dharma quota. During Wichit's term, he indirectly supported the Shin group by giving orders to delay the announcement of the master plan for developing the telecommunications infrastructure, sending it back for further detailed work.[15] Shin Corp also sought to block Telecom Asia's request to operate phones using PHS technology. Once the government changed to that of Banharn Silpa-archa, deputy Communications minister Sombat Uthaisang approved the introduction of PHS phones. He assigned the rights to PCT technology to TA, stating that this was an additional service of landline phones. In addition, his appointment as the foreign minister offered a chance for Thaksin to establish a telecommunications network in Indochina and Burma. Shin's mobile phone and pay TV projects in Cambodia began during this period. Through his appointment, Thaksin was able to get in touch with the Burmese military government, and became close to Khin Nyunt, who at that time was the military officer who worked on Burmese telecommunications issues.[16] Thaksin had to step down from his post as foreign minister because a constitutional clause was about to come into force, forbidding holders of state monopoly concessions to hold public office.[17] Shortly before the 1995 election, he reduced his equity holdings so as to circumvent this consitutional limitation; this allowed him to become a deputy prime minister in the Banharn government. Some of the estimated 1 billion baht raised from the sale of equity was used to support his Palang Dharma Party, but he was also widely reported to have given donations to other parties and factions as well – including some 200 million baht to the Therd Thai faction of Chart Thai.[18] Thaksin's strategy of securing support from political allies apparently began long before he became prime minister.

When granted concessions, these groups saw the opportunity to raise capital through registration on the Stock Exchange of Thailand and this became the major target. But the registration process was difficult because the decision-making power belonged to only one person – the Minister of Transport and Communications. Therefore, these groups needed to build a lot of connections to push their companies into the stock market. Since frequent political changes were the major problem that directly affected telecommunications business, whether to protect their concessions or to register their companies in the stock market, the groups were therefore forced to seek many political alliances at the same time. During this period, ministers and deputy ministers of Transport and Communications typically came from small parties, which were instrumental in helping create a viable coalition government, such as the Social Action Party, Prachakorn Thai Party, Palang Dharma Party and Seritham Party. Thus telecom companies also had to lobby those politicians in charge of the Ministry of Finance, which usually remained in the hands of the major parties.

The clearest example of political instability, troublesome coalitions and mutually beneficial deals done between telecommunications business and political parties was evident in Banharn Silpa-archa's short-lived government, formed in July 1995. Banharn's administration was a seven-party coalition government, whose core partners were the Chart Thai Party, the New Aspiration Party and the Palang Dharma Party. The Ministry of Communications was solely in the hands of the New Aspiration Party. Thus, the Telephone Organization of Thailand and Communicatons Authority of Thailand were under the administration of Muhammad Nor Matha and Sombat Uthaisang, the Minister and Deputy Minister of Transport and Communications. Consequently, Telecom Asia's personal communications telephone (PCT) system[19] was authorized to compete with Shin Corp's AIS, which had been previously granted a large-scale wireless phone concession. In addition, when General Chavalit Yongchaiyudh became Minister of Defence in the Banharn government, he proposed launching the 'Star of Siam' military satellite, worth 27,000 million baht. This proposal was brought about by ministers from the New Aspiration Party, and directly affected Shin Corp's monopolistic satellite project.[20] Ironically, Thaksin Shinawatra was at this time a deputy prime minister in the same Banharn government, having taken over the leadership of the Palang Dharma Party prior to the 1995 general election.

Political instability led to loose but diverse political alliances between telecommunications corporations and politicians. Each large telecom group had various connections with politicians from different parties, depending on which party was overseeing the Ministry of Transport and Communications at the time. For example, CP founder Dhanin Chearavanont was described by *Asiaweek* as a 'key backer' of Chavalit Yongchaiyudh, which helped TA build close ties with the New Aspiration Party.[21]

SHIFTING ALLIANCES

Chavalit had a long-standing reputation for a number of things: he was credited with being a 'political soldier', one of the architects of the policies that had defused Thailand's communist insurgency; and he was also extremely familiar with the illegal business activities (especially logging and smuggling) that thrived on Thailand's borders with Burma and Cambodia. As army commander in chief during the 1980s, he pioneered a new role for the military as an agent of rural development, through projects such as Isan Khiew (the greening of the Northeast) and the New Hope programme in the Muslim-dominated southern border provinces. These projects involved potentially lucrative opportunities for collaboration with big business, and leading agribusiness group CP formed a close working relationship with Chavalit during this period. When Chavalit sought to parlay his military career into a political one by resigning from the army to create the New Aspiration Party in 1990, CP was one of his main backers.[22] But the CP connection went beyond purely domestic concerns. In the aftermath of the 1979 Vietnamese invasion of Cambodia, Thailand had sought to encourage China to balance Vietnamese influence in Indochina by backing and arming the Khmer Rouge. This had been done through personal diplomacy initiated by then foreign minister Siddhi Savetsila. Lacking strong ties with Beijing, Chavalit and Siddhi had asked CP to assist, using Dhanin's personal channels to the Chinese leadership. This was the origin of the connection between Chavalit and CP, and as a result CP gained the trust of both the Chinese and Thai governments. CP members were appointed as advisors to the Thai Foreign Ministry from the time of Siddhi onwards. Subsequently, CP began to establish animal food plants, motorcycle factories and other businesses in China, as well as giving support to Chavalit and the NAP. The clearest political response and business benefits between CP and Chavalit and the NAP were that Sombat Uthaisang, deputy Communications minister in the Banharn government under the NAP quota, approved Telecom Asia's bid to use PCT technology.

When the government changed hands, each group also had to change its alliances. Apart from politicians and parties, these telecommunications companies also had to seek connections with military leaders, who continued to play very significant roles due to the lack of political stability,[23] as well as sustaining good relationships with senior executives of those government enterprises in charge of the communications sector. The period from 1988 to 1997 was therefore an important transition period for the telecommunications business. The companies involved were transformed from being mere sales representatives of communication equipment and computers to new business groups with diverse interests, listings on the stock exchange and enormous actual and prospective income. Such a transformation was brought about through the new BTO concession system by elected politicians from the Chatichai era onwards.

Assessing the 1997–2006 National Telecommunications Master Plan, which envisaged dividing the country into six zones for the purpose of providing telephone services, Cairns and Deunden noted that this kind of suggested market structure was non-competitive, and that 'there may be, especially in the zonal duopoly envisaged in Thailand, arrangements to share the market, rather than to compete'.[24] This was exactly the point: Thailand's Big Four Telecoms greatly preferred non-competitive arrangements, allowing a sharing of the 'cake' of benefits, to arrangements that offered optimal services and pricing to the consumer. The only issue at stake was exactly how the benefits should be shared. Cairns and Deunden stressed the importance of an effective and independent regulator, noting that in the past regulatory mechanisms in the Thai telecoms sector had been captured by special interests.[25] Provisions for an independent regulator were part of the package of reforms agreed in the 1997 constitution. Thaksin is also believed to have made strenuous efforts to become a member of the Constitution Drafting

Assembly, the body that drew up the 1997 constitution. Newspaper reports suggested that he had spent heavily in an unsuccessful attempt to buy his way onto the panel.[26] These efforts doubtless reflected Thaksin's interest in influencing the structure of the regulatory system for telecoms.

Under the pre-reform political system, the acquisition and maintenance of concessions and the capital raising in the stock market of these telecommunications groups were still full of difficulties, because both means of generating profits directly depended on constantly changing ministers, due to the instability of coalition governments during this nine-year period. For these reasons loose and simultaneous alliances with many politicians and parties were essential for each telecom group. However, the structure of the competition between the Big Four Telecoms as well as the system of loose political alliances underwent a change of character when the economic crisis broke out in 1997. This was shaped partly by the business challenges faced by the companies and partly by the emergence of a changed regulatory climate.

THE 1997 ECONOMIC CRISIS AND TELECOMS

The 1997 economic crisis resulted from a combination of global factors and Thailand's internal problems. But the crisis was also an opportunity for large-scale domestic business groups, including those in the telecommunications sector. This crisis led to the recomposition of capital in almost every sector, ranging from the commercial banks to the manufacturing industry to major retailers. This recomposition included the bankruptcy of many large domestic corporations, numerous takeovers by foreign or multinational companies and the internal restructuring of owners and shareholders.[27] This was most evident where Thailand's commercial banks were taken over by foreign banks.[28] But the crisis brought about different types of changes to the telecommunications sector. In short, enormous debts changed the structure of the groups from a position where the Big Four Telecoms – Shin Corp, UCOM, TA and TT&T-Jasmine – had roughly equal levels of capital, technology and political connections, to a position where Shin Corp was economically and politically superior to the other players. Shin Corp was now well-placed to take direct control of the rules of the game, both in terms of telecommunications and in terms of politics more generally.

Crucially, Shin Corp's owner skillfully turned the crisis into an opportunity, by employing his economic superiority to enter politics for the second time.[29] Thaksin Shinawatra founded the Thai Rak Thai Party in July 1998, firstly to protect his business and secondly to help fellow domestic telecommunications groups and other large-scale businesses. These businesses were all under pressure from the forces of globalization, in the form of the liberalization of the telecommunications sector and from the creation of the Office of the National Telecommunications Committee, an independent organization initiated by the 1997 constitution. Thaksin Shinawatra's second entry into politics had a significant effect on the structure of the telecommunications sector; later on, it was to have a parallel impact on Thailand's politics and economy more broadly.

The economic crisis of 1997 left the telecommunications sector heavily indebted. Crucially, these huge debts tore down the former structure of competition between the Big Four Telecoms – Shin Corp, UCOM, TA and TT&T-Jasmine – which depended on the concession system and loose political alliances, and created a new structure where Shin Corp had become a leader whose economic and political status was superior to other players. This meant that all the rules were reconfigured and other telecommunications groups were eventually forced to enter into an alliance with Shin Corp.

The following is a summary of how each of the Big Four Telecoms addressed the post-1997 debt crisis, their solutions and each company's investment in new lines of business.

UCOM

The UCOM group, established in 1956, also began life as a family business. Sutjin Benjarongkakul got together with his wife Kanjana, younger brother Sujit and five local businessmen to create Industrial United. The business of the company in the beginning was small-scale trading and construction materials. In 1961 the American giant Motorola appointed Industrial United as its sole Thailand agent for radio and other communications equipment for the US Army.[30] The company then experienced a phase of rapid expansion and diversification, moving into insurance, investment and hotels, but later hit a low point with the death of Sutjin in 1980. Sutjin's oldest son Bunchai had to implement a plan to clear Industrial United's 300 million baht debts. With his siblings, Bunchai then established UCOM and moved into the communications sector, enjoying considerable early success.

However, after the 1997 crisis, UCOM had the highest liabilities among the telecom groups, amounting to 101,787 million baht (see Table 2.2). In early 1998, UCOM assigned the Union Bank of Switzerland and Lehman Brothers as their financial consultants and reorganized their finance structures. In February 1999, UCOM agreed to undergo restructuring with their creditors in accordance with the following major plans:

1. The postponement until 2003 of the due date for three major debts: a 210-million US dollar loan; Euro Convertible Debentures (ECDs) estimated at 230 million dollars; and baht-dominated Convertible Debentures (CDs) estimated at 3,690 million baht.[31]

2. The ECDs and CDs creditors agreed to convert liabilities total-ling a minumum of 110 million dollars into UCOM stocks. As a result, ECDs and CDs debts amounting to 119.68 million US dollars were converted into the company's 199,266,679 common stocks. After the conversion, the stake of the Benjarongkakul family was reduced from 45 per cent to 26 per cent.[32] This allowed Somers, a British investment enterprise, to become the largest shareholder in UCOM, with a 46 per cent stake.

In May 2002, UCOM made an agreement with its new business alliance, Telenor Asia Pte Ltd,[33] by allowing Telenor Asia to purchase 24.85 per cent of UCOM stocks from Somers, 22 per cent of TAC stocks from UCOM, and 15 per cent of newly released stocks. As a result, UCOM's shares in TAC were reduced from 65 per cent to 41.7 per cent, while the Benjarongkakul family's stake in UCOM remained unchanged. The economic crisis had forced the Benjarongkakul family to sell their shares to foreign telecommunications enterprises from Britain and Norway. Consequently, their shares in UCOM and TAC, their mobile phone division, were drastically reduced mainly to ensure the survival of the company.

Table 2.2: Total liabilities of Thai telecom companies, 1996–2002

	Total Liabilities (Millions of Baht)						
Telecom	1996	1997	1998	1999	2000	2001	2002
TA	62,304	94,415	85,346	86,020	79,757	81,577	86,049
TT & T	30,595	48,453	44,878	44,339	47,726	34,357	32,681
JASMINE	12,784	19,871	20,440	21,743	19,382	17,009	16,129
ADVANC	10,974	23,373	26,751	18,339	31,045	72,517	74,844
SATTEL	8,270	12,927	8,692	6,860	7,594	8,581	13,103
SHIN	27,117	50,800	46,607	11,006	17,775	17,398	20,191
UCOM	48,740	101,787	79,455	68,178	15,070	13,108	13,108
SAMART	7,413	12,626	16,073	12,619	12,328	6,781	8,935
SAMTEL	300	2,627	2,886	2,417	1,790	1,426	1,176
IEC	5,180	4,327	3,184	2,232	960	389	863

Sources: Company annual reports.

Moreover, the company was also forced to cancel the Iridium co-project with Motorola of the US worth an estimated 4 billion dollars, which was designed to develop a global mobile phone network linking 66 satellites in the region covering Thailand, Malaysia, Myanmar, Cambodia, Laos, Vietnam and Bangladesh. This project was launched in November 1998, but due to marketing problems and the company's unresolved debts, it was eventually terminated in March 2000.

TELECOM ASIA (TA)

Telecom Asia is part of the Charoen Pokphand CP group, one of Thailand's most successful conglomerates, and a rare example of a Thai company that has been extremely effective in the wider region, notably in China. Starting out as a seed company, CP moved into agribusiness (becoming especially famed for chicken production) and then diversified into a range of other areas, including telecommunications. This move reflected the changing nature of Asian societies during the rapid period of economic growth from the early 1980s.[34] By 1997, TA had debts totaling 94,415 million baht (see Table 2.2), which took almost two years to resolve. By the end of 1999, the company was successful in signing a deal with financial institutions and various other suppliers to reform the liability structure, valued at 61,790 million baht. The major agreements that TA made comprised the following measures:[35]

- The postponement of the due date of debts with insurance valued at 48,500 million baht, to 2008
- The remaining debts not covered by insurance amounting to 13,290 million baht were in cash and ticket repayment.
- The increase of 7,020 million baht capital by releasing preferred shares to Kreditanstalt für Wiederaufbau Bank (KFW), TA's biggest creditor, of up to 24 per cent of the total shares. TA gained US$150 million from this transaction to repay its unendorsed loaners. The due date for endorsed creditors was accordingly postponed.

As a result of this debt restructuring, TA was able to reduce its total debt to 5,505,000 million baht.[36] Also in 1997, TA underwent a major reorganization through the establishment of Telecom Holding Company Limited (THC) to replace TA as the main company, giving TA the opportunity to carry out the standard phone concession of 2.6 million numbers more easily.

However, negotiations over debt structural reforms alone were insufficient to relieve TA from the 1997 debt crisis, and a number of other measures were also implemented. CP Group had to trade away its shares in minor overseas companies in order to preserve core assets such as TA. The need for CP to create new alliances was clearly seen when the cable TV service UBC, a merger between CP's former UTV and Shin Corp's IBC, was officially launched in May 1998. The 1998 merger between the cable television operations of Shin Corp and CP indicated the nature of the strategic alliance between the two groups. Wingfield stresses that Thai Rak Thai and CP formed a 'new powerful political and business alliance' after the economic crisis: 'Not only does this represent an alliance between old and new capital, but it may have profound implications for the concentration of capital and political power at the next general election'.[37] Among the co-founders of Thai Rak Thai was a son-in-law of CP founder Dhanin.[38]

Apart from the UBC merger, the 1999 launch of PCT, a mobile standard phone service, was also another source of income which helped improve TA's financial standing. Indeed, despite its enormous debts, TA has been increasingly involved in telecommunications businesses. Apart from its core landline phone service – based on a fibre-optic cable network covering greater Bangkok – TA has also ventured into the mobile phone sector. Since June 2001, CP has acquired a 41 per cent share in TA Orange Co., Ltd., which has been granted a concession from the Communications Authority of Thailand to operate GSM 1800 mobile phone services, thus giving TA a 'full set' stake in both landline and mobile phone services. Yet negotiations with creditors and the company's painful restructuring meant that TA experienced a total of five years of post-crisis hardship. TA had to expend considerable time, money and energy to clear up its debts, allowing major rival Shin Corp to leave it far behind.

TT&T-JASMINE INTERNATIONAL

TT&T-Jasmine International, yet another gigantic telecommunications corporation, was also confronted with equally troubled times after the 1997 crisis. TT & T was a consortium led by Jasmine International (JI) and the Loxley Group. In 1992, TT & T won the bid to set up and provide a landline phone service of one million numbers outside Bangkok; this was increased to 500,000 more numbers in 1995.

TT & T began negotiating to restructure its debts in July 1998 with the Debt Restructuring Commission under the supervision of the Bank of Thailand. The company's debt restructuring plan was approved in December 2000, with debts estimated at 95 per cent of the total amount, but was not successfully implemented. The company therefore had to present an alternative plan to the Central Bankruptcy Court in December 2001. The Court approved an agreement to reform TT&T's debt structure totaling 48,453 million baht (see Table 2.2), details of which can be summarized as follows:

- Half of the company's debts were in US dollars.
- 4,000 million baht were due to the Telephone Organization of Thailand (TOT), including the delinquent concession fee.
- Another 25,000 million baht were due to Krung Thai Bank, Credit Lyonnais Bank and Sumitomo Bank. Almost 8,000 million baht were due to the contributors of telecommunications equipment, such as Ericsson and Alcatel.
- The company was to release new common stocks valued at 5,000 million baht. At least 3,000 million baht would be raised in cash, which the company would use to buy back its shares within two and a half years.

In May 2001, TT&T announced the details of its capital expansion plan by increasing authorized capital from 11,250 million baht to 70,000 million baht, calculated as 5,860 million capital expansion stocks. Crucially, however, details of a proposed new business alliance through which 3,760 million newly-released shares were to be offered remained unknown. The company spent more than two years seeking new partners to avoid the possible allocation of the new 3,760 million stocks to the current creditors, which would result in the current creditors over-holding stocks and the threat that the current TT & T shareholders could become a minority. However, this search was abandoned in 2004, when TT & T announced that the process was deterring potential partners.[39]

This is where another problem compounded the initial one. During the time that the company was offering its stocks to its new alliance, parliament passed the Telecommunications Business Act, which limited foreign shareholders to a maximum 25 per cent stake. Consequently, TT & T has not been able to find an alliance to acquire its stocks.[40] TT & T's debt restructuring has proved more difficult and more complex than that of UCOM and TA. While UCOM and TA negotiated restructuring directly with their creditors, TT & T restructured its debt with the Commission under the direction of the Bank of Thailand, and consequently had to appear in the Bankruptcy Court. Moreover, TT & T has still not been able to form a new alliance, because of concerns by foreign firms over the implications of the Telecommunications Business Act. At the same time, the company's current stockholders – Loxley, Jasmine, Italian Thai Development and Phatra Thanakit – were all confronted by the effects of the economic crisis simultaneously, and were all preoccupied with trying to resolve their own problems.

SHIN CORPORATION

Shin Corporation was able narrowly to escape the worst impacts of the 1997 crisis compared to other companies in the Big Four. The three major companies of the group – Shin Corp, Advance Info Service (AIS) and Shin Satellite – had liabilities estimated at 50,800 million baht, 23,373 million baht and 12,927 million baht respectively (see Table 2.2). The total foreign debts of the three companies amounted to approximately 30,000 million baht. It was rumoured that, shortly before the devaluation of the baht on 2 July 1997, Shin Corp had considerable foreign debts, but some debts in US dollars were repaid before their due time.[41] The key to Thaksin's successful weathering of the crisis was that he was largely unaffected by the baht devaluation. As Wingfield argues:

> He had hedged nearly 70 per cent of his group's foreign currency exposure prior to the baht devaluation, leading the Democrat Party to suggest that he had been tipped off by the then Finance Minister, Thanong Bidhya, who he is known to have had a close relationship with (*The Nation,* 27/9/97).

After leaving the government, Thanong was appointed to Shin Corp's internal audit committee, further fuelling speculation about collusion (*Far Eastern Economic Review*, 10/8/00). The price of Shinawatra's telecom shares also rose dramatically just prior to the baht flotation.[42]

Pasuk and Baker also point out that key advisor Bokhin Polakun faced accusations in a subsequent parliamentary no-confidence debate that he had leaked news of the impending devaluation to Thaksin, accusations he firmly denied.[43] In 2001, Shin Corp publicly announced that it had only 92 million dollars or 4,100 million baht of debt remaining (Document on Prefered Share Offering Shin Corporation Plc. 2002: 6).

Being burdened with fewer debts during the economic crisis had a crucial impact on the future of the Shin Corporation Group as well as the structure of the economy, politics and the telecommunications business in Thailand in the post-crisis era. The owners and executives of Shin Corp did not have to waste time or other resources to resolve enormous debts as in the case of the other members of the Big Four. At the same time, Shin Corp's executives also decided to present a new strategy in the telecommunications business, which propelled Shin Corp to an advantageous position over the other three giant companies. According to Wingfield, the economic crisis left the CP group in better shape than before, as a result of the group's rapid restructuring. The same was true of Thaksin:

> Similarly, Thaksin used the crisis as an opportunity to expand his stable of companies and build up a network of political patronage. In 1998, his investment company, the SC Asset Group, spent 7 billion baht acquiring a range of companies involved in property, retail, publishing, leasing and management (*The Nation* 8/6/98). A year later Thaksin came to the aid of the Thai Military Bank, bailing out the interests of senior figures in the military and his colleague Thanong Bidhya (*Far Eastern Economic Review*, 28/12/00–4/1/01).

In 1999, Shinawatra Group changed its name to Shin Corporation for two major reasons. The first was the need clearly to distinguish Police Lieutenant Colonel Thaksin Shinawatra, who had become actively involved in politics, from the telecommunications group;[44] second, the need to reform the Group's structure to strengthen and to stabilize the business. Subsequently, it also proceeded to buy other telecommunications businesses deemed important to the Group in general. Thai Rak Thai positioned itself as the party of domestic capital which had suffered during the crisis, while the Democrats were painted as the party that had defended the banking sector and signed up to the dictates of the international financial institutions.

From the business point of view, 2000 was an important year for Shin Corp to take over important enterprises. First, it bought 39 per cent of the shares in iTV, which had been operating a UHF TV station. Next was the purchase of a 46 per cent share in Samart Group's Digital Phone Company (DPC). This led to a new business alliance with Telekom Malaysia Bhd – a Malaysian telecommunications corporation which held a 49.99 per cent share in DPC. Consequently, Shin Corp Group could control the management of both companies, despite being a minority shareholder. In December 2000, Tele Info Media Co., Ltd., the telephone book publisher in Shin Corp Group, became allied with Singtel Yellow Pages Pte., a move which helped Shin adopt new technology for its internet and e-commerce businesses. During 2000, Advance Info Service Co., Ltd. (AIS) had set up GSM 2 watt networks covering 795 districts throughout the country, as well as developing its market by introducing Wireless Application Protocol (WAP) and International Roaming (IR), covering six continents, 74 countries and 156 networks.

2000 also marked a golden year for Shin Satellite, when Thailand launched its first broadband internet portal site by agreement with equipment suppliers.[45] Shin Corp also established a terminal for the new satellite iPSTAR worth 390 million US dollars,[46] which had the ability to provide extensive service covering several countries such as China, Korea, Japan, Taiwan, the Philippines, Australia, Indonesia,

Malaysia, India and Thailand.[47] 2001 saw another important step for Shin Corp Group when AIS purchased a 97.54 per cent share in DPC, which paved the way for AIS to become the first company in Thailand to operate two mobile phone service systems.

In October 2001, Shin Corp increased the number of iTV shares from the Siam Commercial Bank from 39 per cent to 64 per cent. As a result, Shin Corp gained control of 77.5 per cent of the shares. By the end of 2001, Shin Corp Group established iTV as its major provider of wireless and internet service for the future. Yet Shin Corp's new strategy went far beyond the takeover of iTV, but was also based on a range of new investments, both domestically and regionally.

CREATION OF THE NATIONAL TELECOMMUNICATIONS COMMISSION

The events of May 1992 triggered a wave of criticism of the extent to which control of media, especially electronic media, continued to be dominated by a small number of state agencies and private owners. There was a growing demand for new ways of ensuring a diversification of media ownership and more open access to information. One tangible outcome of these pressures was the establishment of iTV as an independent source of news-based television; a second outcome was Article 40 of the 1997 constitution, which ordained the creation of two new independent bodies: the National Telecommunication Commission and the National Broadcasting Authority. While the NBA was charged with regulating media, especially electronic media, the NTC had the all-important task of setting the rules of the game for Thailand's complex and lucrative telecommunications industry. In theory, these bodies were supposed to override the previous cultures that had seen telecommunications policy politicized by the influence of the Big Four Telecom groups. Members of the NTC were to be drawn from a range of groups: government officials, media representatives, the telecommunications industry, academics, religious groups, cultural groups and NGO representatives. Once a provisional list of fourteen candidates had been produced, a final list of seven was to be determined by the supposedly non-partisan Senate. The creation of the NTC posed a significant challenge to Shin Corp and other telecoms groups: an unsympathetic or outright hostile NTC could block or curtail a group's business opportunities.

The result was that numerous people closely affiliated with telecoms companies or associated interests sought election to the NTC, thereby politicizing the selection process. The initial selection process begun under the Chuan government in 1999 was badly flawed; half of the names of those selected were leaked to the newspapers in advance. It quickly became clear that the NTC would be in the hands of a group of former government officials involved in the telecommunications sector. At the beginning of 2003, the Administrative Court declared the selection process null and void. Yet when a new board of the NTC was announced at the end of the year, it still contained the names of many figures from the original list. More than half had connections with major telecommunications groups. Especially noticeable were Rienchai Riawilaisuk, a former deputy director of the posts and telegraphs department, and Professor Prasit Prapinmongkolkarn of the Faculty of Engineering, Chulalongkorn University and former advisor to the Democrat Minister of Transport and Telecommunications, Suthep Thueksuban. Dr Prasit was the author of research concerning the framework of telecommunications signals decoding, which had been criticized and opposed by the Thailand Development Research Institute.[48] Other members included Goson Pesawan, deputy head of the National Association of Telecommunications of Thailand and former board member of Telecom Asia; Setaporn Khusipitak, former director general of the posts and telegraphs department; and Direk Charoenpon, former deputy director of the TOT and former deputy minister at the Transport and Communications ministry in the Chavalit government, who was criticized as a stooge for Thai Rak Thai. The selection process for the NTC proved a serious challenge for the Senate – a challenge which it failed. Far from acting as an impartial and transparent arbiter dedicated to the public good, the Senate demonstrated that it had been captured by vested telecoms interests.

DOMESTIC SPHERE: TELECOMMUNICATIONS BUSINESS AND SHARE INCOME

The convergence of Thaksin Shinawatra's telecommunications businesses began with the takeover of iTV. This venture signalled a controversial new departure for the group, provoking a bitter conflict between Thaksin, his political rivals, the media and democratic activists. For Thaksin's opponents, the iTV takeover signalled an overt desire to control news content and output and to silence critical voices in the electronic media – something he always strongly denied. In fact, Thaksin's vision for Shin Corp's expansion from 'pure' telecommunications to the entertainment and media business was not about diversifying from one line of business to the other, but about converging telecommunications, the media, television, radio and distant visual broadcasting. If successful, Shin Corp would be the first and only Thai company to operate on such a scale. This decisive convergence strategy was brought about both through Thaksin's own grandiose personal dreams and by renewed pressures created by a new regulatory framework for the telecommunications business introduced in the wake of the 1997 constitution. Most importantly, the political power of Thaksin Shinawatra, both before and after becoming prime minister, was a vital factor in bringing about and ensuring the success of this project. By adopting this new strategy, once the new post-reform rules of the telecommunications business were applied, Shin Corp could sustain its growth ahead of any other rivals in Thailand.

The takeover of the television station iTV was initiated when the station was suffering significant losses in the year 2000. For that reason, Siam Commercial Bank – the major shareholder at the time – sought a new investor in order to reduce its percentage of shares and to sustain its role only as a creditor of iTV. Among many other foreign media corporations, Shin Corp was the only Thai company determined to purchase iTV's stocks. The deal was settled in June 2000. Shin Corp acquired 39 per cent of the stocks for 1,600 million baht.[49] Shin Corp's takeover of iTV at that time also stemmed from political reasons and coincided with Thaksin Shinawatra's rise to power. It signified his negative attitude towards the rights and freedom of the media.[50] The takeover of Thailand's only independent television station, which was accompanied by the dismissal of its most critical and outspoken reporters, corresponded with Shinawatra's acquisition of power before the general elections. Thai Rak Thai had claimed that iTV, and most especially the Nation Group – which was responsible for producing news programmes for the station – had a negative attitude towards the new prime minister. Two major producers of programming for iTV – the Nation Group and the Watchdog Group – were subsequently ditched.

Following the takeover by Shin Corp, iTV enjoyed a better performance. In 2002, iTV had a total income of 1,467 million baht, increasing by 535 million baht from the previous year. In other words, its income rose by 57 per cent, from 932 million baht in 2001 (iTV Annual Report, 2002). Thanks to this growth, the company posted operating profits of 482 million baht, almost ten times more than the 47 million baht profit posted for the year 2001. However, the annual concession fees iTV is obliged to pay the government means that the company has posted a net deficit for several consecutive years. In 2002, when subtracting all expenses and concession fees, the company showed a 770 million baht deficit, decreasing from 979 million baht in 2001.

Once Thaksin's political ambition to own his own television station had been achieved, iTV became the first step in the Group's convergence process. Shin Corp was also able to make money on the stock market through this acquisition: iTV was registered on the Stock Exchange in 2002. GMM Media, Grammy Entertainment's second company, also entered the stock market in November that same year. RS Promotion, the second listing in the entertainment and recreation sector, was registered in May 2003. Two other cinema and film license owners – Major Cineplex Group and EGV Enter-

Table 2.3: Shin Corporation performance 1998–2002 (millions of baht)

Performance		1998	1999	2000	2001	2002
Shin Corp.	Assets	22,432.25	24,368.43	37,879.10	41,356.50	51,248.94
	Income	12,935.31	16,445.51	10,681.58	12,391.78	14,876.20
	Net profits	-1,407.62	10,104.73	2,384.14	2,820.19	5,281.43
AIS	Assets	38,079.39	39,864.16	59,169.96	113,538.39	126,085.37
	Income	17,449.47	25,872.69	39,729.64	60,738.03	81,366.36
	Net profits	1,446.52	2,750.06	6,598.95	3,851.32	11,430.30
Shin Sat.	Assets	10,233.62	10,402.41	11,831.62	14,376.57	20,307.27
	Income	2,375.32	2,909.92	4,016.50	5,161.40	5,430.47
	Net profits	2,508.71	263.18	710.54	1,563.15	1,410.52
iTV	Assets	3,981.26	3,205.96	3,198.33	2,942.34	3,308.97
	Income	815.23	904.04	1,203.18	931.90	1,467.14
	Net profits	-336.71	-768.60	-775.85	-979.18	-770.15
Total	Assets	74,726.52	77,840.96	112,079.01	172,213.80	200,950.55
	Income	33,575.33	46,132.16	55,630.90	79,223.11	103,140.17
	Net profits	2,210.90	12,349.37	8,917.78	7,255.48	17,352.10
Growth %	Assets		4.17	43.98	53.65	16.69
	Income		37.40	20.59	42.41	30.19
	Net profits		458.57	-27.79	-18.64	139.16

Source: Shin Corporation Annual Reports

tainment Company Limited – entered in May 2002 and May 2003 respectively.[51]

Between 2002 and 2003, TV and radio stations, producers, cinema owners, film license holders and the producers and sales representatives of films in VDO, VCD and DVD formats paraded in to register their businesses on the stock exchange, moves that brought enormous profits to members of the Shinawatra Family, the Group's executives and several prominent members of the Thai Rak Thai Party. Among the beneficiaries were Thaksin's only son – Panthongtae Shinawatra – Panthongtae's uncle, Payup Shinawatra, Boonklee Plungsiri, Shin Corp's Executive President, and the Malinont family, whose head – Pracha – served as Deputy Minister of Interior in the Thaksin government. Moreover, Pracha also purchased 300,000 worth of IPO stocks from MIDA Assets.[52]

Pracha and his family, which also owns the Channel 3 TV Station, gained more IPO stocks than any other investors. The five other companies that purchased MIDA Asset's IPO stocks were mostly in the entertainment or mass communication business, such as Major Cineplex, RS Promotion, Asset Plus, Finanza Finance and GMM Media. But the Malinont family was the major purchaser of MIDA Asset's 1.7 million stocks. Within 19 months of the initial offering, the family gained profits estimated at more than 24 million baht from their 38.73 million baht investment. Almost all of the profits derived from the investment in Major Cineplex.[53]

The convergence of telecommunications and TV stations is still in its initial stages. But profits from the stock market – both from the registration of Shin Corp's secondary companies in the market and from the IPO stocks in the entertainment and recreation sector – are a major new source of revenue, demonstrating that Shin Corp Group does not rely on making profits from the telecommunications business. Shin Corp has been trying to avoid limitations within the telecommunications business, which has faced increased obstructions due to internal and external competition. At the same time, the Group is also penetrating the international market through its satellite business. This move has also been aided through Thaksin's visionary emphasis on foreign affairs and diplomacy.

SHIN CORP'S INTERNATIONAL REACH

While other Thai telecommunications groups have withdrawn from regional markets to concentrate on their domestic businesses, Shin Corp continues to pursue a range of business opportunities in the wider Asian region. Shin is not yet a major regional player, yet the capacity of the company to achieve a degree of success in a range of Asian markets testifies to Shin Corp's combination of boldness, tenacity and effective networking

Although Shin Satellite Public Company Limited (SATTEL) has had a customer base in China since 1996, the original number of customers was not significant. In 1999, however, Shin Satellite started marketing the new iPSTAR satellite. This new broadband satellite had the potential and capacity finally to penetrate the Chinese market, which had become the first customer of the iPSTAR project in 2003.[54] Meanwhile, Shin Corp had also been doing business in India since 1997. Clients include public sector bodies such as the Department of Space (DOS), Department of Telecoms (DOT), Doordarshan National TV, Software Technology Park of India (STPI) and a range of private sector customers as well as 30 other TV channels all over the country. Thanks to these clients, SATTEL enjoys the status of being the biggest foreign satellite communication service provider in the Indian market (SATTEL, 2002). Perhaps most surprisingly of all, SATTEL is a major Thai investor that has had access into Burma's market since 1998. The company's customers are Myanmar Posts and Telecommunications (MPT), and Myanmar Radio and Television (MRTV), both of which are public sector entities (SATTEL, 2002).

The regional experience of Thaksin Shinawatra and Shin Corp Group closely corresponds with recent changes in the political economy of the region, especially since Thailand's major reform of foreign policy under the leadership of Chatichai Choonhavan (1988–91). Chatichai had famously called for the ideological pre-occupations of the Indochina conflict to be laid to rest, and replaced by a determination to 'turn the battlefield into a market place'. Coinciding with economic liberalization in Vietnam and Cambodia, Chatichai's policy shift had given the green light for Thai investors to explore business opportunities in the sub-region. Thaksin Shinawatra and Shin Corp became pioneers in Cambodia's TV business from the early 1990s, and Thaksin himself got to know many of Cambodia's top political leaders.[55] However, negotiations were not initially very successful, and their business strategies were adjusted to meet the changing circumstances. The Group invested in the mobile phone market in Cambodia and gained incredibly substantial profits from a country with such a poor economy as Cambodia, whereas other competitors were unsuccessful in the region and were forced to withdraw. For example, Sondthi Limthongkul's Manager Group – which was also granted a concession by the Laotian government – went bankrupt when the economic crisis took place in 1997. Loxley Group and Jasmine International entered the Philippine and Indonesian markets during the Chatichai era but the group's investments crashed, again partly because of the economic crisis. Few Thai telecommunication companies proved able to weather the 1997 crisis to continue their programmes of expansion into Indochina.[56]

SATTEL is Shin's telecommunication company operating in Cambodia under the name of CAMSHIN,[57] covering transmission networks for Digital GSM 1800 MHz mobile phone service. Launched in April 1998,[58] CAMSHIN now has 110,000 subscribers, ranked second in Cambodia in terms of its market share. The company's popularity is steadily growing, challenging CAMGSM, Cambodia's foremost mobile phone service provider – believed to be owned by Cambodia's political leaders[59] – with 250,000 subscribers. This is because CAMSHIN offers comparatively cheap monthly fees and some technical advantages, as well as providing phone rental services in many tourist attractions, such as Phnom Penh, Siem Reap and along the Thai-Cambodian border. It was estimated that in 2003, CAMSHIN would have 24 million US dollars net income and 3 million US dollars net profit, increasing from approximately 18 million US dollars in the previous year.[60]

After becoming prime minister, Thaksin revised Thailand's policies towards the rest of Southeast Asia. At the same time, a remarkable wave of new investment in the region's telecommunication market also took place, especially in three important markets: China, Burma and India. Thus the Prime Minister's official visits have also paved a diplomatic path to introduce Shin Corp into these countries. More interesting is the new large-scale project in the region – iPSTAR – a satellite which will play an important role in linking the domestic and regional convergence of telecommunication and media sectors.

The Thaksin government also promotes regionalist policies emphasizing three aspects of cooperation between Asian countries; a) collaboration with China and the 'Asia for Asians mindset' (February 2001); b) Asian Cooperation Dialogue (ACD) (February 2002); and c) promoting Free Trade Areas (FTA) for bilateral relations with key trading partners such as Australia.[61] Thaksin's government has long tried to combine the business requirements of the private sector and the need for investment in the Asian region. This combination from when Thaksin was still primarily a businessman was strengthened at the time when he established his Thai Rak Thai Party (July 1998), and was further consolidated when he became prime minister. At the time of setting up his party, Thaksin told Zhu Rongji – then prime minister of China – that if Thai Rak Thai won the election and he became prime minister, Asians should rewrite the rules of the game and give preferential treatment to Asian businesses and investors. The Thai tycoon also claimed that China's Prime Minister was quite impressed by his proposals at the time.

This Asia-centred regionalist policy, together with an emphasis on boosting the private sector, bore fruit as Thaksin, in his capacity as prime minister, paid official visits to the following Asian countries: Burma (19–20 June 2001), China (27–29 August 2001) and India (26–29 November 2001 and 1 February 2002).[62] Also relevant was Lieutenant-General Khin Nyunt's visit to Thailand from 3–5 September 2001.

THE ROAD TO BURMA

Thaksin Shinawatra's visit to Burma, which took place during 19–20 June 2001, was the first of its kind by a Thai prime minister. His predecessor, Chuan Leekpai, had consistently refused to visit the country. Thaksin's visit underscored vast differences between the previous and current Thai government's policy towards Burma. The policy of the Chuan Leekpai government emphasized democratic development and human rights promotion in Burma, whereas Prime Minister Thaksin began with a 'good neighbours' policy. His visit took place amidst a host of conflicts between the two nations regarding minority groups, narcotics and drugs, fishing territories and confrontation along the border.

The Prime Minister's first brief visit yielded unexpectedly positive results. Lieutenant-General Khin Nyunt visited Thailand from 3–5 September 2001 as a gesture of reciprocal courtesy following the Thai leader's May 2001 visit to Rangoon.[63] This visit was very significant in the complicated relations between Thailand and Burma, since none of Burma's leaders had set foot in Thailand for 11 years. This thaw in relations also proved beneficial to SATTEL. In May 2002, SATTEL signed a service and procurement contract for purchasing a complete iPSTAR system package.[64]

Bagan Cybertech IDC and Teleport Company Limited are under the supervision of semi-governmental Bagan Cybertech Company Limited (BCT). Its CEO, Dr Ye Naing Win, is the owner of Maykha Group and the youngest son of Lieutenant-General Khin Nyunt.[65] The contract between the two companies was signed at Miet Pat in Rangoon, in the presence of Khin Nyunt as Chairman of Myanmar Computer Technology Development Council Secretary-1 of the State Peace and Development Council.[66] This contract comprised two major parts:

1. The installation of an iPSTAR ground station.
2. The extension of the period of ThaiCOM lease for another five years, including the change from C-Band transponders to Ku-Band transponders, which also support broadcasting.

The installation of a ground system for iPSTAR is composed of a central gateway in Rangoon, which was supposed to have been completed in the third quarter of 2002, and another 5,000 terminals throughout the country, all of which will be completed in 2004. This will provide broadband internet access and communication services. When the contract is completed, the two corporations will also encourage Burma to set up the project's service operators throughout the country, like Thailand's District Internet.

SATTEL helped ensure the success of its plans through developing a close relationship with the semi-governmental ICT Company, closely associated with Burma's political leaders. It was also in charge of installing iPSTAR's communication system and providing exteneded periods of training for 20 IT officers from Myanmar Post and Tele-communications (MPT) and from BCT. The company was paid 15 million US dollars for this project.[67] During the training, the officers also carried out internships at Shinawatra Building III in Bangkok.[68]

This example illustrates that Thaksin's avenues of diplomacy under the concept of 'Asians for Asians' involve much more than the use of diplomacy to reduce tensions between neighbouring countries like Thailand and Burma. It also involves the integration of large-scale investments by SATTEL. Official diplomacy policies helped pave the way for negotiations as well as for the pre-sale and promotion of iPSTAR, a satellite which has not yet orbited.[69] Moreover, Burma offers a new market for telecommunications, which covers basic services throughout the country and links educational, business and especially the banking and public operations together.[70] The pene-tration of this new market in Burma resembles SATTEL's earlier entry into the wireless phone service in Cambodia, which was closely linked to General Chatichai's Indochina policy.

A PASSAGE TO INDIA

During his first year in office, Prime Minister Thaksin Shinawatra twice visited India within a short period of time. The first visit took place on 26–29 November 2001, while the other was a one-day visit on 1 February 2002. The November trip marked the first official visit by a Thai prime minister to India in 12 years. Significantly, Thaksin decided to stop first in Bangalore, India's Silicon Valley – where the country's Space Research Organization is located[71] – before moving on to meet India's political leaders in the capital, New Delhi.

This visit to India was not a mere coincidence, because India was a major business interest of Shin Corp. In the past, Shin Corp had faced certain problems in India. The Corporation had entered the Indian market in the early 1990s, when the Indian government started liberalizing the telecommunications sector; however, Shin was unsuccessful in expanding its investment. Later on, it attempted another investment in the country by establishing a new company, HFCL, which was granted various licenses to operate paging services, standard phone services and mobile phone services in many provinces in India. Faced with the task of having to pay high license fees, the company failed to meet the requisite terms and conditions and was finally forced to relinquish all the licenses it had been assigned. Part of the problem was that the introduction of mobile phone services in the market also gradually forced paging into extinction.[72] Shin Corp thus had no choice but to give up its shares in HFCL.

Shin Corp returned to India's telecommunications market in the late 1990s through the satellite business. The failure of INSAT, India's two satellites, forced the government's Space Research Organization to seek another satellite with sufficient regional bandwidth. SATTEL's ThaiCOM was considered suitable for the project. During the early period, the Indian Space Research Organization therefore leased seven transponders from ThaiCOM, later adding a further ten.

The first lease began in August 1998 and expired in March 2000. In December 1999, India's government decided to extend the period of contract for another six months from March 2000. This decision was brought about by India's Prime Minister Shri Atal Bihari Vajpayee, who was also the chairman of the Department of Space (DOS) under the Space Research Organization.[73] SATTEL's market share in India has since significantly increased, and DOS has consistently expanded its usage in terms of both quantity and duration. Apart from DOS, other customers in the South Asian Region are India's private TV stations, which broadcast programmes to the networks via satellite, Cable TV and national stations of Pakistan, Bangladesh and the Maldives respectively. Also important is the internet service provided through these satellite networks, which has one of the highest numbers of subscribers in the South Asian region. The capability of ThaiCOM satellites has gained an excellent reputation in the subcontinent. SATTEL is a satellite communication service provider with one of the largest market shares in India. ThaiCOM also transmits the highest numbers of local TV channels on three ThaiCOM satellites. Thus, this satellite network has the largest audience in Asia today.[74]

However, Shin Corp's successes in India came under threat at the beginning of 2002. On 24 January, India's DOS succeeded in launching into orbin Insat-3C, India's own new satellite, intended for national TV and telecommunications broadcasting. For this reason, the Thai premier's one-day visit did not come as a surprise. The purpose of his visit was to save the Group's biggest market share in Asia's satellite business when the Indian government decided not to renew the lease with ThaiCOM III when it expired in March 2002. This decision caused SATTEL's stock price to decline by 7 per cent on 29 January 2002, the worst fall in 20 months. However, following Thaksin's February visit, on 18 March 2002, DOS released an official announcement that the lease with ThaiCOM III was to be extended by another six months.[75]

CONNECTING WITH CHINA

Although Thai prime ministers had not officially visited India for as long as 12 years, bilateral relations with China had long been considered extremely important. Since his days in business, Thaksin Shinawatra had shown a keen interest in China's telecommunications market. He had also made contact with Thai-Chinese businessmen who were already operating in China. But Shin Corp had made little headway there, because China already had its own satellite, Apstar1-A, whose orbit also conflicted with SATTEL's ThaiCOM III. This conflict was beyond the scope of the private sector to resolve. Shin Corp therefore needed to depend on negotiations at the governmental level, which began in 1993 (during Chuan Leekpai's first term in office) and continued through Banharn Silpa-archa's term (1995 to 1996) and during Chavalit Yongchaiyudh's term in 1997.

On every official visit to China, government leaders always brought up the satellite issue for discussion, since this was considered important to bilateral relations.[76] However, the conflict over the orbits remained unresolved until after Thaksin himself became prime minister. Negotiations on the satellite issue were an agenda item for the meetings between Thaksin and the Chinese government on his official visit from 27 to 29 August 2001. Also discussed was the possible collision in the future between China's AsiaSat4 and SATTEL's iPSTAR, which were scheduled to be launched in the middle of 2002 and at the end of 2003 respectively.[77] But in the end Prime Minister Thaksin cancelled these discussions, and left the negotiations to the Post and Telegraphs Department of Thailand instead.[78]

Back when Thaksin first founded the Thai Rak Thai Party, he regarded China as a very important nation. During a trip he made as Thai Rak Thai party leader, he proposed the idea of 'Asians for Asians' to then Prime Minister Zhu Rongji. After becoming prime minister, he advocated this idea once again at the 2001 Fortune Global Forum held in Hong Kong in May 2001.[79] This indicates that the Thai premier has long been interested in China and has had many opportunities to meet with China's influential political leaders.

Eventually, the politics and diplomacy of the Thai government with Thaksin Shinawatra at the helm brought about some benefits to SATTEL's telecommunications business. In July 2001, SATTEL revamped 5 per cent of its shares and leased 20 per cent of iPSTAR's total transponders to the China Railway Communication Asia Pacific (CRC-AP), the country's telecommunication public enterprise, in advance. This stock restructuring and transponder leasing marked a significant turning point because CRC-AP had in effect become iPSTAR's first major client in China. Now that iPSTAR has become an asset of both nations, with the Chinese government as a major shareholder, the conflict over possible orbit collision between Chinese and Thai satellites has finally been resolved.[80]

CONCLUSION

Thaksin Shinawatra's telecommunications business vividly illustrated the potent interplay between power and profit in Thailand. Shin Corp, AIS, Shin Satellite and iTV posted impressive results after 1997: assets grew by 16.69 per cent, income grew by 30.19 per cent, net profits increased by 139.6 per cent.[81] The excellent profits and the rapid growth of the company were not solely a result of Shin Corp's relatively low debt levels following the crisis. But before becoming PM, Thaksin was just one player among the Big Four Telecoms group, which had to compete for concessions and benefits with his other competitors. The highly fluid nature of multi-party coalition governments during this period meant that business conditions were very uncertain. Telecom companies had to contend with, and creatively adapt to, frequent changes in the ministers overseeing the Communications and Finance ministries. These changes were accompanied by constant shifts at the level of both policy and implementation in the telecommunications sector. Yet once Thaksin created a political party and became prime minister in a very stable and centralized government, his position completely changed. Thaksin went from being one player among the Big Four Telecoms group to a figure with considerable powers to determine the rules of the political and business game in Thailand.

Once Thaksin became prime minister, and headed a government where Thai Rak Thai controlled a majority in parliament, Shin Corp experienced remarkable growth and a high degree of net profits. The market naturally had confidence in the standing of a telecom company in which the prime minister's family held shares; and Thaksin also appointed loyal adjutants to the posts of Communications minister – heading the newly created Ministry of Information, Communications and Technology – and minister of finance. Wingfield argues that Pitak Intrawityanunt, who served as deputy prime minister in Thaksin's first cabinet, was there as a stooge for the interests of CP, and notes that Adisai Bodharamik, his first commerce minister, was the founder of Jasmine International and a former TOT official.[82]

Capitalizing on the mood of economic nationalism following the end of the IMF programme and the landslide election of Thai Rak Thai, in November 2001 the Thaksin government announced restrictions on foreign ownership in the telecommunications sector. The Telecommunications Services Act created a 25 per cent ceiling on foreign stakes in Thai telecoms companies. This provision left Shin Corp unscathed, but had a substantial impact on rival companies, notably Telecom Asia, in which Orange then held a 49 per cent stake.[83] Thaksin came in for heavy domestic criticism over this move, which explicitly singled out the telecoms sector, apparently reflecting his own special interest in this area. His government failed to address parallel concerns from small retailers over the remarkable expansion of foreign-controlled supermarket chains, such as Tesco Lotus and Carrefour. The new Act also coincided with sharp falls in foreign investment, and in July 2002 the limits on foreign ownership of telecoms companies were rescinded. This policy flip-flop appears to suggest two ambiguities at the heart of Thaksin's thinking. The first involved a love-hate relationship with foreign capital, which Thaksin dreamed of curtailing, but in reality was reliant upon. The second involved an ambiguous approach to his business competitors, on the one hand seeking to weaken them and on the other hand always amenable to cutting them some slack.

The new president of the Stock Exchange of Thailand, Wijit Supinit, was another Thaksin loyalist, who had been an advisor to the premier before his appointment to this post on 1 August 2003.[84] Three new Shin companies were registered on the SET without any problem in the months that followed his appointment: iTV, M Link and SC Assets.

In the period of Thaksin's premiership, Shin Corp had a business strategy to leap ahead of rival telecom companies. Shin Corp did not diversify from telecoms to other forms of business, but sought to bring together telecoms, media, television, radio and long-range satellite broadcasting. In December 2003, iTV boosted the number of stocks it offered on the stock exchange from 6300 million baht to 7,800 million baht. A new shareholder, well known Channel 3 presenter Traipop Limphapat, took on a 10 per cent stake, and the Kanthana Group a further 10 per cent. At the same time, iTV also announced that they would offer more entertainment programmes to increase their business competitiveness,[85] to fit in with the company's plan to launch the new iPSTAR satellite, which would come into service in 2004.

To consolidate the telecoms, media, TV and radio and long-range broadcasting businesses more efficiently, an ombudsman who was appointed on the request of iTV concerning the reduction of the license fees payable to the state, decided in February 2004 on two important issues: 1) to amend the 44 per cent representative fee to 6.5 per cent, and reduce the guaranteed minimum representative fee from the present level to that of Channel 7, 230 million baht a year for the rest of the contract, and 2) to give the Office of the Perman-ent Secretary of the Prime Minister's Office the right to change the allocation of different types of programming for iTV, by reducing the number of documentaries and news programmes from 70 per cent to 50 per cent, and removing the existing restrictions on showing only knowledge-based programmes during prime time from 7 pm until 9.30 pm.[86] It seems rather a coincidence that all these favours done for iTV happened just before the increase in the stock-holding. This sequence of events was reminiscent of the support Shin Satellite received in the case of the iPSTAR satellite, which was granted an eight-year tax holiday with Board of Investment (BoI) support. Shin Sat received this favour at a time when the BoI was under a Minister of Industry, Suriya, who was Thai Rak Thai's secretary general and who came from Thaksin's inner circle. Both issues raised questions among political commentators concerning potential conflicts of interest.

The consolidation of telecoms, media, TV, radio and long-range broadcasting from 2001 onwards was a development specific to Shin Corp, arguably resulting from its influence over both rules and mechanisms, in terms both of politics and of the telecoms business.[87]

A similar consolidation strategy has not been followed by any other telecommunications company, and thus Shin Corp has left its old rivals – TA, UCOM and Jasmine – far behind. Shin Corp, through Shin Satellite, has been successful in simultaneously opening three large markets – India, China and Burma – reflecting Thaksin's active international policy as both a regionally-minded prime minister and telecommunications magnate. Official visits by Thaksin were frequently associated with the resolution of tricky business problems for Shin Corp. Thaksin's official visits to India led to an extension of Shin Corp's contract to provide satellite services to the Department of Space. Thaksin's official visit to China coincided with Shin Satellite's resolution of the decade-long issue of overlapping satellite footprints. Following Thaksin's official visit to Burma, Shin Satellite won the state concession to provide a basic nationwide telephone network, in collaboration with a semi-governmental Burmese agency, the major shareholder of whom was the son of a senior Burmese politician. None of Shin Corp's rivals could match such international successes. While the extent to which Thaksin's occupancy of Government House was responsible for Shin Corp's domestic and regional success was difficult to measure, there seemed little doubt that the two were intimately related.

At the same time, it would be highly misleading to suggest that after 1997 Shin Corp adopted a simple strategy of assuming market dominance, with the aim of squeezing out competition in the telecoms sector. Nothing is ever so simple. Rather, their strategy involved forming strategic alliances with other telecoms companies, especially Telecom Asia and Jasmine. Senior figures from these companies backed the formation of Thai Rak Thai and the creation of the Thaksin government, and were rewarded accordingly with government posts and with sympathetic treatment for their business activities. Thaksin used a strategy of informal mergers and acquisitions, in much the same way as he incorporated political parties such as New Aspiration into the government fold. It was not necessary for Shin Corp formally to control the entire telecoms sector, so long as Thai Rak Thai played a crucial mediating role in the nexus of connections between the sector and the state. As Dixon puts it: 'Thaksin and Thai Rak Thai appear to be increasingly exposed as representatives of the small group of Thai-Chinese corporations in which business power is becoming concentrated'.[88]

NOTES

1   Sorakon Adulyanon, *Thaksin Shinawatra: asawin khloen luk thi sam* [Thaksin Shinawatra, Knight of the Third Wave], Bangkok, Matichon, 1993, pp. 32–33.

2   Sorakon, *Thaksin Shinawatra*; Yingyord Machevisith, 'Still on very firm ground. Thailand's tycoons: winners and losers', *The Nation Mid-Year Review*, July 1998, p. 27.

3   The Thai computer industry became highly profitable in the early 1990s, averaging more than 20 per cent growth for several consecutive years; for a discussion see http://www.siam-star.com/computer4.html

4   In 1981, Thaksin and his wife Pojaman invested in a condominium project in Rajawat, Bangkok. The project involved the demolition of the Rajawat Theatre, which they bought using an 18-million-baht bank loan. The couple set up PT Corporation Company Limited, with Pojaman as the managing director. However, the company eventually went bankrupt with debts amounting to 50 million baht. Thanawat Suppaiboon, *26 nakthurakit chin phu mi prasoprakan* [26 Experienced Chinese Businessmen], Bangkok, Pimkum, 2003, p. 212.

5   Thanawat, *26 Experienced Chinese*, p. 212; Ukrist Pathmanand, 'The Thaksin Shinawatra Group: a study of the relationship between money and politics in Thailand', *The Copenhagen Journal of Asian Studies*, 13, 1998, pp. 67–68.

6   Ammar Siamwalla, *Thailand's Boom and Bust*, Bangkok, Thailand Development Research Institute, 1997, p. 37.

7   Gene Mesher and Thawatchai Jittrapanun, 'Thailand's long road to telecom reform', *ASEAN Economic Bulletin*, 21, 1, 2004.

8   Tom Wingfield, 'Democratization and economic crisis in Thailand', in Edmund Terence Gomez (ed.), *Political Business in East Asia*, London, Routledge, 2002, pp. 279–280.

9   Natthapong Thongpakdi, *General Agreement on Trade in Services (GATS) and The Thai Telecommunication Industry*, Bangkok, Thailand Development Research Institute,1996, p. 64.

10 For a relevant discussion, see Gene Mesher and Thawatchai Jitrapanun, 'Early telecom reform under Thaksin: Can Thailand meet its WTO commitment to liberalize by 2006?', paper presented at the ITS Biennial Conference, Seoul, 14-18 August 2002, http://www.its2002.or.kr/pdffiles/papers/199-Gene.pdf, especially pages 6–9.

11 The eight governments during this period were: 1. General Chatichai Choonhavan's government (1988–1991); 2. Anand Panyarachun's first government (February 1991–April 1992); 3. General Suchinda Kraprayoon's government (April–May 1992); 4. Anand Panyarachun's second government (June–September 1992); 5. Chuan Leekpai's first government (September 1992–July 1995); 6. Banharn Silpa-archa's government (July 1995–November 1996); 7. Chavalit Yongchaiyudh's government (November 1996–November 1997); and 8. Chuan Leekpai's second government (November 1997–February 2001).

12 Tom Wingfield, 'Democratization and economic crisis in Thailand', in Edmund Terence Gomez (ed.), *Political Business in East Asia*, London, Routledge, 2002, p. 267.

13 *Phujatkan*, 8 August 1996.

14 *Phujatkan*, 19 August 1996 and Table 2.1.

15 Nualnoi Treerat and Noppanan Wannathepsakul, *Setthasat kanmuang torakhomanakhom:kanpraesanan sampratan torakhomanakhom: phon prayot khong krai?* [The political economy of telecommunications: who benefits from the allocation of telecommunications concessions?], Bangkok, Political Economy Centre, Faculty of Economics, Chulalongkorn University, 2001, p. 20.

16 Information from interview, 4 February 2003.

17 Wingfield, 'Democratization', p. 280.

18 Wingfield, 'Democratization', p. 280.

19 New technology generally known as PHS (Personal Handy Phone) was launched in Thailand under the abbreviation PCT. PCT allows landline subscribers to receive calls on their landline numbers via portable handsets. Since PCT shares many characteristics of a mobile phone, arguably the concession should have been granted to mobile phone operators Shin Corp or UCOM instead. But the government claimed that PCT was an additional service based on a standard landline phone, and therefore TA and TT & T were awarded this concession (*Phujatkan*, 24 July 1996).

20 *The Nation*, 28 December 1995.This project was later aborted.

21 Julian Gearing, 'All out in China', *Asiaweek*, 29 August 1997.

22   James Ockey, 'Thailand: the struggle to redefine civil-military relations', in Mutiah Alagappa (ed.), *Coercion and Governance: The Declining Political Role of the Military in Asia*, Stanford, Stanford University Press, 2001.

23   For examples, TA was a good friend of Chulachomklao Military Academy Class 5 (the clique behind the 1991 military coup) and former prime minister General Prem Tinsulanond was appointed the honorary chairman of its parent company, the CP group. Air Chief Marshal Siddhi Savetsila, former head of the Social Action Party, was appointed their honorary consultant. Shin Corp was close to General Sunthorn Kongsompong, from Chulachomklao Military Academy Class 1, who was the former Supreme Commander and the chairman of the National Peace Keeping Council (NPKC), the formal body behind the 1991 coup.

24   Robert Cairns and Deunden Nikomborirak, 'An assessment of Thailand's new telecommunications plan', *Telecommunication Policy*, 22, 2, 1998, p. 150.

25   Cairns and Deunden, 'An assessment', p. 148.

26   Wingfield, 'Democratization', p. 280.

27   Kevin Hewison, 'Thailand's capitalism: development through boom and bust', in Garry Rodan et al. (eds), *The Political Economy of South-East Asia: Conflicts, Crises and Change*, Melbourne, Oxford University Press, 2001, p. 92.

28   Pasuk and Baker point out that many Thai commercial banks were taken over either by the state or foreign banks. Pasuk Phongphaichit and Chris Baker, *Thailand's Crisis*, Chiang Mai, Silkworm, 2000. Ukrist's work, on the other hand, argues that there was a recomposition of old shareholders and owners, especially during the major restructuring of these organizations. Ukrist Pathmanand, *Wikrit sethakit kap kanpraptua khong thanakan panit nai prateth thai* [Economic Crisis and the Adaptation of Commercial Banks in Thailand], Bangkok, Institute of Asian Studies, Chulalongkorn University, 2003.

29   Or the fourth time, if his three previous government roles are counted separately.

30   United Communications Industry plc, Annual Report 1999.

31   United Communications Industry plc, Annual Report, 1999.

32   United Communications Industry plc, Annual Report, 2000.

33   Telenor Asia Pte. Ltd. is a telecommunications enterprise owned by the Norwegian government whose investment is based in Singapore.

34 See http://www.cpthailand.com/webguest/faq.aspx

35 TelecomAsia Corporation Public Company Limited Annual Report, 1998 and 1999.

36 TelecomAsia Public Company Limited Annual Report, 2000.

37 Wingfield, 'Democratization', p. 276.

38 Wingfield, 'Democratization', p. 278.

39 *The Nation*, 4 February 2004.

40 This is also the reason why the company's former ally, Nippon Telegraph and Telephone (NTT), hesitated to increase its stake in TT&T.

41 See *Thaicoon*, January 1999. The exact amount of the Group's US dollar liabilities still remains confidential. Also unknown are the reasons why Shin Corp repaid its foreign debts before the due date, and why the company decided to cover some of its foreign debts against currency exchange risk, while other companies did not.

42 Wingfield, 'Democratization', p. 281.

43 Pasuk Phongpaichit and Chris Baker, *Thaksin: The Business of Politics in Thailand*, Chiang Mai, Silkworm, 2004, pp. 58–59. Thaksin later made Bokhin Interior Minister.

44 *The Nation*, 22 June 1999.

45 See www.shinbroadband.com.

46 *Bangkok Post*, 13 December 2002, and *Krungthep Thurakit*, 16 September 2002.

47 *The Nation*, 28 August 2001.

48 *Nation Weekend*, 29 December 2003 to 4 January 2004

49 iTV Public Company Limited Annual Report, 2003.

50 However, Thaksin Shinawatra had argued that certain factions in the media had disliked him personally because he was still in business. Besides that, he further argued that his political rivals used such scandalous issues as the violation of media rights and his rumoured conflict with the royal family to attack him – all because they could not confront him in parliament.

51 Information from Office of the Securities and Exchange Commission, 2003.

52 *The Nation*, 17 July 2003.

53 *The Nation*, 17 July 2003.

54 From SATTEL's document regarding the explanation about the company's involvement and how it was exploited for political means.

55   Walaya (Phumtham Vetchayachai), *Thaksin Shinawatra: ta du dao thao tit din* [Thaksin Shinawatra: Eyes on the Stars, Feet on the Ground] Bangkok, Matichon, 1999.

56   Interview with Dr Sakarin Niyomsilp, senior researcher, Thai Farmers' Bank Research Centre, 28 June 2003.

57   Originally, CAMSHIN was a joint venture with the Ministry of Posts and Telecommunications of Cambodia in the proportion of 70:90. Later on, SATTEL took over 100 per cent of the stocks. The service also changed into a license granted by the Cambodian government. According to this format, CAMSHIN pays 20 per cent tax and 11 per cent profit shares (www.efinance.com, 30 January 2003).

58   *Bangkok Post*, 23 June 2003.

59   According to interviews with many Cambodian businessmen, Cambodia's Prime Minister Hun Sen owns CAMGSM. The corporation's report, however, indicates that the Danish company Millicom is the owner. The company was established in March 1997, and has 250,000 subscribers (Prasit Saengrungruang, 'Telecom business in Cambodia', *Bangkok Post*, 23 June 2003).

60   Interview with Dr Damrong Kasenset, President of SATTEL executive committee, www.efinance.com, 30 January 2002.

61   Ukrist Pathmanand, 'Prathet thai kap kanprianplaeng yai nai phumiphak: kan topsanong khong rat lae ongkon mai chai rat' [Thailand and major changes in the region: the response of state and non-state actors], *ASEAN in the New Millennium Project*, Bangkok, Institute of Asian Studies, Chulalongkorn University, 2003.

62   These are www.mfa.go.th and www.thai.go.th.

63   *The Nation*, 3 September 2001.

64   *Myanmar Times*, 20–26 May 2002, and *Bangkok Business*, 16 May 2002.

65   *Irrawady*, June 2002, and *Financial Times*, 24 April 2002.

66   *Myanmar Times*, 20–26 May 2002.

67   *Myanmar Times*, 15 July 2002.

68   Interview source, February 2003.

69   The launch of iPSTAR was repeatedly delayed.

70   The technology of iPSTAR will provide for telecommunications infrastructure development throughout Burma, covering four main projects: 1) Rural telephony services covering 3,000 villages still in need of telephone services throughout the country; 2) E-Education services. Burma's government aims to connect 300 schools all over the country

to the multimedia networks in the first year, and increase the number of schools in following years; 3) Provision for the expansion of broadband internet services, now covering only Rangoon and Mandalay, to outlying areas; 4) Internet Protocol (IP) services to users in the business sector and large-scale organizations. (Interview with Dr Ye Naing Win, Chairman of BCT, quoted in *Bangkok Business*, 16 May 2002.)

71 *Bangkok Post*, 1 February 2002.

72 *Bangkok Post*, 2002.

73 *Bangkok Post*, 2002.

74 *Matichon*, 19 March 2002.

75 Interview with Mr Yongsit Rojnasrivichaikul, Marketing and Sales Assistant Director of SATTEL, quoted in *Matichon*, 19 March 2002.

76 SATTEL Plc Annual Report, 2002.

77 *The Nation*, 28 August 2001.

78 The Prime Minister cancelled the agenda at the last minute before his flight departed. He insisted that the item had been initiated by the Ministry of Foreign Affairs off icials, and not by Shin Corporation (*Matichon*, 27 August 2001). Negotiations on the issue were left to Mr Sethaporn Kusripitak, director-general of the Post and Telegraph Department, who went to negotiate on this issue twice: first, one week before the Prime Minister's visit, and second, in September 2001. (Quoted in *The Nation*, 28 August 2001.)

79 Thaksin stated at the forum that Asia needed to re-examine its own standpoint in development strategy together, after the experience of the economic crisis. 'The Prime Minister's Speech in 2001 Fortune Global Forum', Government House Press Release 05/09, 9 May 2001.

80 *Matichon*, 27 August 2001.

81 Shin Corp Annual Reports,1998–2002.

82 Wingfield, 'Democratization', p. 285.

83 Chris Dixon, 'Post-crisis restructuring in Thailand: Foreign ownership, corporate resistance and economic nationalism in Thailand', *Contemporary Southeast Asia*, 26, 1, pp. 63–64.

84 *Bangkok Post*, 26 August 2003.

85 *Matichon*, 22 December 2003.

86 *Prachachat Thurakit*, 12 February 2004.

87 This section draws on research from Ukrist Pathmanand, 'Sethasat kanmuang khong khlum thun torakomanakhom rang wikrit sethakit

thai' [Political economy of telecom capital groups in post-crisis Thailand], unpublished research report for Professor Pasuk Phongpaichit's Thailand Research Fund project 'Khongsang lae phonrawat khong khlum thun rang wikrit sethakit thai' [The structure and dynamics of capital in post-crisis Thailand], presented at Faculty of Economics, Chulalongkorn University, 29 January 2004.

88 Dixon, 'Post-Crisis Restructuring', p. 64.

CHAPTER 3

Thai Rak Thai: A New Form of Thai Party?

Democracy is a vehicle. We can't drive a Rolls-Royce to a rural village and solve people's problems. A pickup or a good off-road car will do. We just need to think carefully and make the right choices. – Thaksin Shinawatra[1]

THAI RAK THAI WAS HAILED by some observers as a new kind of Thai political party, changing the rules of the game and paving the way for a more policy-based party system that would offer voters genuine electoral alternatives. Other commentators were guilty of underestimating or even ridiculing the ambition and determination of the new party and its leader, Thaksin Shinawatra. Developments since 2001 have made simplistic summaries of the Thai Rak Thai phenomenon impossible, since the party is clearly a substantial and complex force, which has changed Thai politics in numerous respects. But to what extent was Thai Rak Thai a new phenomenon, and how far was it simply a repackaging of earlier political forms? Answering this question involves reviewing the way in which Thai political parties had been analysed and understood before the ground-breaking 2001 general election. Prior to the emergence of the Thai Rak Thai Party in 1999, political parties in Thailand had been broadly viewed through three alternative approaches: political economy approaches, political sociology approaches and political science approaches.

POLITICAL ECONOMY APPROACHES

The political economy approach, popularized by writers such as Sungsidh Phiryarangsan, Pasuk Pongphaichit and Kevin Hewison, emphasized the extent to which the nature of Thai politics was determined by the country's underlying socio-economic realities. In other words, the emphasis was very much on an intimate relationship between political activity and business activity – politics was simply the continuation of business by other means.[2] Central to any understanding of Thai parties was the idea of political factions: parties were alliances of different factions, brought together not by a common ideology, but rather through shared financial interests, personal ties and opportunism. Factions varied in character – some based on particular regions of the country, others on religious ties (such as the Southern Muslim Wadah group, which migrated from the Democrats to New Aspiration, then later to Thai Rak Thai) – but most were highly pragmatic.[3] Factions were typically organized around key individuals who supplied leadership and financial support; these individuals could readily move their faction from one party to another in search of greater opportunities and benefits, thereby destabilizing political parties, causing them regularly to fragment and then reconstruct. Central to parties was the role of power brokers and 'fixers', individuals (almost always men) who worked to bring together coalitions of factions to create parties, and then to create larger coalitions of parties in order to form administrations. The ultimate political fixer of the 1990s was Democrat Party secretary-general Sanan Kachornprasart, who brokered the creation of the 1992–95 and 1997–2000 Democrat-led coalition governments, before himself falling victim to accusations of corruption and being banned from politics for five years.

Where parties and coalitions were brokered by political fixers, typically party secretary-generals with less than respectable public images, there was a necessity for these organizations to be 'fronted' by a more reputable leadership figure. Such was precisely the case during the two Democrat administrations of the 1990s, during which Chuan Leekpai served as prime minister. A highly regarded and personally incorruptible lawyer of academic inclinations, Chuan was a completely different figure from secretary-general Sanan. Chuan had little day to day control over many aspects of the government – Sanan played a crucial role in assigning ministerial portfolios, for example – but served as a highly plausible public face for the Democrats.[4] In this way the underlying political economy of the administration, while widely understood by political insiders, was concealed from the public through a 'dual structure'. The party leader acted as prime minister, while the secretary general was the principal financier and broker of the deals, including some less than transparent and legitimate deals. A self-declared exception was Chaturon Chaisang, a former 1970s student leader who served for a time as secretary-general of New Aspiration, who asked rhetorically 'But what would people want a secretary-general to have money for? Not being rich is my strength instead of my weakness'.[5] Perhaps because of this weakness, Chaturon did not remain in his post for very long.

The reason for wealthy secretary-generals was that the key to electoral success in Thailand's prevailing political economy was money politics:[6] party buying of electoral candidates, buying support from influential figures to facilitate their election, and then directly buying votes from the electorate.[7] Money politics involved industrial-scale operations, using elaborate networks of vote-canvassers and all manner of sophisticated ploys. In some places, for example, illegal lottery sellers were used to dispense funds, and voters were given 'tickets' which they could redeem after the election if the chosen candidate won. A vast range of merchandising was produced, ranging from t-shirts to fish-sauce bottles marked with the name and number of the favoured candidate. Those displaying posters in support of candidates would be paid 'rents' for the use of their wall or window space. Accompanying such practices were various modes of violence and intimidation, ranging from hired thugs loitering near polling stations, to the actual murder of canvassers who failed to deliver votes they had promised. By 1995, a serious candidate for election in the provinces needed to be able to spend at least 20 million baht (at the time, close to a million US dollars). Under such conditions, it is unsurprising that mediocre and corrupt individuals were frequently elected to parliament, producing growing demands for political reform led by urban-based elites.[8] Since respectable people were reluctant to involve themselves in dirty and violent election campaigns, parliament was increasingly populated by those with questionable qualifications. This reinforced a sense amongst political reformers that Thailand's parties were simply pragmatic interest groups that served to badge and credentialize political undesirables. Interestingly, these were views that Thaksin Shinawatra himself appeared to support soon after creating Thai Rak Thai, telling the *Far Eastern Economic Review* in 1999, 'After the next election you will see a totally different scene from what you see now. What you see now is the last honeymoon for corrupt politicians'.[9]

POLITICAL SOCIOLOGY APPROACHES

Political sociology approaches see Thai political parties in terms of the wider structure of Thai society, which they see as characterized by the formation of groups and cliques (best rendered in Thai as *phuak*), linked to wider social networks through a complex web of personal contacts and obligations. Earlier approaches saw these *phuak* in terms of patron-client relations.[10] More recently, it has been argued that patron-client relations have become highly commercialized and divorced from traditional Thai social constructs. These approaches underly some of the work of Jim Ockey, but are most clear in the writings of Michael Nelson and Daniel Arghiros.[11]

Under the faction-based system, cabinet posts were allocated on a quota basis, reflecting the size and number of political parties joining the coalition. Jobs in turn were assigned by parties on the basis of internal factional considerations: a faction leader who had delivered, say, 10 MPs to his party, had a claim to a ministerial position of some kind.[12] The holder of this ministerial position would then be obliged to repay the faction through recovering some of the faction's electoral 'investments', normally through some form of corrupt practice. In other words, there was a direct relationship between the factional basis of party politics and the structural nature of political corruption in the Thai order, a relationship that shared much in common with Japan under the Liberal Democratic Party.[13]

The net result was that parties themselves were essentially irrelevant. Parties were not associated with formal policy platforms: manifestos were essentially interchangeable, as were so called 'government policy statements' announced with great fanfare following the opening of a new parliament. In the run-up to the July 1995 general election, considerable media attention was paid to comparing the details of the various party manifestos. Yet on the very night of that election a completely opportunistic and patently preassembled seven party coalition emerged to form a government, and their supposed policy differences were thrown unceremoniously to the winds.[14] Under such circumstances, it did not matter how many members or branches a given party claimed to have, since parties were in no sense accountable to their memberships, but were run entirely on behalf of the leadership and the financial interests underwriting them. This phenomenon of the sham party was most clearly seen in the Sammakhi Tham Party, an ad hoc alliance assembled by supporters of the 1991 coup group. This entirely pragmatic grouping became the largest single party following the March 1992 general election, and was instrumental in making coup leader Suchinda Kraprayoon prime minister – though only, as it turned out, for 48 days. But while Sammakhi Tham was the most blatant example of political opportunism, it is arguable that other parties and governments of the 1980s and 1990s were fundamentally similar in their orientation and outlook. For political sociologists, Thai parties were nothing more than collections of *phuak*, groups of personalized factions.

POLITICAL SCIENCE APPROACHES

All this is anathema to the mainstream political scientist, for whom parties are driven essentially by politics and are only secondarily influenced by considerations of business or clientelist ties. Thai political scientists have been very reluctant to accept the views of the political economy school; indeed, this school, largely based within the Political Economy Centre of Chulalongkorn University's Faculty of Economics, threatens the academic jurisdiction of political scientists over their own sphere of teaching and research. Since the late 1980s, political science as a subject has been in a weak condition in Thailand, as prominent and internationally recognized political scientists have pursued alternative careers.[15] Local political scientists have consistently argued that Thai parties ought to be comparable with those in other countries (a central plank of Kramol Tongdhama-chart's pamphlet on Thai parties). As early as August 1932, analysts had been suggesting that ideally, Thailand should move towards a two-party system like those of Britain and the United States.[16] Coalition political systems, though widespread in Western Europe, have been consistently seen as unsuitable for Thailand. Ultimately, this seems to be a matter of status: Thailand ought to aspire to the status of a two party system, which is the ultimate reflection of party politics in a democratic order. It is also necessary that political parties possess two key elements: ideology (closely associated with specific policy platforms, stances and manifesto pledges) and organizational complexity (involving mass membership and a network of branches).

Political scientists such as Kramol Tongdhamachart have served as advisors to numerous Thai parties, notably the United Thai Peoples' Party (UTPP) in the 1960s, for which Kramol drew up blueprints based on the Taiwanese KMT.[17] Proposals of this kind reflect a curious mixture of academic expertise and normative idealism: the idea that the KMT was either a desirable or a possible model for a party created by the Thai military in the 1960s can only strike the detached observer as profoundly curious. But underlying this and other proposals (Kramol was also one of the many academics who advised Chavalit Yongchaiyudh during the creation of the New Aspiration Party) lay a pervasive belief that a certain kind of party could be brought into being through a top-down process of organization and management. This mode of party is what the leading Italian political scientist Angelo Panebianco terms the 'mass bureaucratic party' (after Duverger's 'mass party'), a party that emphasizes formal structures above all else.[18] Its attractions for political scientists, both Thai and non-Thai alike, lie in its complete rejection of the totally informal and personalized connections and networks that underpin the political economy view of parties. The mass bureaucratic party has members all over the country (in a country the size of Thailand, this is taken to mean millions of members), members who represent a significant proportion of voters, and who enable more direct communication between politicians and the electorate. Such a party is disciplined, following clearly defined rules and procedures; the leadership has legitimacy and support derived from party members and MPs.

Elements of the mass bureaucratic party can be seen in various Thai parties. References to such parties are pervasive in Thai political discourse: it is simply not possible for a Thai politician to declare publicly that parties do not really need members or branches. To this extent, the discourse of the mass bureaucratic party is hegemonic in Thailand, despite the fact that no such party has ever existed. The New Aspiration Party, founded in 1990, is a classic example of an attempt to build a mass bureaucratic party: from the outset, the NAP was characterized by elaborate formal structures and claims of a huge membership. Chavalit saw it as emulating Suharto's Golkar,[19] populated by large numbers of ex-bureaucrats and military people. Similarly, Chamlong Srimuang's Palang Dharma Party aspired to create a sophisticated network of regional branches, and placed emphasis on building up a strong membership base. Both parties sought to stake out their own distinctive ideological positions. Though in practice their policy manifestos were rather anodyne, Chavalit's party was characterized by an appeal to national security ideas and conventional approaches to economic development, while Chamlong's was associated in the public imagination with an opposition to corruption and money politics and a strong determination to resist the dictatorial tendencies of the military. Ultimately, however, both parties were too closely linked with the personalities of their founders to pass the test as mass bureaucratic parties: rules and procedures were always subordinated to the concerns of the leadership. James Putzel has argued that developing countries urgently need to promote programmatic political parties, suggesting that the current vogue for 'civil society' pays insufficient attention to the need to strengthen 'political society', and to offer the poor a range of legitimate political alternatives.[20]

ELECTORAL PROFESSIONAL PARTIES

In 1997, McCargo argued that the key trend in Thai political parties was neither the continuing centrality of money politics nor the ever-present myth of the 'real' mass bureaucratic party. Rather, the emerging reality was the 'electoral professional party',[21] a new mode of Thai party in which the leadership sought to establish a direct connection with voters through the media and through a variety of marketing techniques.[22] This argument reflects the view that mass membership organizations are in general decline throughout the world – Westerners are increasingly 'bowling alone'[23] – and that political parties typify this trend. Mass membership parties such as the socialist parties of Western Europe emerged through a particular set of historical circumstances, but new parties of this kind are no longer being created, and existing mass parties are gradually transforming themselves into something else. Even where mass membership is still salient, it is not usually the decisive variable underpinning electoral success, which more typically reflects the public images of party leaders and their ability to craft messages that are easily communicated through television and other media. In most developed countries, an ever-contracting segment of the electorate considers itself permanently aligned with a particular political party. Floating voters, swayed by short term 'valence issues', have become increasingly central to electoral outcomes. Membership and branches play a largely subordinate role to party images, profiles and policies espoused by a national leadership. The politics of Britain, the US, most Western European countries and Japan can all be analysed in similar terms.

On the face of it, Thailand is quite different from these examples: whereas in 'developed democracies' political parties formerly played a more important role than they do now, in countries such as Thailand they have never played a crucial role in determining electoral outcomes. Thais like to see themselves as more group-oriented than Westerners, are highly sociable and typically form themselves into competing cliques or factions in all sorts of settings. Thai political parties are likely to be rather different from Western parties: much more factionalized, and more based on personal networks.

The argument here, however, is that the lack of any historical roots for the mass bureaucratic party in Thailand make the electoral professional party an even more important alternative. Electoral professional parties are characterized by the dominance of a small core leadership, who work closely with a group of professional political organizers who include media, marketing and advertising specialists. Polling and focus groups are typically extensively used to help shape party responses to current issues. Such parties make direct appeals to the electorate, without concern for formal party structures such as conferences, which have limited relevance to the 'core business' of the party – winning elections. They have policies and ideas, but no ideology as such: they are the product of a post-ideological age, a world of 'third ways' and pragmatic compromises. Formal membership is of secondary importance, nice if you can get it, but not crucial for mobilizing votes. Professionals who run the party need not be politicians at all – their backgrounds may be in relevant fields such as journalism, advertising or marketing. Such parties are a product, images to be sold to the electorate. The most crucial element for success for such parties is a highly marketable leader, around whom election campaigning is centred. Electoral professional parties travel light: they have little baggage, historical or ideological, to encumber them. They are thus free to adopt those pragmatic policy positions that best serve their purposes in any given election.

Elements of electoral professionalism began to emerge even prior to the creation of Thai Rak Thai. Palang Dharma, especially during its later years, showed a predilection for clever television commercials that proved a precursor of later features of Thai Rak Thai. Similarly, the Democrat Party used cheeky English slogans in Bangkok posters for the September 1992 election, and used good-looking Abhisit Vejjajiva as a poster boy for campaigns in the capital. Baker argues that in the 1990s the Democrats successfully 'reengineered' themselves to reflect the changing nature of Thai society; they brought in technocrats and 'showcased a new generation of young urban professionals who symbolized urban aspirations for modernization'.[24] In this way, they were able to build support in Bangkok, as well as strengthening their traditional base in the South. This Southern base was consolidated partly because of the immense personal popularity of Chuan Leekpai in the region. The regional hold that the Democrats achieved in the South was not matched by other parties, despite their best efforts, and there were generally weak links between regions and national level electoral politics.[25] But the key to Democrat success in dominating Thai politics for most of the 1990s lay in the combination of Southern strength and 'electoral professional' attempts to appeal to a Bangkok electorate.

The emergence of Thai Rak Thai, however, arguably saw the first serious contender for the title of electoral professional party set out its stall in Thailand. The party contained most of the elements of the electoral professional party: it was marketing-led, featured a focus on leadership, had various policies but no ideology, and a core group of professionals underpinned the Party's operations. In order to assess and review this claim, various features of Thai Rak Thai will be reviewed here: the role of MPs and factions; members and branches; policies and programmes; the role of advisors and technocrats; marketing and electoral campaigning, local elections, the parliamentary party and the role of the party leader.

ROLE OF MPS AND FACTIONS

In traditional Thai parties, gathering together political factions was the primary means by which a viable electoral machine could be assembled: parties competed to woo personalized factions under their umbrellas, creating a transfer market in electable candidates, which operated both individually and in blocs. This approach was part of Thai Rak Thai's strategy: by September 2000, it was reported that Thai Rak Thai had already recruited as many as 100 incumbent MPs.[26] *Phujatkan Weekly* referred to Thai Rak Thai as *'phak dut',* 'the sucking party', because of its penchant for vacuuming up prospective winning candidates.[27] But Thaksin did not confine himself to wooing existing or former MPs; many new figures were recruited to stand as Thai Rak Thai candidates, many of them provincial councillors who had a ready-made local support base.[28] While former local politicians could be presented to the voting public as 'new faces' in parliamentary terms, they were hardly idealistic advocates of new thinking and policy initiatives; most were seasoned log-rollers and pork barrelers, who had typically made their money in the contracting business.

Nevertheless, Thai Rak Thai sought to project itself as a new kind of party, stressing the extent to which its MPs had emerged from non-traditional sources. The change to a party list system was important in this respect: because only those parties securing more than 5 per cent of the popular vote were entitled to any party list seats, senior figures running on the party lists of small parties found themselves wiped out. As Baker notes, this was most clearly illustrated by the humiliation of the Asavahame family in Samut Prakan.[29] As intended by the constitution drafters, this change worked in favour of larger parties, weakening party proliferation.

It could be argued, however, that Thai Rak Thai is more electoral than professional. Factions still persist and are highly salient. This continuing reality forms the basis of Thai Rak Thai's 'grand coalition' strategy.[30] Money politics still plays a huge role in Thai Rak Thai's election victories, and alliances with 'rural network' politicians remain crucial.[31] One way of explaining this paradox would be to argue that Thai Rak Thai is actually two parties in one, adopting a new form of 'dual structure': the electoral professional party plays in Bangkok, while the rural network party operates in the countryside.[32] This may be true to some extent, but it also belies the complexity of the situation. Baker suggests that Thai Rak Thai MPs comprised two similar-sized groups: 'first time MPs, with an average age in their late 30s', and those who had defected from other parties, whose average age was in the mid 50s.[33] It would be tempting to see the first group as the 'Thaksin MPs', and the second group as the warhorses with whom Thaksin had been obliged to make a tactical alliance. The implication here is that over time, traditional electoral politicians would give way to a new generation of professional politicians. According to this argument, Thaksin is a technocrat and a reformer who privately despises old-style politicians such as kingmaker Sanoh Tienthong, who made and broke the Banharn and Chavalit governments and serves as his chief political advisor. This is an argument which Thaksin presents to certain audiences; shortly before the 2001 general election, he told interviewers:

> We have 75 per cent new people, 25 per cent old-face politi-
> cians. During the transition, there is no way you can take
> only all brand new. This is not really a totally new era, it's the
> transition to a new era. So when it's a transition you need the
> experience of the old and the ideas of the new people. We can
> blend them to work together.[34]

This statement echoed an interview he gave immediately after the creation of Thai Rak Thai, in which he said that the ratio of new to old politicians in Thai Rak Thai should be 75: 25, generating the view that the final proportions would be a benchmark to determine how far Thai Rak Thai was a new alternative.[35] In practice, however, the distinction was not so clear-cut, since many of the younger MPs elected in 2001 enjoyed close patronage or even familial relations with the more senior group. Members of the old political groupings did take on major cabinet roles, though it is significant that the main economic portfolios were given to Thaksin's close associates and senior people from the business community, while areas such as education and health were given mainly to reformers and civil society activists.[36] It could well be argued that Thaksin was extremely comfortable with old-style politicians who did not challenge his authority, and had trouble trusting technocrats and reformers who showed signs of resisting his attempts to interfere in the working of their ministries.

What was the factional structure of Thai Rak Thai? The party had two large competing factions: Snoh Thienthong's Wang Namyen faction, and the northern faction led by Thaksin's sister, Yaowapha Wongsawat. Wang Namyen was believed to have expanded from around 40 MPs at the time of the election to around 65, mainly comprising central and Northeastern representatives.[37] Snoh was something of a mixed blessing for Thaksin, since his problematic political image made him unsuited to cabinet office. Designated the prime minister's 'chief political advisor', Snoh proved a thorn in Thaksin's side, improbably claiming to control the majority of votes in parliament and seeking to ensure that the prime minister could not challenge the vested interests of his supporters.[38]

Yaowapha was widely seen as a force to counterbalance Snoh's influence: in July 2001, members of her faction occupied 14 government positions, compared with 13 members of Snoh's faction.[39] She gained much of her following through serving as Thai Rak Thai's northern campaign manager, playing a key role in candidate selection in the northern provinces. As Crispin observed 'Although new to the game, Yaowapha seems to have already mastered the nuances of entourage politics'.[40] Yaowapha was believed to have at least 60 MPs in her faction, mainly from northern provinces, and was instrumental in having Suriya Jungrungruengkit made secretary-general of Thai Rak Thai. She chaired the House Industry Committee and sat on several other key committees, as well as playing a key role in the 'one tambon, one product' programme, a local development initiative which helped firm up her power base. OTOP was an important project for the government in terms of creating new networks of local support.[41] Yaowapha is very close to her brother: when Thaksin briefly doubled up as education minister in 2001, she acted as his secretary. At the same time, she had substantial business interests related to some Shinawatra telecommunications companies.[42]

Other elements in the party included Purachai Piumsombun and his supporters, and a small group of reform-minded academic MPs – known as the 'twenty doctors', on account of their holding PhDs – who wanted to restructure the party and curtail Snoh's influence. The twenty doctors, who were led by Rawang Netpokaew, quickly met with a strong reaction from Snoh, adopting a lower profile when he accused them of a holier-than-thou attitude and suggested they leave the party if they were over-qualified for their jobs.[43] There were also tensions between Snoh and some former NAP MPs, whom he had publicly criticized as 'Nazis': the overall effect of the merger between NAP and Thai Rak Thai was to reduce Snoh's influence, since Thaksin now relied less on his support.[44] A further element in Thai Rak Thai, the group of former student and social activists such as Chaturon Chaisang and Sutham Saengprathum, was not a unified force and appeared to become progressively marginalized as Thaksin's term went on. While factionalism was in one sense the feature of a weak and disunited political party, the factionalism of Thai Rak Thai allowed the leadership to engage in 'divide and rule' tactics: when the coalition controlled over 300 seats, even a sizeable faction with over 60 MPs counted for relatively little.

Thaksin's majority in 2001 was so large that he had no real need to bring the old-style Chart Thai and New Aspiration parties into his government: had he favoured technocratic reformist professionalism over simple parliamentary arithmetic, surely he would not have done so. He initially won 248 of parliament's 500 seats, and could even have established a single-party government had he wished (especially once he had absorbed the small Seritham Party, with 14 seats). Nor did he really need to incorporate New Aspiration into Thai Rak Thai at the beginning of 2002. Indeed, it can be argued that old-style politicians were useful to Thaksin in counterbalancing the other forces in his government, allowing him more scope to adjudicate and to get his way on all manner of crucial issues. Thaksin did more than tolerate these politicians: he actively wooed them and welcomed them into his own party. He also worked hard to build alliances with sympathetic figures in the supposedly non-partisan Senate.[45] As Chang Noi pointed out, this form of incorporationist political control was an expensive business – paying Thai Rak Thai MPs a monthly allowance of 200,000 baht per month was costing 0.72 billion baht per annum, and other party expenses probably meant that a budget of a billion baht a year was needed.[46] Such an expensive policy was clearly part of a systematic strategy.

A long analysis of Thaksin's first year in office homed in on the issues facing Thai Rak Thai.[47] Whereas previous Thai governments had been characterized by unstable coalition politics and the lack of a clear policy direction, this government was quite different. Yet despite the 325 seats commanded by Thaksin and his allies, 'the political condition of the government still did not satisfy prime minister Thaksin, because any movement of coalition government partners would still be able to rock the ship of state'. Jim Ockey has suggested that Thaksin's desire to build a grand coalition – thereby marginalizing the role of faction leaders – is the most innovative feature of Thai Rak Thai.[48] At the same time, he cautions that 'in the long term, a grand coalition is less stable than a minimum winning coalition': this is a political strategy replete with risk. By trying to bring the elements of the grand coalition inside his own party, Thaksin sought to manage and control that risk as best he could. He was helped in this by the 1997 constitutional changes which made party-hopping extremely difficult, so strengthening the hand of an incumbent prime minister.

Indeed, Thaksin was reported to have told Thai expatriates in Los Angeles that Thailand was moving towards a two party system: but whereas in the USA power alternated between two parties, in Thailand Thai Rak Thai would retain a monopoly of power, opposed by a permanently isolated Democrat Party.[49] He suggested that after the general election, Thai Rak Thai would form a single party government, increasing from his current level of 294 of the 364 coalition seats in the 500 member house. Clearly, this goal would be achieved partly through the cooptation of MPs from other parties into Thai Rak Thai, replicating the strategy adopted both prior to the 2001 election, and indeed since the election had taken place. Another element would involve increasing Thai Rak Thai's share of the 100 party list seats. By this point, Thai Rak Thai was claiming 15 million members. Elsewhere he declared that Thai Rak Thai hoped to gain 400 seats after the next election. Thepchai Yong argued that Thaksin was willing to 'roll back the spirit of political reform in order to remain in office', replacing checks and balances with an overriding preference for political stability.[50] The party held a major gathering to begin planning for the election campaign as early as August 2003, targeting 130 of the total 138 seats in the Northeast, and 400 overall. Deputy party leader Thammarak Isarankura urged party activists not to attack politicians from coalition partners Chart Thai and Chart Pattana, given that either party might yet merge with Thai Rak Thai.[51] This meeting was significant for the presence of Thaksin's wife Pojamarn, who said nothing but was widely credited with exerting behind-the-scenes influence over the management of both party and government.

Chai-Anan Samudavanija, speaking at a seminar on the thirtieth anniversary of the 1973 student uprising, suggested that 'politics has taken a turn in favour of strong leadership personalities, whereas political parties as an institution will be less important in winning upcoming votes'.[52] He went on to predict that the other parties would be left as nothing more than regional interest groupings if Thai Rak Thai won 400 seats in the 2005 general election. MPs were being bypassed under the Thai Rak Thai dominated system, which allowed the government's programmes to reach voters directly rather than via local mediation, and in future party policies would be more important: small groups of MPs would no longer be able to bargain for a ministerial post in return for supporting an administration.[53]

Thai Rak Thai's factions had a variety of origins and orientations, including regional groupings (Yaowapha) and ideological elements (the former leftists). Thaksin himself sought to argue that a generation of new MPs was displacing older, more traditional politicians, but the reality was rather more complex. Thaksin and his party represented a synthesis of the old and the new, and while the organization of

Thai Rak Thai had numerous electoral professional features, the parliamentary party was rather more electoral than professional.

MEMBERS AND BRANCHES

Thai Rak Thai retains an attachment to ideas of a mass bureaucratic party in terms of branches and membership, partly because no Thai politician dares to challenge this mythology. Baker notes the party's efforts to create a network of local branches and its claim to have enrolled 8 million members by the end of 2000.[54] Despite party claims that creating a membership base allowed Thai Rak Thai to bypass traditional patronage politics, Nelson is sceptical.[55] Arguably these moves were in no way central to the party's success, which hinged on the image of the leader, the electoral platform, the mobilization of old-style canvasser networks and the massive use of money to buy both candidates and votes. Nelson also notes that securing membership numbers involved paying applicants, either in kind or in straight cash: 'I had never before seen so many people wearing t-shirts, jackets, and aprons sporting a party's name and logo'.[56] Apart from the public relations value of claiming large numbers of members, there were practical benefits to establishing a sizeable membership base, since political parties received state funding from the Election Commission (EC) determined partly by their membership levels and by the number of branches they maintained. These stipulations reflected the way in which the 1997 constitution had sought to create structural incentives for the emergence of mass bureaucratic parties.

Numbers of party members were an important means by which EC grants were allocated. In 2003, Thai Rak Thai had 10.86 million members, 2.33 million of whom were found by the EC also to be members of other political parties.[57] In other words, for all the talk of 15 million members, Thai Rak Thai had only 8.5 million 'real' members in 2003, the same order of membership as the party had claimed before the 2001 general election. Accessed in May 2004, the party website claimed 13 million members. According to the EC, the

Democrats had 3.82 million members, 1.37 million of whom were members of other parties: Chart Pattana had 3.7 million, 1.474 million of whom were 'dual' members. Thai Rak Thai received Bt 103.54 million from the EC in 2003, while the Democrats received Bt 54.4 million, Chart Thai Bt 17.4 million and Chart Pattana 18.9 million.

In its first five years of existence, the EC paid out Bt 940 million to political parties, but was unable to account for exactly how the money was used; more than half of all 1,464 party branches in the country did not meet requirements, many being used as houses or shops.[58] The EC was in the process of changing regulations so that rents and utility charges for such branches would no longer be covered by grants. The only activities supported would be 'those activities leading to political development such as providing knowledge on political issues, holding seminars or admitting new party members'.[59] *Nation* reporters found clear evidence of abuses. The Khonkhopbondee Party, which had no MPs, purported to have 218 branches nation-wide, but reporters were unable to contact any party officials at all. However, the changed rules would clearly have a major impact on the Democrat Party, which maintained a very large number of longstanding branches –152 in 1993,[60] and around 192 in 2003 – and could be construed as politically motivated.

Partly because of Thai Rak Thai's dominance over the state and the media, the Democrats sought to revive their rather neglected net-work of branches after Banyat Bantadtan took over the leadership in April 2003. Acknowledging that branches had enjoyed little importance outside election times, Banyat promised to use the network to try and generate renewed support for the party.[61] Prasarn Niyomsap, a Kanchanaburi branch director, claimed that government officials in the provinces were shunning their attempts to maintain contact:

> 'Those officials are scared that political clout will be wielded to harm their families', Prasarn said, adding that they preferred him to act on their behalf as an ordinary citizen rather than a representative of the opposition. Prasarn said his branch had published copies of newsletters promoting the party's

activities and cautioning people against the government's populist policies. But he said it had not proven highly effective, because people were inevitably lured to the government's big spending ways.

The message here was that even for the Democrat Party – with a far better-developed system of branches than Thai Rak Thai – membership structures were a second order priority, a fallback plan when other sources of voter mobilization proved unavailable. Thai Rak Thai's highly centralized structure, and overwhelming emphasis on the image of the party leader, meant that branches had little real function, and that processes of consultation were highly superficial. In an editorial, *The Nation* argued that Thai Rak Thai's February 2004 annual convention would reflect the party's leadership-driven approach:

> Input from party members is supposed to filter through to the party's top echelon, which then gives shape to ideas through policy formulation, provides effective leadership to translate policies into actions and exercises communicative skills to inspire the masses.

In reality, however, Thai Rak Thai had a top-down corporate culture that did not respect democracy 'nor a tradition of tolerating dissenting voices'.[62] Nelson asserts that the party has failed to create the branch networks and organizational structures to allow members to participate in decision-making, and asks rhetorically:

> Will the members have any meaningful part in the party's internal political decision-making when they have probably been considered as merely a tool for promoting a leadership-oriented political model in which party members and voters entrust a patron-style leader with their welfare and refrain from interfering in 'his business'?[63]

Pasuk and Baker have similarly argued that Thai Rak Thai's populist polices were part of a broader agenda, dedicated to reordering the political system so as to create 'a powerful executive and a centralized party supported by business firms', and also to curb civil society as part of an authoritarian programme to create greater social order.[64] To borrow Panebianco's terms, the creation of a structure of party branches with local memberships was part of a party policy of 'territorial penetration' underpinned by the financial incentives of Election Commission funding. They were not an example of what he calls 'territorial diffusion', a natural spread of voluntary activity in support of the party. Thai Rak Thai engaged in a membership drive primarily for financial and presentational reasons, paying lip service to mass bureaucratic ideas of the political party. Fundamentally, however, Thai Rak Thai's attitude to membership was that of an electoral professional party, in which all activity is subordinated to the creation of a centralized campaign machine.

POLICIES AND PROGRAMMES

The electoral success of Thai Rak Thai in 2001 was closely associated with the party's so-called 'populist policies', especially the proposals for a farmer's debt moratorium, a million baht development fund for every village and a 30-baht healthcare programme. Many observers, including prominent columnists in *Matichon* and *Krungthep Thurakit*, credited them with a crucial role in the Thaksin landslide.[65]

Political scientist Sukhum Naulsakul declared that this illustrated the public's demand for a new mode of politics: 'People vote for the big picture and principles instead of for individuals like they used to'.[66] Even Thepachai Yong – the Nation group editor who quit his post as news director of iTV when Thaksin took over the station – argued that, 'For the first time, people voted with judgement… people went out there to cast votes believing in the platform of a political party. This is unprecedented, no matter how populist you may say Thaksin's policies may be'.[67] Arguably, this was the beginning of a political landscape in which policies could gain the upper hand over traditional money and patronage politics, thereby vindicating the post-1997 political reform process.

Were Thai Rak Thai's 'populist' programmes actually policy initiatives, or simply alternative means of vote-buying or gaining attention? Analysts were divided, but before the election some financial experts argued that measures such as relieving farmers debts and providing village development funds were not really workable. IDEAglobal.com described the moves as 'simply old-style politics from a party that claims to be ushering in a new order'.[68] Kenneth Ng, head of research at ING Barings, was even sceptical that a change in the ruling party would see any shift in economic policy: 'we believe a change in government is unlikely to result in a significant change in current reform measures, although perhaps they will be implemented with a little less enthusiasm'. Some analysts saw a fundamental difference between the Democrats and Thai Rak Thai in terms of their attitudes to globalization and free trade. Pasuk argued that the Democrats were more free market oriented, reflecting their strengths in Bangkok and the South, while Thai Rak Thai's more sceptical view of globalization mirrored the position of farmers in the North and Northeast of the country.[69] Dr Thanavath Ponvichia suggested that while Thai Rak Thai was also market oriented, 'Many initiatives, whether farm debt suspension of Internet development, will be led by the government'. In other words, there was a top-down, statist character to Thai Rak Thai's thinking and rhetoric – this was a party led by a business leader whose career had been built on working closely with the state.

Another populist policy was the creation of the 'People's Bank', or bank for the poor, a bank to make business development fund loans at low interest, for amounts of no more than 15,000 baht.[70] Speaking to a gathering of Asian political parties in November 2002, Thaksin declared that competition between parties should be based on 'winning the hearts and minds of the people through their actions', rather than on the basis of ideological differences. Given that parties had never competed in Thailand over ideological differences, this was not a particularly surprising assertion. Michael Nelson suggests that these 'populist policies' actually offered little concrete benefit to the ordinary voter, and viewed them as a means of creating a patron-client relationship between the party leader and the electorate.[71]

But what was the core of Thai Rak Thai's policy platform? For all the talk of populist policies and social programmes, there was little evidence of these from a quick search of the Thai Rak Thai website, www.thairakthai.or.th, which contained a lot of outdated press releases and non-functioning links.[72] An English language book comprising 96 pages of information on the party, apparently released around the time of APEC in October 2003, contained a rather different discussion of the party's policy priorities than the vague platitudes to be found on the website. The first page of the book declared that the party's principal policy platform was based on three wars: the war on poverty, war on drugs and war on corruption.[73] This alarming emphasis on all-out warfare gave way to a more familiar list of five 'new' policies designed to solve economic hardships and create opportunities for the common man: the 30-baht healthcare scheme, three year suspension of farmers' debt, million baht village development fund, SME support and the creation of the Thai Asset Management Corporation. It was unclear exactly how this last initiative was likely to benefit the common man.

The book went on to offer three alternative formulations of party policy: a 12-page section entitled 'Nation building through 11 national agendas'; 22 pages devoted to the three wars (poverty, corruption and drugs); and then 36 pages headed 'Policy of the government', an unofficial translation of the policy statement Thaksin had presented to the Thai parliament on 26 February 2001, shortly after taking office. There were numerous overlaps, contradictions and inconsistencies between the three main sections of the book, none of which corresponded to the summaries of party policy given on the website. It is difficult to avoid the conclusion that Thai Rak Thai was not terribly clear about its policy positions, and in this respect did not differ greatly from other past or present Thai political parties. The 'populist policies' sounded clearer and more attractive than they were in reality, perhaps because Thaksin and those around him were frequently changing their minds about the best policy options and directions.

In November 2003, Thaksin announced a new plank of his populist policies, a promise to eradicate poverty within six years – a pledge which attracted some criticism as an unrealistic, top-down initiative. Rather than focusing on those living below a certain income level, the anti-poverty programme emphasized seven key groups – 'landless farmers, the homeless, needy students, people heading for bankruptcy, labourers who have been victimized by overseas job scams, low-income earners who lack housing, and those engaged in the underground economy'.[74] These ideas were criticized for generating publicity and appealing to troublesome sectors of society rather than concentrating on sectors suffering from the greatest real deprivation. However, government plans to register poor people all over the country so that benefits could be targeted directly towards them offered Thai Rak Thai a means of building up a new support base centred on the estimated 8.2 million people concerned. In mid-2004, Thaksin announced a follow-up programme to inject a further round of village development funds, proposals widely criticized as an electoral ploy.

Thai Rak Thai's policy platform created a new challenge for the opposition Democrats, who had previously traded on their overall image as a long-established party rather than a specific policy pro-gramme.[75] Chumpol Sungthong, a Democrat Party branch director in Chaiyaphum, argued that people were now voting mainly according to policies and were rejecting the old style of patronage politics. Somkiat Pongpiaboon of Rajabhat Insitute Nakhon Ratchasima argued that Thai Rak Thai policies now led local people to expect help from the central government rather than local officials and politicians.[76] Such views put pressure on the opposition party to counter with populist policies of its own. Abhisit Vejjajiva, who was defeated for the Democrat Party leadership in April 2003, argued that the party needed to 'get together to count down for the future', stressing that 'to win voters we need to come up with a policy at a time and not rush all of them out at once'.[77] Clear-cut and effective policies were needed. However, the new Democrat leader Banyat Bantadtan declared that his party would not engage in 'destructive ways' to compete with the populist policies of Thai Rak Thai. 'We will not promise that we will give each village Bt 2 million or launch a Bt 15-per-visit health-care scheme to compete with them'. He insisted that the party would not create quick-fix projects that lacked popular participation. However, less than a year later the Democrats were producing policy proposals that sounded remarkably like attempts to upstage Thai Rak Thai: at the Democrat Party conference in April 2004, Banyat announced plans to reduce tuition fees at state universities by 50 per cent, to forgive farmers' debt, to provide farmers with 5000 baht a month to help them improve their productivity, to pay 1,000 baht a month to people over 60 who did not receive a government pension and to provide free healthcare for those in this category.

However, Sombat Thamrongthanyawong, a political scientist at NIDA, argued that attempts by Thai Rak Thai and the Democrats to claim that people now voted on the basis of policies were untrue: the basis of politics remained local patronage, and all Thai Rak Thai had done was move patronage from local society to the national level. Thai Rak Thai voters backed the party simply to gain benefits from populist policies, something unrelated to faith or loyalty.[78] The cynical view was that Thaksin's policy promises were hollow, a vote-winning package with little to do with the core concerns of the Thai Rak Thai administration. By extension, this was not really an electoral professional party, and the rules of the Thai political game had been slightly modified rather than fundamentally changed by the emphasis on policies which had characterized the Thai Rak Thai campaign for the 2001 general elections. A more positive view is that by voting for attractive party policies, Thai voters were behaving as rational actors, and that Thai Rak Thai's election platform had helped raised the quality of the Thai political process.

ADVISORS AND TECHNOCRATS

One characteristic of the electoral professional party is its reliance on a relatively small group of technocrats to guide policy and pre-sentational issues. Thailand experienced an analogous idea during the Chatichai government of 1988–91. Chatichai had employed his own team of academics as advisors, referred to as the Ban Phitsanulok group because of their location in the official residence of the prime minister, close to Government House. Thaksin's version was different: while Ban Phitsanulok was concerned with government policy and not the activities of the ruling Chart Thai Party, Thai Rak Thai advisors played a combined role in strategic thinking for both party and government. At the core of Thaksin's advisory group was Pansak Vinyaratn, former head of the Ban Phitsanulok team, who had worked closely with rival media magnate Sondhi Limthongkul to establish the now-defunct newspaper *Asia Times*. Pansak, co-founder of Thai Rak Thai,[79] was closely associated with Thaksin's rise to power.

Described by Suranan Vejjajiva as 'an ideas man ... the intellectual firepower behind the prime minister's business acumen that makes our government work',[80] Pansak was believed to be Thaksin's chief spin doctor and English speech writer. Given to jumping from one topic to another, Pansak's main themes were how Thailand fitted into the world economy, and the importance of fostering SMEs. Highly critical of the Washington consensus, he argued that Thailand should position itself as the 'Italy of the East', that Western capitalism was largely driven by nationalism, and that the USA and Japan were examples of 'failed economies'. His views on nationalism as the engine of capitalism were apparently influenced by American academic Liah Greenfeld's book, *The Spirit of Capitalism: Nationalism and Economic Growth*, to which he and Thaksin made various references.[81] Pansak argued that Thailand should move away from a free-market economy towards what Crispin terms 'more welfare-oriented economics, a departure aimed at strengthening the country's grassroots economy, while providing a buffer against the global one'.

Speaking at the Central Party School of the Chinese Communist Party in 2002, Pansak declared:

> I would like to emphasize that we in Asia should not replicate the West in our economic model. This does not mean we should reject historical and scientific facts, but rather we should provide alternative models of development, alternative and

appropriate time frames to achieve our objectives. The world will be richer if there is more than one model of development.[82]

Briefly jailed after October 1976 because of his critical journalism, Pansak embraced a curious mixture of socialistic ideals and capitalist leanings. He was in his element playing behind-the-scenes roles in the courts of rich and powerful men with large egos, serving as head of Chatichai's Ban Pitsanulok team from 1988 to 1991, then as editor-in-chief of Sondhi's grandiose and ill-fated *Asia Times* newspaper in the mid-1990s, a post which he held concurrently with the editorship of the monthly English-language *Manager* magazine. At *Asia Times*, he began to advocate the peculiarly Sondhian mixture of globalization and Asian values which he later transmuted into a kind of pseudo-ideology for Thai Rak Thai.[83] As Sondhi argued at the newspaper's launch:

> *Asia Times* is the first Asian owned, Asian regional business newspaper. This is the first time that Asians can hear the voices of other Asians. The launch of *Asia Times* demonstrates the first time Asians are breaking the western media monopoly in Asia.[84]

Asian nationalism is in some ways an ironic stance for a Western-educated intellectual said to write better in English than in Thai. Described as 'known for creativity as well as extreme arrogance', Pansak was also renowned for his proclivity for swearing.[85] Along with Prommin Lertsuridej (who later became finance minister) and Padung Limcharoenrat, he formed the 'gang of three', close aides who shielded Thaksin from criticism and provided a buffer for his day-to-day activities. Pansak was widely credited with having coined the election slogan 'Think new, act new', and with promoting the government populist policy programmes. He was unpopular with many cabinet members, however, who saw him as undermining the prime minister's position by restricting policy debate, and encouraging him to overreact to press criticism.

Pana Janviroj argued that Thai Rak Thai's top strategists, led by Somkid and Pansak, had introduced some new thinking, stressing that Thailand did not to accept the economic dictates of the Anglo-Saxon world, and that unchecked market forces could undermine Thailand's global competiveness.[86] Instead, in conjunction with the NESDB, they advocated a plan known as 'Thailand's Dream', based around seven aspirations:

> Being a country which thrives on growth with stability through small and medium-sized enterprises; is an active international player; is a world leader in niche markets; is an innovative nation with its own wisdom and learning base; is an entrepreneurial society; is a nation of cultural pride but with a global sense; and is a land of decent living standards and environment.

These ideas were opposed by sceptical traditionalists, who themselves 'are loathed by the Thai Rak Thai elite, who see them as unadventurous and, perhaps wrongly, as servants of an Anglo-Saxon-dominated world'.[87] Thai Rak Thai's advisors sought to stake out a distinctive intellectual territory which formed the basis of government policy, a territory in which Pansak played a central role.

Thaksin's advisory team also worked with foreign consultants and was believed to be the first Thai political party to use Westerners to assist with its electoral strategy.[88] They also used foreign advisors as public relations strategists, particularly in dealing with the foreign press, whose questions Thaksin sometimes detested.[89] Michael Nelson has described a personal encounter with some of these Western consultants:

> Shortly after TRT was registered, I had a talk with a Briton and an American in my office at the Faculty of Political Science, Chulalongkorn University. They wanted to know how the Thai election system worked and what I thought of Thaksin. Money did not really matter to them, they told me, and handed me 20,000 baht in cash for about two hours of intensive conversation. When I asked them if they were

working for a political party, one of them answered, 'Not yet. We are collecting data and then may offer our services'.[90]

He added that when he checked the website of their organization, he could not find out who was behind it; there were no names given. Nelson goes on to describe how not long afterwards, there were press stories saying that a well-funded foreign 'NGO' was hiring Thai academics to conduct political research.

> A professor at the above-mentioned faculty was hired, and he recruited scores of research assistants to collect data in every district in Thailand. (One may recall that TRT takes pride in having done 'in-depth' research on and in every Thai district to get to know in detail the socio-economic situation of people in the countryside).[91]

The foreign 'NGO' turned out to be an international consultancy organization, which closed its office and went to ground after receiving unwelcome press coverage. Nelson actually suggests that employing foreigners to help a political party gain electoral advantage may be illegal under Thai law. Interestingly, however, it illustrated the party's love-hate relationship with the outside world – 'loving Thais', but buying in Western expertise where this proved useful.

Whereas under Chatichai the advisory team comprised only seven core members, the Thaksin team had 40 or 50 and was able to conduct performance checks on all policies approved by the cabinet.[92] Two advisory teams were created, one at Ban Phitsanulok and another based at Ban Manaangkhalisa. Pansak was said to have chaired personal weekly macroeconomic meetings with key policy advisors, meetings which were not attended by finance minister Somkid Jatusripitak.[93] Asked about rumours that he and Pansak were at loggerheads, Somkid dismissed them as 'virtually groundless' – a less than convincing denial.[94]

Somkid was in fact one of Pansak's main rivals in Thaksin's court, described by Achara Deboonme of *The Nation* as 'one of the chief architects of Thai Rak Thai's landslide election victory'. Somkid was the natural choice to implement the party's 'contractual socialist policy', since he had helped develop this 'New Deal', which aimed 'to recreate the domestic economy through support of rural enterprises and small- and medium-scale companies'.[95] Somkid, who holds a doctorate in marketing and management from Northwestern University, was widely credited with overseeing the village-level surveys that helped generate the ideas for the 30-baht healthcare programme, the farmers' debt moratorium and the Village development fund. Nelson, however, suggests that much of the detailed oversight was done by an international consultancy company.[96] Somkid credited the American marketing guru Philip Kotler – with whom he had co-authored two books – as a crucial influence on his thinking.[97]

Another key advisor on these policies was Prapat Panyachatiraksa, a former student leader from the 1970s, who had started a successful organic orange farm in Lampang. In 1999, he had faxed Thaksin a policy statement that inspired part of the Thai Rak Thai programme, and was rewarded with the post of deputy agriculture minister when the party took office.[98] Another former activist was Prommin Lertsuridej, who served first as Thaksin's secretary, then in October 2002 assumed the role of deputy premier overseeing economic affairs. *The Nation* described him as 'the shadow, if not the alter ego, of the prime minister'.[99] Prommin had spent four years fighting with the CPT in the jungle after 6 October 1976. While the Chuan government had worked closely with the bureaucracy to suppress grassroots protest and dissent, Thai Rak Thai sought to enlist support from the popular sector. However, the warm relations Thaksin enjoyed with the NGO community in his early days as premier did not endure. As prominent activist Pibhop Dhongchai declared in October 2001:

> We thought this government would make a difference as it has under its wings quite a number of former October 14 activists. We did not have blind faith in those former activists, but we did expect them to convince the government to choose the right solution for poor people .... But we have found out that we were too optimistic.[100]

He added that he believed the former leftists in the government were likely to lose influence to more conservative advisors. By March 2002, northern farmers were once again protesting outside Government House. Nevertheless, Thaksin continued to employ the rhetoric of social inclusion, even quoting from Rousseau's *Social Contract* in a November 2002 speech to a gathering of Asian political parties.[101] Clearly, Thaksin did not write this speech himself, and it tells us little about his real political attitudes.

Thai Rak Thai did emulate the electoral professional model in its use of a small group of 'ideas men' working closely with the party leader as political advisors. To a significant degree, these were different from the political advisors of earlier parties and governments – a mixture of technocrats, hangers-on and tame academics. The Thai Rak Thai administration was essentially run by the prime minister in conjunction with a small team of trusted advisors, who were closely involved in both the formulation and presentation of policy. These advisors helped empower the party leadership and the office of prime minister, at the expense of the faction bosses and cabinet ministers who had typically played central roles in previous governments. They helped to professionalize the decision-making process, insulating Thaksin from other political and social forces ranging from parliament to the electorate.

MARKETING AND ELECTORAL CAMPAIGNING

One of the distinctive characteristics of the Thai Rak Thai Party was its strong emphasis on polling, marketing and modern, business-style approaches to electoral campaigning.[102] Yet for all this talk of sophisticated marketing campaigns, the continuing salience of traditional methods of electioneering was very evident in all parties, especially in the provinces: vote-buying, electoral manipulation with the connivance of government officials, mobilization of traditional patronage networks and straightforward violence and intimidation, continued to be major features of the 2001 election; numerous Thai Rak Thai candidates were 'yellow carded' by the Election Commission and forced to engage in electoral re-runs.[103] Whether or not marketing activities and policy pledges contributed more than marginally to the final election outcome is highly debatable.

Between elections Thai Rak Thai was engaged in a continuing, if lower-key, marketing drive. Political marketing differs from the marketing of consumer products and services, since 'customers' of political services only make significant 'purchases' at election times, which may be years apart. Thai Rak Thai sought to devise ways of keeping supporters engaged with their 'product' between elections. This involved reaching out to a wide range of social groups and devising programmes aimed at instilling loyalty to the party brand. These included the so-called 'Youth Councils', involving miniature political forums for hundreds of primary, secondary and university students each year. Participants had the option of doing voluntary work for Thai Rak Thai or writing for *Krati Khon* (cream of the crop), a party publication sent out to schools all over the country every two months. These activities aimed to engage young people with party activities, as well as parents and teachers. Other community activities also involved older people in training and brainstorming programmes: it was estimated that over 100,000 people took part in various Thai Rak Thai programmes in 2002. These people were given the chance to volunteer to train as party activists or volunteer canvassers.[104] As *The Nation* put it: 'When you sell mobile phones, you have to make sure that kids get cool applications while adults, who may not be totally happy with your brand, have lesser alternatives and your rivals are not allowed to grow'.[105]

Suthichai Yoon described Thai Rak Thai strategy for the forthcoming 2005 elections as one of 'shock and awe',[106] based on a target of 20 million votes compared with the 12 million the party gained in 2001. 20 million votes would ensure Thai Rak Thai 70 party list seats; combined with 340 of the 400 constituency seats, this would give the party 410 seats in total. Suthichai claimed that Thai Rak Thai MPs had been ordered to ensure that they boosted the number of Thai Rak Thai members in each constituency to 50,000, or risk being de-selected. Their performance would be evaluated every two months, and the target date was set for July 2004.

> Thailand Inc's CEO had let it be known that if the customer base isn't jacked up and sales targets aren't met, the sales and marketing departments will come under severe 'appraisal'. Direct-sales teams are being readied to take their place if the results of constant marketing research so demand.

At the same time, Suthichai argued that this was largely a psychological ploy to encourage members of other parties to defect to Thai Rak Thai: the party remained unable to make a decisive breakthrough in the South, and still faced formidable opposition in areas such as Korat. Nor was the party secure in the capital city. Despite this, Thaksin was confidently predicting not just a landslide but an 'avalanche' victory in the forthcoming election. Michael Connors has persuasively argued that Thaksin's determination to secure 400 seats reflects his desire to avoid facing no-confidence debates, since under the 1997 constitution at least 100 votes are required to call a censure motion.[107]

Summarizing discussions from a roundtable in Khon Kaen, Pana Janviroj argued that no less money would be spent in the Northeast region at the next election, though smaller amounts might be given out in the direct form of vote-buying. He argued that the dominance of the party had created 'the politics of Darwinism': intense competition between rival party factions, which was eroding patronage politics. Local politicians were emulating the policies of the national government, with some SAO's creating 300,000-baht development funds which operated very much like a smaller-scale version of the Thai Rak Thai village development funds.[108] While the 30-baht health scheme and the CEO governor system were quite popular, the village development fund was more controversial, excluding the very poor, with much of the funds typically allocated to committee members. Some community leaders argued that Thai Rak Thai policies had created a culture of passivity, in which people simply waited for help from the government.

Thai Rak Thai's hopes of sweeping Isan, and its stated ambition to win 130 of the region's 134 seats, could not be realized so long as Chart Pattana and Chart Thai refused to merge with the party. Thai Rak Thai won 80 Northeastern seats in the 2001 general election, expanding this to 104 by absorbing Seritham and New Aspiration. For the 2005 election, Thai Rak Thai was targeting a further 27 seats – those held by Chart Thai and Chart Pattana – but the chances of winning them were quite slim.[109] The party faced similar problems in the South, where it was seeking to oust incumbent Democrats and was targeting 20 of the region's 54 seats, having gained only 20 in 2001. In 2001, only 400,000 of the party's 11 million party list votes came from the South. Traditionally, southerners were regarded as 'the most politically-savvy voters', less swayed by practices such as vote-buying, and often very loyal to the Democrats.[110] But deputy Thai Rak Thai leader Sutham Saengprathum argued that Thai Rak Thai's populist policies, plus southerners' admiration for Thaksin's strong, decisive image, would lead to a much better showing in the region in 2005.[111] Thai Rak Thai believed that they were very popular with Muslim voters in the South, a view contested by the Democrats, who insisted that the government's handling of conflicts and violence in the area had alienated Muslim support. The decisive victory of the Democrats in a Songkhla by-election in February 2004 illustrated just how difficult the region remained for Thaksin's party.

Marketing alone could not determine the outcome of Thai elections, which were still substantially determined by issues such as choice of candidate, the effectiveness of local canvassers, and the use of money, fraud and intimidation. Nevertheless, the emergence of Thai Rak Thai did mark a substantial step in the direction of a more professionalized political market place in Thailand: never before had a Thai political party engaged in such elaborate and sophisticated marketing. This development was testimony to the extent to which Thai Rak Thai was a centralized political machine, containing many elements of the electoral professional party.

LOCAL ELECTIONS

Local elections – for these purposes, elections for provincial administrative organizations, sub-district administrative organizations, municipalities, the Bangkok governor and city council, and for village headmen – posed a challenge for Thai Rak Thai. Given that Thaksin sought to operate with an overarching national mandate and political agenda, local elections of all kinds posed more of a threat than an opportunity. One of his first instincts was simply to distance the party from these processes. In September 2003, Thai Rak Thai issued a directive that banned those standing for local elections from using the party banner, or large posters of Thaksin, as part of their campaigns. Because of numerous defeats for Thai Rak Thai candidates running under the party banner, Thaksin wanted to dissociate himself from this pattern of political failure.[112] Snoh Thienthong, whose influence as a faction leader was rapidly declining, told members of his Wang Namyen faction:

> The notion that the party can 'sell' well with the current populist trend could be just wishful thinking. Individuals and canvassers still count when it comes to what can influence the decisions of the voters.

In other words, at the local level, old-fashioned tactics such as vote-buying and canvasser networks remained the key to electoral success. Thaksin was eventually forced to bow to political realities on the ground: the party rescinded the order and allowed local election candidates to run in association with Thai Rak Thai's brand. The first test came with the 2004 provincial administrative organization elections.

The provincial administrative organization (PAO) elections of March 2004 illustrated the emergence of political tensions between the Thai Rak Thai leadership and constituency MPs. For the first time, mayors of provincial administrative organizations were directly elected. This was an interesting development for two reasons. First, immediately after the 2001 elections Thai Rak Thai had apparently given serious consideration to the idea of abolishing PAOs – notorious for having been captured in many provinces by cabals of corrupt construction contractors – altogether.[113] By strengthening the organizations instead of dissolving them, the party had done an about-turn. Second, the idea of elected provincial mayors seemed directly to challenge the prime minister's idea of putting all provinces under the jurisdiction of 'CEO' governors.[114] Significantly, a number of current and former MPs expressed interest in running for these posts, perhaps suspecting that they could have greater power and influence as PAO mayors than as backbench MPs.[115]

Because government programmes such as the Village Development Fund established a direct connection with voters, the role of MPs as middlemen had been seriously curtailed.[116] MPs were reduced merely to supporting Thaksin and his initiatives. Provincial administrative organizations were of declining importance to the government, which had effectively bypassed them by giving provincial governors 'CEO' powers. However, many MPs put considerable efforts into supporting PAO candidates from their own *phuak* (cliques) – in some cases leading competing candidates to claim Thai Rak Thai endorsement – in the hope that they could gain influence over PAO budgets and so procure some political advantage for themselves. Such MPs hoped that using the same teams of canvassers in the general election could yield dividends, ensuring they could retain their seats whatever happened to the prime minister's popularity.

However, these tactics produced some bitter outcomes, as in Phayao province, where former minister Ladawan Wongsriwong found that MPs from a neighbouring province backed a rival PAO candidate instead of the one endorsed by her as the official party representative.[117] Michael Nelson notes that at a Thai Rak Thai training seminar on PAO elections held in Chiang Mai in December 2003, one of the party's deputy leaders endorsed party candidates in some northern provinces, but not the incumbent in Chiang Mai itself. As he argues:

The problem remains, however, that provincial politics are still based on *phuak* rather than party. This means that normally there are a number of informal political groups in any given province, mainly centered in different MP constituencies. TRT thus may have most MPs in a province without those MPs being party-oriented in their provincial-level politics. As a result, each of these groups may wish to enter its own candidate for the position of PAO *nayok*.[118]

PAO elections had effectively become proxy contests between members of rival factions of the Thai Rak Thai. Nelson suggests that since the two main parties have a vested interest in seeing well-run PAOs operate under their banner, 'provincial politics may thus become increasingly party-politicized' – and the same might eventually apply to municipal elections. However, this politicization might apply not just to PAOs, but to provincial election commissioners. It was striking that, while politicians close to Thai Rak Thai won PAO contests in most provinces, the Election Commission showed little willingness to punish winners suspected of electoral abuses.

One solution to problematic local elections was simply to abolish them; in February 2004 Thai Rak Thai announced plans to abolish direct elections for village headmen and *kamnan* (subdistrict heads), an act of re-centralization that would amount to a substantial reversal of political reforms enacted in recent decades.[119] This proposal illustrated Thai Rak Thai's lack of enthusiasm for the political reform process, and lack of concern with the needs of village communities: local elections were seen as a potential challenge to the dominance of a hegemonic national party. In this sense, Thai Rak Thai's views closely resembled the views of Interior Ministry bureaucrats, who opposed local elections that weakened their authority over the country's rural population. Thai Rak Thai's overwhelming concern with parliamentary elections and the central authority of a state dominated by a single party was in this sense highly conservative. The government later backtracked on these plans, but this flip-flopping nevertheless testified to Thaksin's lack of commitment to a consistent stance on decentralization.

THE PARLIAMENTARY PARTY

For Thaksin's party in government, parliament was very much subordinated to the executive power of the prime minister's office. This was illustrated by the poor attendance of Thai Rak Thai MPs in parliament. The speaker sometimes had to close business early because parliament was inquorate, and five times between 2002 and 2004 House sessions were actually halted following head counts. Given that MPs had to attend only two half-day sessions a week, this was a lamentable state of affairs. At one point Thai Rak Thai whips proposed paying MPs meeting allowances to encourage their attendance – despite the fact that they already enjoyed high salaries by Thai standards.[120] Yet this reluctance to attend parliament also characterized Thaksin himself, who in 2002 failed to present the required annual parliamentary report on the government's performance in person. Sophon Ongkara wrote in *The Nation*:

> Throughout the past year the chief executive has rarely shown up and is remembered only once for giving a brief response during question time. He has not come to thumb his nose at House motions, but he has made it plain enough that being there and listening to harangues was just a waste of his time. … In his view, it must be that he does not regard himself as being accountable to the House.[121]

Thaksin had a longstanding aspiration to create a 'super-party', bringing together all the parties in his coalition government under a single banner. His spokesman, Suranan Vejjajiva, claimed early on in Thaksin's term that mergers between large and medium-sized parties were a positive step: 'That was the intention of the drafters of the constitution. Now we are moving in that direction naturally'.[122]

In an extraordinary move in April 2004, Chart Pattana and Chart Thai apparently agreed to become 'subsidiaries' of Thai Rak

Thai.[123] Subsidiary parties would retain nominal independence, yet take policy instructions from Thai Rak Thai – they would, however, be free to decide whether or not to support particular policies. This structure would mirror Malaysia's Barisan Nasional, in which smaller parties took their cue from UMNO. Banharn Silpa-archa, leader of Chart Thai, expressed support for such an idea, though he said he was not clear whether his party wished to become a subsidiary of Thai Rak Thai, even hinting that they might align themselves with the Democrats.[124] Thaksin himself denied that any such plan existed. Banharn also suggested the media ask the Buri Ram faction of his own party whether they planned to defect to Thai Rak Thai, since they would not tell him – a clear indication of the persistence of factional politics in the Thai party system. Nophakhun Limsamarnphun argued that a 'holding company' political party structure was now emerging as an alternative to mergers and acquisitions.[125] Whereas Thai Rak Thai had successfully acquired both Seritham and NAP, Chart Thai and Chart Pattana were still resisting full incorporation, and a holding company structure was a good alternative from Thai Rak Thai's point of view. By suggesting that he could also align his party with the Democrats, Banharn was seeking to negotiate from a position of strength, a strength which would be largely surrendered if he were formally to embrace Thai Rak Thai. Chart Pattana, however, gradually weakened their resistance to Thai Rak Thai's advances.

Thaksin's fondness for incorporating other parties into Thai Rak Thai laid him open to charges of 'parliamentary dictatorship' – a curious Thai political felony that had been cited as a justification for both the 1991 military coup and the introduction of the reformist 1997 constitution. This was illustrated by the appointment of Suchart Tancharoen as deputy house speaker in February 2002; Suchart, a former member of the infamous 'Group of 16' parliamentary heavies, was an entirely inappropriate choice for a sensitive post traditionally reserved for MPs who carried a high degree of public respect. In 1999, Thaksin himself had described Suchart as the most dubious provincial politician in Thailand.[126] As such, Thaksin's failure to block the move could be judged as demonstrating his willingness to subordinate all political principles to the goal of creating a completely unassailable mega-party.[127] Unveiling a statue of former premier Chatichai Choonavan in Korat in August 2004, Thaksin called upon everyone interested in helping the country to stop squabbling and simply join Thai Rak Thai. His was becoming the ultimate catch-all political party.[128]

Thaksin's preoccupation with expanding the parliamentary party – despite his complete lack of interest in parliamentary politics itself – illustrated his willingness to compromise on the quality of his party, demonstrating the extent to which Thai Rak Thai was a vehicle for his own dominance of Thai politics rather than a coherent and focused political organization. In effect, he sought to drive a wedge between elected MPs – who provided him with electoral legitimacy and were the source of his political authority – and the policy-making machine based on his own advisors and political priorities. MPs and parliament were to be tolerated and subordinated rather than appreciated and encouraged.

THE ROLE OF THE PARTY LEADER

The extent to which Thai Rak Thai and the Thaksin government were highly personalized is emphasized by numerous commentators. Criticism of the prime minister was rarely voiced, and those who dared to express it risked excommunication. A prime example was Ammar Siamwallar, one of Thailand's leading economists and the head of the Thailand Development Research Institute, the country's most respected policy think tank, who then took a vow of public silence on the subject of Thaksin.[129] Another was former Bank of Thailand governor Vijit Supinit.

Thaksin was not solely concerned with rebutting criticism: he devoted considerable attention to promoting favourable images of himself. An English book published in 2003 describing Thai Rak Thai's policies began with a hymn of praise to the leader's family life:

> In terms of his personal life, Thaksin enjoys a happy and
> warm family with his wife, Khunying Potjaman Shinawatra,

and three children – one son and two daughters. He has often stated in the past that the family is the most important foundation of our lives and that building warm and strong family would provide the best immunity for children from all social problems.[130]

Some of this could certainly be read as a side-swipe at former prime minister and Democrat leader Chuan Leekpai, whose irregular family situation had always been a window of vulnerability; but it also testified to the extent to which Thai Rak Thai was explicitly organized around social values said to be epitomized by the party leader himself.

Senior Thai Rak Thai advisor Sanoh Thienthong hinted at his alienation from Thaksin when he suggested that 'the prime minister's thoughts run faster than the Consitution, so it might be necessary to change the law to keep up with him. He's a commander who moves faster than his army'.[131] Thaksin's dominance of Thai Rak Thai was such that he personally controlled a wide range of policy areas, and typically announced new developments himself rather than delegating them to ministers and senior party officials. This was exasperating for veteran politicians and deal-makers such as Sanoh, who were used to participating in extensive backroom discussions before decisions were made public.

In a rare example of critical self-awareness, Thaksin had told *Asian Business* magazine in a 1995 interview: 'I'm the Ghengis Khan type of manager'. He went on:

> 'When you start a company, you need someone to propel it, to set a vision and force everyone to work like barbarians. But after a certain point you need a builder, who must be professional, so they don't need someone like me any more, who might push too hard.'[132]

In a somewhat generous gloss, *The Nation* argued that Thaksin could become over-sensitive when under pressure: 'He delegates well, but at the same time does not easily trust people, and lately, because of anxiety over the election, he became sensitive and reacted excessively to perceived criticism'.[133] However, it soon became apparent that mistrust of others, concentration of power in his own hands and intense intolerance of criticism were all standard features of Thaksin's normal operating procedure as prime minister and party leader: Thai Rak Thai, like the government it led, was an organization centred entirely around a single man. That man's confidence did not diminish as his term of office wore on: in April 2003, Thaksin declared that he expected to be prime minister himself for a further term, and that Thai Rak Thai would remain in power for at least 20 more years, leading the government long after he had stepped down.[134] While many agreed that Thaksin would be able to win and complete a further term, the notion that his party would continue on without him at the helm met with widespread scepticism.

While an electoral professional party does give a central role to leadership, Thaksin's role in Thai Rak Thai was so dominant and so personalized that it undermined the party's claim to be a new political force. Like other recent parties such as Chamlong Srimuang's Palang Dharma and Chavalit Yongchaiyudh's New Aspiration, Thai Rak Thai was a one-man show. Thaksin's determination to boost the number of Thai Rak Thai MPs failed to conceal the fact that however large Thai Rak Thai became, it would owe its existence solely to his own participation and leadership.

CONCLUDING REMARKS

Thai Rak Thai is a new kind of Thai political party in the sense that it is run by a highly professional core group of advisors and managers, using the latest polling and marketing methods, and placing much more emphasis on policy initiatives than previous Thai parties. Thai Rak Thai has sought to bypass the existing linkages between ordinary voters and local politicians and MPs, creating a direct connection between the electorate and the government. At the same time, Thai Rak Thai does not meet all Panebianco's criteria for the status of 'electoral professional' party: despite its strategies and rhetoric, the party remains fundamentally reliant on traditional Thai forms of campaigning and canvassing, many of them illegal. Furthermore, the sense in which the party is simply a political vehicle for its leader undermines its credibility: no one seriously believes that the party would survive a change of leader-ship, since the party appears to lack any wider institutional identity or coherence.

Much of the success of Thai Rak Thai in its early years was based on 'feel-good' factors: during the 2001 election the positive image of Thaksin compared with Chuan and the Democrats; and following the election, the economic recovery presided over by the new prime minister. How far the party could survive an economic downturn or some other political crisis remained to be seen. Although to date Thaksin's coalition appeared secure, there was always the danger that disgruntled former allies might join forces with the Democrat Party, and that following a drop in Thaksin's popularity other parties could use similar marketing strategies to emulate the successes of Thai Rak Thai. This possibility appeared less likely following the revival of the Mahachon Party, by former Democrat secretary-general Sanan Kachornprasart, in mid-2004. Sanan led a team of Democrat defectors, including former Thammasat University political scientist Anek Laothamatas, in setting up a new political outfit that would be well placed to form an accommodation with Thaksin following the forthcoming election. The new party was widely rumoured to have received financial support from sources close to Thai Rak Thai.

For adherents of political economy approaches, Thai Rak Thai is not an electoral professional party. Baker has argued that Thai Rak Thai is a party of the business elite. Finally, the Sino-Thai nouveau riche have given up working through front men and intermediaries, and used the political system to take direct control of the Thai economy: 'big domestic capital has come right into the core of Thai politics'.[135] Ockey, who sees Thaksin's attempts to build a grand coalition as the most distinctive feature of his political strategy, suggests that Thai Rak Thai's grand coalition contains 'inherent

economic paradoxes'.[136] Building a grand coalition is ultimately a
means of bypassing faction leaders; this has involved deploying considerable financial resources and employing 'legal forms of patronage
on a vast scale'. Given that Ockey still believes factions and their
associated local electoral networks remain the key to political power
in the Thai context, he argues that Thai Rak Thai's expensive experi-
ment may be inherently unsustainable – quite apart from wider
questions about Thailand's oppositional political culture, or whether
Thaksin could successfully hand over the party leadership to anyone
else.

Michael Nelson similarly questions the extent to which Thai Rak
Thai was capable of institutionalizing itself into a more plausible
political party:

> It seems the jury is still out on whether TRT will indeed de-
> velop into the first full-blown Thai electoral professional party,
> or whether merely is a modernized version of the personalized
> and temporary ad hoc parties, such as Chart Thai, Chart
> Pattana, New Aspiration, Samakkhi Tham, Social Action, and,
> to a large degree, Palang Dharma.[137]

The acid test for Thai Rak Thai concerns the extent to which the
national appeal of the party and its leader, fostered through
marketing campaigns and policies calculated to reach out directly to
rural voters, can transcend the traditional political realities of *phuak*-
based local canvassing and campaigning. There are two ways in
which this could happen: traditional canvassers could be incorporated into a new party-led system; or local networks could be
completely bypassed by a different mode of political participation.
So far, the evidence for either of these trends is patchy. Rather, Thai
Rak Thai takes old-fashioned *phuak*-based politics to new heights,
transforming political factions into extensive and complex networks
centring on Thaksin himself.

NOTES

1   *Straits Times*, 12 December 2003.

2   The best 'political economy' discussion of Thai parties is to be found in Sungsidh Phiryarangsan and Pasuk Phongpaichit, *Jitsamnuk lae udomkan khong khabuankan prachatipatai ruam samai* [Consciousness and Ideology of the Contemporary Democracy Movement], Bangkok, Political Economy Cente, Chulalongkorn University, 1996. The volume is especially useful for its excellent histories of various political parties.

3   See James Ockey, 'Political parties, factions and corruption in Thailand, *Modern Asian Studies*, 28, 2, 1994, pp. 251–277. Ockey's stress on factions reflects the influence of political economy approaches, though he also draws on culturalist readings of Thai politics.

4   Other examples of plausible public faces as prime minister were Prem, Chatichai and, to a much lesser extent, Chavalit. Suchinda and Banharn had short terms as prime minister, in part precisely because they were unable credibly to front their administrations.

5   Rodney Tasker and Prangthip Daorueng, 'New-age leader', *Far Eastern Economic Review*, 17 June 1999.

6   It may be objected that electoral politics even in developed democracies is overshadowed by issues of campaign finance; while this is certainly true, it hardly excuses the abuses practised routinely by most Thai politicians.

7   For background on these issues, see Sombat Chantornvong, *Luektang wikrit: panha lae tang ok* [Elections in Crisis: Problems and Solutions], Bangkok, Kopfai, 1993; William A. Callahan and Duncan McCargo, 'Vote-buying in Thailand's Northeast: the case of the July 1995 general election', *Asian Survey*, 36, 4, 1996, pp. 376–392; Surin Maisrikrod and Duncan McCargo, 'Electoral politics: commercialization and exclusion', in Kevin Hewison (ed.) *Political Change in Thailand: Democracy and Participation*, London, Routledge, 1997, pp. 132–148; William A. Callahan, 'The ideology of vote-buying and the democratic deferral of political reform', presented at Trading Political Rights: The Comparative Politics of Vote Buying, International Conference, 26–28 August 2002, Massachusetts Institute of Technology, Cambridge MA http://web.mit. edu.cis/pdf/Callahen.pdf; and Allen D. Hicken, 'The market for votes in Thailand', presented at Trading Political Rights (as above), http:// web.mit.edu.cis/pdf/Hicken.pdf; and various chapters of Michael H. Nelson, *Central Authority and Local Democratisation in Thailand: A Case Study from Chachoengsao Province*, Bangkok, White Lotus, 1998.

8   On the background to Thailand's reform process, Duncan McCargo, 'Alternative meanings of political reform in Thailand', *The Copenhagen*

Journal of Asian Studies, 13, 1998, pp. 5–30; and Duncan McCargo, 'Introduction: understanding political reform in Thailand', in Duncan McCargo (ed.), *Reforming Thai Politics*, Copenhagen, Nordic Institute of Asian Studies, 2002, pp. 1–18.

9   Tasker and Prangthip, 'New-age leader'.

10 For a classic statement of this position, see James C. Scott, 'Corruption in Thailand', in Clark D. Neher (ed.), *Modern Thai Politics: From Village to Nation*, Cambridge MA, Schenkman, 1979, pp. 297–299.

11 See Ockey, 'Political parties'; Nelson, *Local Authority*; and Daniel Arghiros, *Democracy, Development and Decentralization in Provincial Thailand*, Richmond, Curzon, 2001.

12 Ockey, 'Political parties'.

13 Duncan McCargo, *Contemporary Japan*, Basingstoke: Palgrave 2004, pp. 114–118.

14 Duncan McCargo, *Politics and the Press in Thailand: Media Machinations*, London, Routledge 2000, p. 103.

15 Examples include the two Chulalongkorn University political science professors who were best known internationally at the beginning of the 1990s: Chai-Anan Samudavanjia pursued a series of new careers, including newspaper columnist, Chair of Thai Airways International and principal of a high-class secondary school; while Suchit Bunbongkarn became a member of the Constitutional Court.

16 Duncan McCargo, 'Thailand's political parties: real, authentic and actual', in Kevin Hewison (ed.), *Political Change in Thailand: Democracy and Participation*, London, Routledge, 1997, pp. 115–116.

17 Kramol Tongdhamachart, *Towards a Political Party Theory in Thai Perspective*, Singapore, Maruzen Asia, 1982, p. 19.

18 Angelo Panebianco, *Political Parties: Organisation and Power*, Cambridge, Cambridge University Press, 1988.

19 McCargo, 'Thailand's political parties', p. 128.

20 James Putzel, *The Politics of 'Participation': Civil Society, the State and Development Assistance*, Discussion Paper 1, Crisis States Programme, London School of Economics, January 2004, p. 10. http://www.crisis states.com/Publications/dp/dp01.htm.

21 Panebianco, *Political Parties*, p. 264.

22 McCargo, 'Thailand's political parties', pp. 130–131.

23 See Robert D. Putnam, *Bowling Alone: the Collapse and Revival of American Community*, London, Simon & Schuster, 2001.

24 Chris Baker, 'Pluto-populism: Thaksin and popular politics', in Peter Warr (ed.) *Thailand Beyond the Crisis*, London, Routledge, forthcoming.

25 See Allen D. Hicken, 'From Phitsanulok to parliament: multiple parties in pre-1997 Thailand', in Michael H. Nelson (ed.), *Thailand's New Politics: KPI 2001 Yearbook*, Bangkok, White Lotus, 2002, pp. 157–164.

26 *Bangkok Post*, 17 September 2000.

27 *Phujatkan Weekly*, 31 July to 6 August 2000, cited in Michael H. Nelson, 'Thailand's house elections of 6 January 2001: Thaksin's landslide victory and subsequent narrow escape', in Michael H. Nelson (ed.), *Thailand's New Politics: KPI 2001 Yearbook*, Bangkok, White Lotus, 2002, p. 288.

28 Michael H. Nelson, 'Thailand's house elections', pp. 289–290.

29 Baker, 'Pluto-populism.'

30 James Ockey, 'Change and continuity in the Thai party system', *Asian Survey*, 43, 4, 2003, pp. 663–680.

31 Philip Robertson, 'The rise of the rural network politician', *Asian Survey*, 36, 1996, pp. 924–941.

32 This argument reflects Anek Laothamatas's conception of Thai electoral politics – see Anek Laothamatas, 'A tale of two democracies: conflicting perceptions of elections and democracy in Thailand', in Robert H. Taylor (ed.), *The Politics of Elections in Southeast Asia*, New York, Cambridge University Press, 1996, pp. 201–223.

33 Baker, 'Pluto-populism'.

34 Rodney Tasker and Shawn Crispin, 'How to save Thailand', *Far Eastern Economic Review*, 6 November 2000.

35 *The Nation*, 15 July 1998.

36 Baker, 'Pluto-populism'.

37 Shawn Crispin, 'Bigger party, bigger risk', *Far Eastern Economic Review*, 30 August 2001.

38 Nelson, 'Thailand's house elections', p. 289.

39 *Nation Weekend* 9–15 July 2001, cited in Nelson, 'Thailand's house elections', p. 411.

40 Crispin, 'Bigger party'.

41 See Marwaan Macan-Markar, 'Thailand – government promotes village handicrafts scheme', Inter-Press Service, 22 May 2002.

42 *Bangkok Post*, 4 March 2002.

43 *The Nation*, 9 July 2001.

44   Michael Vatikiotis and Rodney Tasker, 'Prickly premier', *Far Eastern Economic Review*, 11 April 2002.

45   The proximity of many supposedly neutral senators to the ruling party was made clear in June 2003, when Kasem Rungthankiat quit the Senate on the grounds that he had grown too close to Thai Rak Thai (*The Nation*, 8 June 2003). Similarly, 26 senators who had previously supported a petition for the review of two controversial telecom decrees abruptly changed their minds around the same time, suggesting that the ruling party was systematically lobbying senators to toe the government line. They were widely believed to be among a group of between 30 and 40 senators who had been considering resigning en masse to join Thai Rak Thai. This sort of tendency illustrated the extent to which the aims of the 1997 constitution-drafters were being flouted in spirit. Such tendencies were confirmed when Thaksin, who had publicly urged senators to cooperate with the government, attended the birthday party of Srimuang Charoensri, a senator who had been instrumental in ousting controversial senate speaker and former coup leader Manoon(krit) Roopkachorn (*The Nation*, 15 July 2003). At the party, Thaksin was told that senators sympathetic to Thai Rak Thai would soon seize control of the chairmanship of the Senate Committee on Public Participation, which had often criticized the government under current chair, the outspoken former academic and broadcaster Chermsak Pinthong. The February 2004 election of a new senate speaker was characterized by 'alleged rampant vote-buying, blackmail and intimidation', so ensuring that a candidate with close ties to the Thaksin administration was chosen (*The Nation*, editorial, 2 March 2004). 'Self-respecting senators who perform their duty honestly are few and far between and thus have little if any impact on the working of the Senate as a whole'.

46   Chang Noi, 'Thaksinomics is all the rage', *The Nation*, 5 January 2004. Pasuk and Baker cite newspaper sources suggesting that Thai Rak Thai MPs collected large monthly allowances in cash from a party office in the Shin Corp building. Pasuk Phongpaichit and Chris Baker, *Thaksin: The Business of Politics in Thailand*, Chiang Mai: Silkworm, 2004, p. 192.

47   'Testing times for Thaksin', *Bangkok Post*, 30 December 2001.

48   Ockey, 'Change and continuity', p. 679.

49   *The Nation*, 19 June 2003.

50   *The Nation*, 29 July 2003.

51 *The Nation*, 21 August 2003.

52 *The Nation*, 22 August 2003.

53 The bypassing of constituency MPs helps explain the growing interest of local *phuak* in provincial and sub-district council elections, which could grant access to substantial local development budgets.

54 Baker, 'Pluto-populism'. In practice, Thai Rak Thai has so far set up nine regional coordination branches.

55 Nelson, 'Thailand's house elections', pp. 290–291. Nevertheless, some of those who have been given party jackets and membership cards may be encouraged to vote for Thai Rak Thai, especially if there is follow-up on these initial contacts.

56 Nelson, 'Thailand's house elections', p. 291.

57 *The Nation*, 24 November 2003.

58 By November 2003, 52 of the 88 parties in existence in 1997 had been dissolved by the Constitutional Court following complaints from the Election Commission (*The Nation*, 5 November 2003). Many had failed to register the required 5,000 members within 180 days, while others failed to submit annual reports to the EC or to account for grants they received.

59 *The Nation*, 5 November 2003.

60 McCargo, 'Thailand's political parties', p. 122.

61 *The Nation*, 22 January 2004.

62 *The Nation*, 29 February 2004.

63 Nelson, 'Thailand's house elections', p. 292.

64 Pasuk and Baker, *Thaksin*, p. 229.

65 Duncan McCargo, 'Thailand's January 2001 general elections: vindicating reform?', in Duncan McCargo (ed.), *Reforming Thai Politics*, Copenhagen, Nordic Institute of Asian Studies, 2002, p. 253.

66 Prangthip Daoreung, 'Obstacles await next premier', Inter Press Service, 8 January 2001.

67 *The Australian*, 8 March 2001.

68 *Bangkok Post*, 24 August 2000.

69 *Bangkok Post*, 3 October 2000.

70 *Bangkok Post*, 1 July 2001.

71 Nelson, 'Thailand's house elections', pp. 293–294.

72 Accessed 5 May 2004.

73 *Thai Rak Thai Party*, Bangkok, Thai Rak Thai, 2003, p. 1.

74 Marwaan Macan-Markar, 'Premier's anti-poverty drive is under fire', Inter-Press Service, 20 November 2003.

75 For an interesting discussion of the Democrat predicament following Banyat's election to the party leadership, see Michael Kelly Connors, 'Thaksin's Thailand – to have and to hold: Thai politics in 2003–2004'. Paper presented at the Thailand Update Conference, Macquarie University, 20–21 April 2004. http://www.latrobe.edu.au/socsci/staff/connor.thaksin.rtf.

76 *The Nation*, 28 July 2003.

77 *The Nation*, 29 June 2003.

78 *The Nation*, 29 June 2003.

79 *The Nation*, 18 January 2001.

80 Shawn Crispin, 'Ideas man', *Far Eastern Economic Review*, 1 May 2003.

81 For a critical discussion, see Chang Noi, *The Nation*, 1 March 2004.

82 *The Nation*, 21 August 2002.

83 Pansak angrily rejected allegations by senator Chermsak Pinthong that he had lobbied for the government to bail out Sondhi's M Group in 2002, insisting that he had not talked to Sondhi for years. See *The Nation*, 3 May 2002.

84 Business Wire, 5 December 1995.

85 *The Nation*, 16 March 2002.

86 *The Nation*, 9 April 2003.

87 *The Nation*, 9 April 2003.

88 *The Nation*, 16 August 2000.

89 *The Nation*, 8 January 2001.

90 Nelson, 'Thailand's house elections', pp. 286–287.

91 Nelson, 'Thailand's house elections', p. 287.

92 *The Nation*, 17 January 2001.

93 *The Nation*, 10 October 2001.

94 *The Nation*, 21 May 2001.

95 *The Nation*, 9 February 2001.

96 Nelson, 'Thailand's house elections', p. 286.

97 Nelson, 'Thailand's house elections', pp. 409–410.

98 *The Nation*, 23 March 2001.

99 *The Nation*, 14 October 2002.

100 *The Nation*, 19 October 2001.

101 Pasuk and Baker, *Thaksin*, pp. 137–139. We do not share Pasuk and Baker's views on the significance of this speech.

102 For a relevant discussion, see Nichapha Siriwat, *Branding Thairakthai*, Bangkok, Higher Press, 2003 (a Thai language book with an English title).

103 See McCargo, 'Thailand's January 2001 general elections', pp. 249–251, and Duncan McCargo, 'Democracy under stress in Thaksin's Thailand', *Journal of Democracy*, 13, 4, 2002, p. 117.

104 *The Nation*, 29 April 2003.

105 The marketing offensive engaged in by Thai Rak Thai posed challenges to the opposition Democrats. While deputy leader Anek Laothamatas argued that the Democrat Party used its 192 branches to involve local people and listen to the voices of the grassroots (*The Nation*, 22 June 2003), he did not rule out slicker marketing by the Democrats at the next election. He told an interviewer, 'We have to accept that in this day and age of politics, good policies need good marketing to drive forward'. In practice, however, matching Thai Rak Thai's marketing skills proved beyond the Democrat Party throughout the 2001 to 2005 parliament.

106 'Thai Talk', *The Nation*, 15 January 2004.

107 Connors, 'Thaksin's Thailand'.

108 *The Nation*, 10 March 2004.

109 *The Nation*, 4 September 2003.

110 *The Nation*, 24 February 2004.

111 *The Nation*, 3 December 2003.

112 *The Nation*, 7 September 2003.

113 Nelson, 'Thailand's house elections', pp. 250–253.

114 Nelson, 'Thailand's house elections', p. 257.

115 Michael Nelson, 'Politicizing local governments in Thailand: direct election of executives', *KPI Newsletter*, December 2003, p. 9.

116 *The Nation*, 12 March 2004.

117 *The Nation*, 19 March 2004.

118 Nelson, 'Politicizing local governments', p. 9.

119 *The Nation*, 3 February 2004.

120 *The Nation*, 29 March 2004.

121 Sophon Ongkara, 'Why is Thaksin hiding from the House?' *The Nation*, 3 March 2002.

122 Quoted in Crispin, 'Bigger party, bigger risk'.

123 *The Nation*, 13 April 2004.

124 *The Nation*, 15 April 2004.

125 *The Nation*, 18 April 2004.

126 Pasuk and Baker, *Thaksin*, p. 189.

127 Suthichai Yoon, 'Umno-isation of Thai politics has begun', *The Nation*, 12 February 2002.

128 *Matichon*, 9 August 2004.

129 Pasuk and Baker, *Thaksin*, p. 156. Ammar ended his silence in 2004.

130 Thai Rak Thai, p. 3.

131 *The Nation*, 11 December 2003.

132 Quoted in *The Nation*, 8 January 2001.

133 *The Nation*, 8 January 2001.

134 *Bangkok Post*, 28 April 2003.

135 Baker, 'Pluto-populism'.

136 Ockey, 'Change and continuity', p. 679.

137 Nelson, 'Politicizing local governments', p. 9.

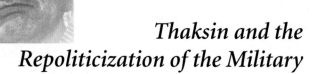

CHAPTER 4

Thaksin and the Repoliticization of the Military

The leaders of the Armed Forces are very disciplined. They support the Government firmly, especially myself, since I come from the Armed Forces academy. We have very good relations. So we have no problems. – Thaksin Shinawatra, New Straits Times, *10 July 2003.*

We adhere to the no-interference-with-politics principle. At present, the armed forces don't interfere with politics, anyway. Yet, as the military and the armed forces are one of the government's instruments, we have to collaborate with the government. Nowadays, the military is already in order. Politics and government are two different things and you have to learn to distinguish them. – General Chaisit Shinawatra, Army Commander-in-Chief, from the army official policy statement, 10 October 2003, quoted in Matichon Weekend, *17–23 October 2003.*

THAKSIN SHINAWATRA HAS BEEN WIDELY CREDITED with political decisiveness, for his determination to advance his own agenda, and with a desire to bring the market discipline of the private sector to bear on the sometimes lumbering bureaucratic machinery of the Thai government. Curiously, however, some sacred cows remain. Thaksin has practically never mentioned the military during his Saturday morning radio programmes to the nation, and he has yet to articulate a clear vision for military reform. Indeed, under

Thaksin the military has been engaged in a subtle process of trans-formation, which has amounted to a repoliticization of Thailand's armed forces. Thaksin's approach to the military reverses the trend towards de-politicization which began following the violence of May 1992, in which the armed forces were responsible for numerous civilian deaths. This chapter will examine why Thaksin has supported the potentially dangerous process of military repoliticization, a process that reflects his own background and political experience. It will sketch out the methods he has used for this repoliticization and explore the implications for the changing nature of civil-military relations during his own premiership and beyond.

Although he rarely speaks publically about the military, Thaksin is deeply interested in military matters, an interest which reflects his political ideas, his personal and political experiences, and his own goals and objectives. Recent studies of Thaksin have focused on parallels between his administration and those of previous Thai prime ministers.[1] One obvious example is the military strongman, Field Marshal Sarit Thanarat, whose authoritarian rule (1958–63) was characterized by an emphasis on state-led economic develop-ment, and who adopted a hard-line approach to law-and-order issues. This parallel gained credence during the 2003 'war on drugs', characterized by a wave of extra-judicial killings that seemed to emulate Sarit's methods of operation. Like Thaksin, Sarit was given to asserting his willingness to take sole personal responsibility for the solution of apparently intractable problems. Another candidate for a Thaksin prototype was Field Marshal Plaek Phibulsongkram (1932–44 and 1947–57), who was in many respects a more radical thinker than Sarit, and subscribed to a highly nationalist discourse. Like Thaksin, Phibun subscribed to ideas of an assertive Asian regionalism – though these were initially articulated under Japanese sponsorship. Whereas Sarit built up the monarchy as a political instrument of his regime, Phibun had a more antagonist relation-ship with the palace.

Despite certain parallels with both Phibun and Sarit, Thaksin differs from both men in his background. Whereas Phibun and Sarit were military men whose power was based on their positions in the army, Thaksin is a civilian political leader who has gained power through an electoral process. Thaksin emerged from the 'post-Prem' political system during the 1990s, when Thai politics was led by party politicians operating in an emerging, unstable and somewhat disorderly parliamentary system. Popular politics was strong, civil society groups were vocal and critical, and the military and bureaucratic elites which had retained a dominant voice until 1992 were being gradually displaced from power. Successive army commanders were distancing themselves from politics. Following the violence of May 1992, there were growing demands for reform of the Thai political system – demands that culminated in the passage of a relatively liberal new constitution in 1997. Thaksin was the first prime minister elected under the post-reform framework, and he had to co-exist with a range of independent bodies set up to check and balance the power of the executive. In other words, his power was far less absolute than that of Phibun or Sarit, and exercising it required a different range of strategies and skills.

While the political context that framed the Phibun and Sarit regimes was dominated by abrupt transitions of power in 1932, 1947, 1957 and 1958, coupled with the Second World War, the Cold War and the anti-communist movement, all of these events and issues are far removed from Thaksin's own experience and concerns. Thaksin is a creature of the social and political context of the 1980s and 1990s, a largely peaceful period of economic boom. His life has been shaped by a dominant culture of consumerism, and his primary interests – computers and mobile phones – more resemble those of a typical MBA-holder than the concerns of most army officers. His lack of interest in history is reflected in the books he recommends to his cabinet, most of which are best-selling business books published in the United States.[2]

In the end, Thaksin's own political stances are not readily reducible to analogies with previous Thai leaders. Rather like a cocktail waiter, he mixes together a blend of ingredients to create apparently new concoctions with a slightly familiar taste. These diverse ingredients are reflected in the circle of people around him, which includes business people, politicians, police officers, military men, high-ranking civil servants, academics, intellectuals and social activists. Prominent in that circle are those who have directly shared Thaksin's political experiences, including former prime minister Chavalit Yongchaiyudh, Pansak Vinyarat, Surakiart Sathirathai, Bowornsak Uwanno, Pitak Intrawithyanunt,[3] Banharn Silpa-archa and Sanoh Thienthong. These people have been drawn together around Thaksin for a variety of reasons, but all played significant roles in the ill-fated Chatichai Choonavan government. Chatichai brought together a range of talented and creative people, yet his innovative government suffered from factional instability, and was ended by the 1991 military coup amid allegations that it had become deeply corrupt. Before becoming premier, Thaksin described Chatichai as one of his two favourite politicians.[4] While Thaksin admired Chatichai's qualities as a modern leader, characterized by vision and decisiveness, he must also have been well aware of the former prime minister's failings. Chatichai's government lost power because he was unable to control his fractious political allies, and because he fatally antagonized the military. Thaksin clearly set out to avoid both of these mistakes, subordinating his party and the ruling coalition firmly under his own authority and humouring the military at all costs. In other words, Thaksin's basic attitude to the military was a pre-May events, pre-reform approach; in this respect, Thaksin was turning back the Thai political clock to the late 1980s, 'doing a Chatichai' without making Chatichai's mistakes.

But some of Thaksin's political lessons were learned even earlier, reflecting the experiences of another talented but ill-fated prime minister, MR Kukrit Pramoj (1975–76). This was because Thaksin's most important political mentor had his own formative experiences in Kukrit's government. The mentor in question was the well-connected former Chiang Mai MP, Preeda Pattanathabut, who had served as a Minister in the Prime Minister's Office during the short-lived Kukrit administration. Preeda knew Thaksin's father, Lerd Shinawatra; during his early career as a police officer, Thaksin was assigned to shadow Preeda.[5] In practice, Thaksin served as a kind of personal secretary to Preeda, who taught him how to deal and liaise with politicians, how to conduct negotiations and how to draft speeches and broadcasts.[6] He is also said to have served as a bagman for Preeda, delivering loans and payments on his behalf.[7] This political education was clearly central to moulding Thaksin's outlook, and the lessons were similar to those of the Chatichai period: a highly capable prime minister could be quickly toppled if he lacked the authority to unite his coalition partners. Thaksin once observed that Kukrit was only able to maintain control over his fractious coalition by using an ingenious range of tactics and negotiating ploys.[8] Like Chatichai, Kukrit had struggled with a hostile military, who had eventually brought an end to civilian rule in October 1976.[9] Again, the lesson was clear: a successful civilian prime minister needed to find a way of accommodating the military and retaining the upper hand over them.

THAKSIN'S VIEW OF PARTY POLITICS

In the mid-1990s Thaksin reached the conclusion that he could not achieve a stable position of political leadership in Thailand through engaging in party politics. His hundred days as foreign minister in the Chuan 1 government were mired in controversy, and he was strongly criticized by elements within the Palang Dharma Party itself. Thaksin returned to Palang Dharma to assume the leadership of the party in June 1995, and served a controversial spell as a deputy prime minister in the Banharn government. This episode is memorable mainly for Thaksin's grandiose but unfulfilled promises to 'solve' Bangkok's traffic woes. By vocally supporting the unpopular and incompetent Banharn government, Thaksin frittered away his party's remaining electoral credibility and political capital. Palang Dharma gained only one MP in the 1996 general elections. In August 1997, Thaksin became a deputy prime minister under the New Aspiration quota, but the Chavalit government soon collapsed because of the Asian economic crisis. His fingers burned by three consecutive inept entanglements with the prevailing political order, Thaksin was now deeply frustrated by the problems of joining an existing political party, with its own image, history and traditions. He became increasingly convinced that he could only make a successful political career by founding a new party, which he could organize entirely to his own liking. Ironically, the 1997 constitution – full of provisions designed to reduce party-switching and stabilize ruling coalitions – helped create the opportunity for Thaksin to re-enter politics, this time on his own terms.

Thai Rak Thai, founded by Thaksin in July 1998, acquired much of its political base by recruiting former MPs and members of existing political factions, including those of prominent political barons such as Sanoh Thienthong. In this respect, Thai Rak Thai resembled earlier modes of Thai political parties. Where it differed was in Thaksin's determination to achieve a hegemonic control of the Thai parliament, a determination reflected in his persistent pursuit of mergers and acquisitions. The Seritham and New Aspiration Parties were absorbed into Thai Rak Thai following Thaksin's 2001 election victory, and he persisted in his attempts to bring on board Chart Pattana and Chart Thai.[10] By the sheer scale of his operations, Thaksin hoped to override the problem of instability which had vitiated pre-reform coalitions: Thai Rak Thai quickly became the only serious political game in town, and there was room inside for everyone who wanted to join. This inclusive approach addressed the first Chatichai-Kukrit lesson about controlling the coalition. But his desire to form a one-party government after the 2005 election,[11] plus his determination to stay in power for two terms – until the beginning of 2009[12] – meant that Thaksin needed to secure other long-term allies. Extending the benefits of his rule to major institutions such as the police and the military was one means of trying to ensure his political longevity. The only recent Thai premier to survive for eight years was Prem, who was known to enjoy the blessing of both the military and palace.

Although Thaksin's family were silk-traders,[13] he was interested in the military from an early age. He had always dreamed of studying at the Armed Forces Academy Preparatory School, passing the entrance examination at his second attempt.[14] He went on to study at pre-cadet school before entering the police academy, but many of his school friends entered military service. As a boy, he dreamed of becoming a pilot: this was not to be, though he did briefly fly in an F-16 after becoming prime minister. Thaksin had an uncle in the military, four of whose sons also studied at the Armed Forces Academy Preparatory School. After he became prime minister, Thaksin was to appoint one of these cousins to the top position of Army Commander.

Thaksin's business has always made use of good contacts in the uniformed services. When Thaksin started out in his business, his company sold computers to the Police Department.[15] Most importantly, Thaksin's immense business success in the 1990s was significantly predicated upon the launch of Shin Satellite's Thaicom 1, Thailand's first ever satellite project. This project was first approved by the Chatichai government, but the contract was never signed. The National Peace-Keeping Council (NPKC) reviewed and re-approved the project following the February 1991 military coup.[16] Thaksin later told an interviewer that without support from General Sunthorn Kongsompong, the head of the NPKC, the Thaicom project would never have materialized. Thaksin was more than willing to do business with the military, where doing so could prove mutually beneficial. A similar attitude shaped his approach to the military when he gained political power.

THE MILITARY NEVER DEPOLITICIZED

Prior to the February 1991 military coup, many academics and commentators argued that the military had lost its appetite for political power, and had supported Thailand's gradual transition towards democracy. Some of Thailand's leading political scientists went so far as to declare that the military would never again seize control of the government.[17] These arguments had to be revised in light of the events of 1991 to 1992, which saw a coup d'etat, systematic attempts by the military to secure their own power and privileges, the installation of former coup leader Suchinda Kraprayoon as prime minister (with the connivance of a supine parliament) and a violent crackdown by the military culminating in the deaths of scores of unarmed civilians in May 1992.

After May 1992, familiar arguments about the military's supposed willingness to de-politicize itself resurfaced. The inability of the military to retain power supported the view that the 1991 coup was simply an aberration, an anachronistic intervention. Some academics regarded the May 1992 protests as a crucial event, permanently ending the military's leading role in Thai politics.[18] Certain of these interpretations were over-optimistic, making premature assumptions that the military had simply abandoned all political aspirations and would be completely displaced by new social forces.[19] Perhaps the most persuasive version of this reading was a 1997 chapter by Chai-Anan Samudavanija, in which he argued that the military was simply being 'bypassed' by complex socio-economic changes.[20] According to this view, the May 1992 events had seen the playing out of a decisive struggle between the rising tide of Sino-Thai capital and conservative bureaucratic and military elements struggling to retain the vestiges of power. Over time, the military would simply succumb to the inexorable logic of globalization. This was a beguiling picture, but in the event the position turned out to be far more complex. Even when the triumph of Sino-Thai capital was complete – as seen in Thaksin's 2001 landslide election victory – a powerful prime minister whose power base lay in the private sector continued to woo the military, seeking to co-opt the men in uniform rather than to confront them and strip them of their privileges.

Had the military really been thoroughly depoliticized, Thaksin would have faced difficulties in establishing such strong links between his own political and economic interests, and those of the military. In fact, Thailand's military did not really depoliticize itself in the wake of May 1992. Samuel Huntington defined a professional military as one which 'recognizes the limited functions of the military and is compatible with civilian control'.[21] Yet the Thai military has never recognized clear limits to its functions, nor has it genuinely subordinated itself to civilian control. Since 1992, it has instead been willing to pretend to accept limits and controls, on condition that it remained unreformed, with its privileges essentially intact. Jim Ockey has suggested that while the Thai military did resolve to depoliticize, it did so reluctantly and with considerable regret.[22] John Girling takes a harder line, arguing that the Thai military remains a 'wild card', whose ideology remains essentially unchanged despite the need to project a different image.[23] Duncan McCargo has argued that the Thai military has simply engaged in a discursive turn, preferring the language of development and participation to the old rhetoric of national security.[24] In other words, the military adjusted itself to changing socio-political conditions, maintaining a low profile until conditions were right for a reassertion of influence. That opportunity emerged when the Chuan and later Thaksin governments sought military help with projects of social control, including managing protests in rural areas which arose from rapid and inequitable socio-economic change, and from an expanded and assertive popular sector. The state found itself placed on the defensive and sought support from the military and police to suppress dissenting voices on issues ranging from the Pak Mun dam to the Thai–Malaysian gas pipeline.[25]

Immediately following the May events, the military attempted to protect their major sources of benefits, opposing all requests for change. Documents such as the 1994 Defence White Paper sought to rationalize requests for new weapons as essential to create a more technically sophisticated and professional military – despite all the evidence that the more weapons the Thai military received, the greater the tendency for corruption and de-professionalization.[26] Privileges acquired decades ago, supposedly on the basis of national security needs, remained intact. There was considerable pressure from social activists and consumer protection groups for the military to surrender their control over the country's radio airwaves;

yet there was no real progress on this issue after 1992, clearly because successive governments lacked the political will to tackle it. Large numbers of troops remained stationed around Bangkok – where there were no security issues to tackle – and the military controlled much of the underdeveloped prime real estate in the capital. Most seriously of all, the Thai armed forces suffered from a culture of chronic over-promotion, with the result that they probably included more serving generals – around 1,400 – than any other military in the world. It was an open secret that many senior officers had little or nothing to do.[27]

Military privilege is nothing new and long predates Thaksin's rise to power. General Prem Tinsulanond, the former prime minister, is the consummate example of the military insider. After stepping down from the premiership in 1988, Prem became a privy councillor and elder statesman, yet continued to exert significant influence in military and bureaucratic circles. This partly reflected his position as a figure who had the trust of the palace, and many of his behind-the-scenes interventions were widely assumed to reflect royal preferences. As a non-party figure, Prem was generally considered to be above the political fray and independent of political parties. Yet he also developed his own distinctive network of contacts, linking high-ranking military officers, large business conglomerates, leading politicians (notably from the Democrat and Chart Thai parties), high-ranking civil servants and politically influential newspapers. Prem is supported by some of the largest business conglomerates in Thailand. He enjoys close ties with the Bangkok Bank; he formerly served as the chairman of the New Imperial Hotel conglomerate; and in April 1996, he was also appointed the President of the Advisory Committee of the Charoen Pokphand Group. Prem had close political ties with Democrat and Chart Thai parties. This network, which gradually developed from around 1980 onwards, gave him considerable influence: Chai-Anan even called him Thailand's 'surrogate strongman'.[28] Prem's status received a further boost in 1998 when he became president of the privy council. During the 1990s, Prem was not above orchestrating cabinet appointments or the creation of political coalitions.[29] Nevertheless, Prem's privileged position began to decline after Thaksin became prime minister in February 2001. Thaksin set himself the task of dislodging Prem's dominant political network and replacing it with a new network of his own devising.

Prem's creation of a network of connections illustrates the military's process of adaptation during a period when they could not foster their own strong leaders or powerful internal groups.[30] The military needed to seek new connections both at the institutional and personal levels through the creation of a new patronage network. To ensure their institutional relationship with the elected government, military leaders established strong personal ties with leading politicians, often mediated by Prem's network. These personal and institutional ties were mutually beneficial for politicians and the military alike. Although such connections were not clearly visible to the wider public, they illustrated the extent to which the military still acted as significant players in the political and economic life of Thailand.

Immediately after the events of May 1992, there was a strong popular backlash against the military, whose leadership faced considerable pressures. Their strategy was to go to ground during the first Chuan government, making far fewer public statements, tolerating scrutiny from the media and even accepting parliament's decision to reduce the 1993–94 military budget.[31] General Wimol Wongwanich, who became Army Commander-in-Chief immediately following the May events in August 1992, adopted a new approach to the job, declining to comment on political matters and consistently declaring that the military would not interfere in politics.[32] Wimol came under pressure to reduce the size of the armed forces, which had grown increasingly bloated. He agreed to implement force reductions of 50,000 men, to improve and shorten training programmes and keep arms purchases to a minimum. His ideas were supported by then Lieutenant General Surayud Chulanont, who argued that weapons purchases needed to be linked to Thailand's needs. It has been suggested that Chuan never intervened in the military promotions exercise during his first term, simply endorsing what was submitted to him; this changed during the Banharn and Chavalit governments, which saw a more interventionist approach to the process.[33]

During the second Chuan government (1997–2001), Prime Minister Chuan Leekpai took the unusual step – especially for a civilian who had never served in the military – of also assuming the post of Defence Minister. In September 1998, Surayud Chulanont unexpectedly became the new Army chief. Prem's support was widely believed to have been the crucial factor leading to his appointment.[34] During his tenure as Army chief, Surayud actively pursued a programme of military reform and led a crackdown on 'mafia colonels' who abused their rank to engage in criminal activity. Equipment procurement was to be centralized under the Defence Council, and there were attempts to reduce the number of military officers sitting on this important body.[35] This change, however, met with strong resistance and was never fully implemented. Similarly, proposals for a unified joint command structure met with fierce resistance.[36] A new plan to reduce overall troop levels was introduced, involving reductions of 72,000 men over a 12 year period.[37] Plans were made to reduce salary costs to around 30 per cent of the budget, freeing up more resources for capital investment. Chuan and Surayud also attempted to expand an early retirement project for senior officers. Though there were few takers, the programme illustrated a degree of political will on the part of the government to tackle the thorny issue of military reform.

At the same time, it is debatable just how much credit Chuan deserves for his military reform efforts, since they were introduced in special circumstances as part of the government's attempts to address the aftermath of the 1997 economic crisis. Ockey notes that Chuan did not take a consistently hard line with the military, supporting them over a controversial decision to make former prime minister Thanom Kittikachon an honorary royal guard.[38] The reform measures introduced in Chuan's second term were as much about cost savings as about subordinating the military to civilian political control. Measures introduced included cuts in the defence budget as well as the number of military attachés serving abroad.[39] The relative acquiesence of the military leadership, attempts to reduce force levels, the introduction of a new policy on weapons procurement, Surayud's surprise promotion and the support of Wimol and later Surayud for programmes of reforms during Chuan's two administrations all testified to the military's adaptations to the post-May 1992 political environment. Crucially, however, they were also underpinned by the close links between the military, the Democrat Party and Prem, who acted as a mediator and facilitator in negotiating these policy initiatives.

Wimol had been hand-picked for the post of Army Commander in order to improve the image of the military in the wake of the May 1992 events. Although a member of Class 5, he had long been estranged from Suchinda and the clique behind the 1991 coup. Both Wimol and Surayud had served previously as commander of the special combat division, and were on excellent terms; most importantly, both were known to be close associates of Prem. Surayud had a particular interest in Cambodia, having worked in a secret team conducting operations directed by Prem on the Cambodian border during the 1980s.[40] This close and longstanding connection between Prem and Surayud led many to assume that Surayud's appointment as Army Commander-in-Chief was a 'special' appointment, intended to oversee the military during a delicate period following the economic crisis and political reform movement. Surayud was seen as closely aligned with the Thai monarchy through his links with Prem.[41] This illustrated the special relationship forged by the Democrat Party with the military, a relationship in which Prem played a central role. Chuan's approach to the military may well have been shaped by the odd circumstances that allowed him to become prime minister in 1997: no election was fought, Chavalit stood down and Chuan was installed by a mysterious elite pact, apparently arranged by Prem with the blessing of the palace. Both Chuan and Surayud assumed their posts in unusual circumstances. In other words, the military never ceased to have a political role during the 1992 to 2001 period, but it was a low-key role shaped by close connections with the Democrats, and reflected Chuan's need for alternative sources of political support beyond the parliamentary arena.

THAKSIN AND THE REPOLITICIZATION OF THE MILITARY AFTER 2001

The persistence of strong connections between the military and the civilian political order during the 1990s, mediated primarily by Prem's patronage network which linked business groups, political parties, senior civil servants and powerful newspapers in a complex web, actually served to facilitate the wholesale repoliticization of the military that occurred after Thaksin came to power in 2001. However, Thaksin's relationship with the military was rather less subtle: he set out simply to convert the military into a direct source of political support, a major component of his power base.

The repoliticization of the military during the Thaksin era began to take shape since the appointment of his first cabinet in February 2001. Thaksin's first administration was a melting pot of former politicians of various other parties who gathered under the name Thai Rak Thai, as well as owners of large businesses and former political activists. At the same time, Thakin's team included a surprisingly large number of men with high-ranking military backgrounds, including the following: General Chavalit Yongchaiyudh (who became Defence Minister), General Thammarak Isarangkura na Ayudhaya (who became Deputy Defence Minister), General Thawal Sawaengphan (former Deputy Army Commander), General Pallop Pinmanee, General Rattana Chalermsanyakorn, Admiral Suravuth Maharom, ACM Sermyuth Boonsiriya, former Army Commander-in-Chief General Chetta Thanajaro, and General Yuthasak Sasiprapha (former permanent secretary for defence, who became deputy defence minister).[42]

General Thammarak is a former intelligence officer who discreetly worked for Thai Rak Thai while still serving in the armed forces, prior to the January 2001 elections. He masterminded the party's highly successful campaign in the Northeast. Chavalit and Yuthasak

were former military officers with longstanding business connections; Chavalit was very familiar with the arms, gems and logging
trades along Thailand's borders with Burma and Cambodia.[43] His
appointment as Defence Minister in the Thaksin government could
be seen as a reward from Thaksin for the benefits he gained during
his brief participation in the Chavalit government,[44] and a quid pro
quo for Chavalit's permitting New Aspiration to merge with Thai
Rak Thai.

Chavalit was the kind of ex-soldier who hankered after the
restoration of the military to its former status as a major and open
player in the politics and economy of Thailand. Immediately after
his appointment as defence minister, Chavalit called for the restoration of the traditional seniority system of military promotions – a
proposal greeted with dismay by many observers, who saw it as the
beginning of the end of serious attempts to implement reforms of
the military structure.[45] Yuthasak, by contrast, was more low-key,
but maintained connections with the former military clique of his
father-in-law, Field Marshal Prapas Charusathira, and had various
business interests of his own. Given that Thaksin started out with a
defence minister and deputy minister who were sympathetic to the
idea of symbiotic links between the military and the business sector,
it was unsurprising that after 2001 the rhetoric and reality of
security sector reform was downplayed. The military no longer had
to be so discreet or defensive about its relationships with the holders
of economic and political power; the period of quasi-penance
following the May 1992 events was now over, and Thailand was back
into a pre-reform mode of civil-military relations.

The first annual military reshuffle under Thaksin took place in
August 2001. With the agreement of Chavalit and Yuthasak, promotions were made more on the basis of political contacts than questions
of equity, ability or seniority.[46] Yuthasak did well out of the
reshuffle, which saw the promotion of General Somdhat Attanand,
one of his in-laws, from First Army Commander to Chief-of-Staff of
the Army.[47] But Thaksin did even better, promoting Lieutenant
General Uthai Shinawatra, deputy director of the Defence Ministry's

Planning and Policy Office, to the rank of General and appointing him as Chief of the Defence Ministry's Planning and Policy Office. Lieutenant General Chaisit Shinawatra, special advisor to the Army, was named deputy commander of the Armed Forces Development Headquarters. Uthai and Chaisit were both Thaksin's cousins. In the same reshuffle, Thaksin reportedly insisted on the appointment of General Songkitti Chakrabart as Fourth Army Deputy Commander. Thaksin apparently wanted Songkitti to act as his eyes and ears with regard to southern border issues. This was despite the fact that Songkitti had been commissioned into the Supreme Command and had never previously served in the Fourth Army.[48] Major General Suriyo Inthabamrung was named commander of the Chiang Mai-based Third Army Division responsible for the Chiang Mai and Chiang Rai areas, although he had never previously served in the Third Army. However, both men had been classmates of Thaksin, graduating from Class 10 of the Armed Force Academies Preparatory School.[49]

Those who received political preferment were given sensitive political tasks to perform in return. Uthai was put in charge of drafting a bill providing an amnesty for people who had avoided military service, on the orders of General Chavalit Yongchaiyudh. The bill formed part of a mutually beneficial deal agreed between Chavalit, Thaksin and veteran politican Chalerm Yubamrung (then a deputy leader of New Aspiration), because Chalerm's sons were being prosecuted for submitting counterfeit conscript papers.[50] The 2001 military reshuffle was a return to a much more overtly politicized form of reshuffle than those of the 1990s, and illustrated Prem's loss of control over the military promotions process. Whereas previously Prem was widely believed to have been extensively consulted on important promotions decisions, he was now marginalized.

The 2001 reshuffle was a sign of things to come, but the clearest indication that Thaksin intended to transform the military directly into a personal power base came with the September 2001 reshuffle. Surayud, tainted by his reformist credentials and close ties to Prem, was kicked upstairs to the largely ceremonial post of Supreme Commander of the Armed Forces. He was replaced as Army Commander by General Somdhat Attanand, a politically-oriented soldier closely associated with Thai Rak Thai, and related by marriage to deputy defence minister Yuthasak: both were sons-in-law of former dictator Field Marshal Prapas.[51] Somdhat had extensive business activities, owning a number of companies;[52] and he had worked closely with Chavalit during his time as Army Commander.[53]

The appointment of Somdhat to the top Army post was carefully planned and had various political implications. First, Surayud's ouster was an indication that Prem's influence was declining and that the reformist policies associated with Chuan's two premierships were now out of favour. Second, the change reflected attempts by Thaksin to bring the military into line with his government's policy on Burma. Whereas Thaksin and foreign minister Surakiart Sathirathai favoured a policy of constructive engagement with Burma, which entailed playing down sensitive issues such as border clashes, refugee and minority concerns and questions such as drug-trafficking, Surayud had long insisted on a more hard-line approach. He had been particularly determined to confront the United Wa State Army (UWSA), believed to be the main source of the amphetamines widely sold and abused in Thailand. The UWSA, whose activities were extremely lucrative, were tacitly supported by the Burmese military regime. The Army's tough line on Burmese border issues – closely associated with the policies of Third Army Commander General Wattanachi Chaimuanwong, a classmate of Surayudh – had infuriated Thaksin and Surakiart, who felt it undermined their attempts to develop better business and diplomatic links with the Burmese military regime. Furthermore, Somdhat's appointment was widely regarded as a stop-gap appointment; once Surayudh reached retirement age in 2003, Somdhat could succeed him as supreme commander – leaving the top army post vacant for Chaisit Shinawatra, who became deputy army commander in the 2002 reshuffle. By installing one of his cousins in the position of Army Commander, Thaksin would be well placed to position more of his relatives and

Chart 4.1: Assignments of Class 10 memberss, 2004

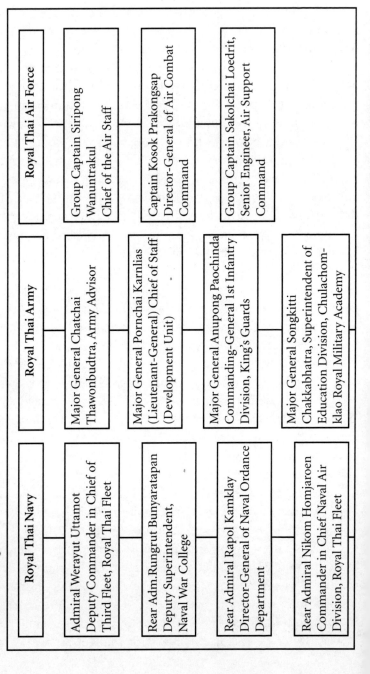

Royal Thai Navy	Royal Thai Army	Royal Thai Air Force
Admiral Werayut Uttamot Deputy Commander in Chief of Third Fleet, Royal Thai Fleet	Major General Chatchai Thawonbudtra, Army Advisor	Group Captain Siripong Wanuntrakul Chief of the Air Staff
Rear Adm. Rungrut Bunyaratapan Deputy Superintendent, Naval War College	Major General Pornchai Karnlias (Lieutenant-General) Chief of Staff (Development Unit)	Captain Kosok Prakongsap Director-General of Air Combat Command
Rear Admiral Rapol Kamklay Director-General of Naval Ordance Department	Major General Anupong Paochinda Commanding-General 1st Infantry Division, King's Guards	Group Captain Sakolchai Loedrit, Senior Engineer, Air Support Command
Rear Admiral Nikom Homjaroen Commander in Chief Naval Air Division, Royal Thai Fleet	Major General Songkitti Chakkabhatra, Superintendent of Education Division, Chulachom-klao Royal Military Academy	

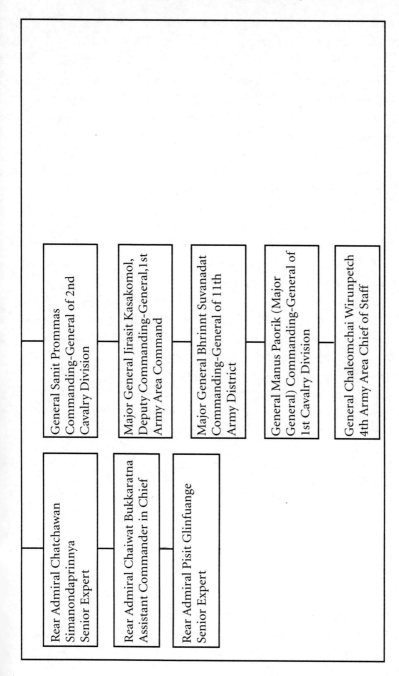

Rear Admiral Chatchawan Simanondaprinnya
Senior Expert

Rear Admiral Chaiwat Bukkaratna
Assistant Commander in Chief

Rear Admiral Pisit Glinfuange
Senior Expert

General Sanit Prommas
Commanding-General of 2nd Cavalry Division

Major General Jirasit Kasakomol, Deputy Commanding-General,1st Army Area Command

Major General Bhrinnt Suvanadat Commanding-General of 11th Army District

General Manus Paorik (Major General) Commanding-General of 1st Cavalry Division

General Chaleomchai Wirunpetch 4th Army Area Chief of Staff

friends from Class 10 of the Armed Forces Academies Preparatory School in a range of key military posts.

The plan worked, and Somdhat proved a very responsive Army Commander from Thaksin's point of view. Soon after taking up his appointment, Somdhat announced that under his leadership the military would strictly adhere to national policies and do nothing that could damage Thai-Burmese relations.[54] He told an interviewer that political imperatives now took priority over military concerns, and so the Army had to follow the orders and policies of the civilian government. He would therefore consult the prime minister before drafting rules for the army to follow. On the Burma issue, he made efforts to ease tensions with Rangoon by building a personal rapport with the Burmese leadership.[55] Accompanied by a team of military officers, he travelled to Rangoon in mid-January 2003, bearing gifts of high-class wine and Monthong durians for Burmese leaders General Maung Aye and Lieutenant-General Khin Nyunt. During their meeting, they held talks on developing collaboration in respect of drugs suppression, joint military patrols of the border and solving border demarcation disputes. No previous Army Commander had been able to negotiate successfully with the Burmese on these topics.[56] Furthermore, and much more importantly, Somdhat proved highly cooperative in supporting Thaksin's desires to entrench a strong network of his own friends and relatives in key positions within the army.

THERE ARE NO STUPID SINAWATRAS

'…The Shinawatras, none of them are stupid'.
Headline, *Nation Weekend*, 28 October 2002

The September 2002 military reshuffle clearly illustrated the extent to which Thaksin was succeeding in politicizing Thailand's armed forces. When Chaisit became Assistant Army Commander in 2002 – taking charge of the Army's finances[57] – 15 more of Thaksin's Class 10 classmates were also promoted. It is significant that Thaksin first placed Chaisit in a position with oversight of the military budget, an issue in which he took considerable interest. Though willing in principle to support military requests for increased spending, Thaksin sought to gain personal control of such allocations, ensuring that all such requests would be channelled through himself. Although by 2002 Thaksin seemed to have significant military support, appearances were somewhat deceptive. Somdhat rather meekly and obediently did Thaksin's bidding, but was serving only as an interim Army Commander, keeping the seat warm for Chaisit's planned elevation a year later. Somdhat, and his allies Yuthasak and Akaradej Sasiprapha, sought to increase their power through negotiations with Thaksin's faction, but were thwarted. In October 2002, Yuthasak was ousted as deputy defence minister, when Thammarak Isarangkura na Ayudhaya replaced Chavalit as defence minister. Thammarak was a Thaksin loyalist and co-founder of Thai Rak Thai. Chavalit was given the important-sounding post of deputy prime minister for security affairs, but in practice the cabinet reshuffle aimed at central-izing all decision-making powers relating to the military in the hands of the prime minister. These moves were followed by a further seven Class 10 promotions on 18 March 2003, reflecting Surayudh's removal from the decision-making processes of the Army.

All seven March 2003 promotions were politically significant, since the officers concerned were all placed in charge of major forces of the Army: Major General Songkitti Chakrabart was appointed as the Fourth Army Region commander; Major General Manas Paorik was named First Cavalry Division commander; Major General Pornchai Kranlert was named Chief of Staff for Development Unit. Major General Chalermchai Wirunpetch was named the Fourth Army Region Chief of Staff; Major General Jirasit Kesakomol was named Commander-General of the First Infantry Division; and Major General Anupong Phaochinda was named Commanding-General of the Eleventh circle. In addition Major General Phicharnmet Muangmanee, General Chaisit's Armed Forces Academies Preparatory School Class 5 classmate, was elevated to the post of Third Army Regional Commander, directly responsible for implementing the government's policy towards Burma (see Table 4.1). This round of promotions included two other appointments not considered significant in purely military terms, but clearly illustrative of Thaksin's designs and preferences: Major General Trairong Indharathat was named special advisor to the prime minister and Major General Chatchai Thavoraburt was named aide-de-camp to the prime minister. Both were fellow members of Class 10 (see Table 4.1).

Later in 2003, Thaksin quickly pushed ahead with the firming up of his political base in the military. With Chavalit removed from the Defence Ministry, it was easy for him to ensure the promotion of his cousin Chaisit to Army Commander in August 2003, despite the fact that Chaisit had little experience of top Army posts. Appointing a relative to this position was a risky strategy, likely to provoke criticism, suspicion and resistance, but Thaksin clearly saw it as an essential part of his long-term game plan to install his classmates into key positions. He seized the initiative by announcing Surayud's move to the Supreme Command in August, a month before the usual date. Chaisit himself was not an inherently strong figure; as a Signals officer who had served in low profile posts attached to Development Headquarters and the Supreme Command, he lacked any substantial power base within the armed forces. An officer from the provinces,[58] Chaisit hailed from a middle-class family, and had been posted mainly to rural areas, especially in the South.[59] The financial status of his family could be considered average, but all his siblings performed well in the Armed Forces Academies Preparatory School, serving in the military,[60] and marrying into military families.[61] His wife started out as a nurse, but later on invested in a publishing company with friends, and also worked for a while for Shinawatra Thai Silk.[62]

Although Chaisit had served as assistant army chief, he was in post for less than a year, and his position did not place him in command of any troops. His responsibilities concerned logistics, budgets and weapons purchasing. Chaisit's power base lay mainly outside the armed forces, where he had a large circle of friends and contacts, including some 'influential' people – a Thai euphemism

Table 4.1: Rotation and appointment of military officers connected to Thaksin Shinawatra

Order	Name	App't order	Appointment	Relation-ship
1.	Gen. Uthai Shinawatra	1	Dep. PSec., MoD	A
2.	Gen. Chaisit Shinawatra	1	Asst C in C, Royal Thai Army	A
		3	C in C, Royal Thai Army	
		4	Supreme Commander	
3.	Gen. Somdtat Attanand	1	C in C, Royal Thai Army	B
		3	Supreme Commander	
4.	Lt-Gen. Sombat Muangklum	1	Senior Expert to PSec., MoD	C
5.	Major Gen. Pongtut Svetsreni	1	Dep. Cdg-Gen., Weapons Production Centre, Defence Industry and Energy Centre	C
6.	Major Gen. Surapol Puanaiyaka	1	Asst D-G Office of Defence Budget, Defence Industry	C
7.	Major Gen. Chumpod Sritham	1	Senior Expert to PSec., MoD	C
8.	Major Gen. Teera Bhuranakasipong	1	Senior Expert to PSec., MoD	C
9.	Major Gen. Nakorn Kumsuntorn	1	Senior Expert to PSec., MoD	C
		4	Dir., Special Devpt Office, Armed Forces Devpt Cmd	
10.	Gen. Bhirddh Suvanadat	1	Chief of Staff, Defence Industry and Energy Centre	C
11.	Major Gen. Worawat Indharathat	1	Staff Officer to MinD Dep. Cdg-Gen., Royal	C
		4	Military Academy	
12.	Major Gen. Somkiat Masomboon	1	Dep. Dir. of Joint Personnel	C
		4	Dep. Inspector General	
13.	Major Gen. Anop Sombatthawee	1	Dep. Director of Joint Intelligence	C

Table 4.1: Rotation and appointment of military officers connected to Thaksin Shinawatra *(continued)*

Order	Name	App't order	Appointment	Relation-ship
14.	Major Gen. Eakachai Srivilas	1	Senior Expert, Supreme Command Headquarters	C
		4	Asst. Dir., National Defence Studies Institute	
15.	Gen. Surapan Srisakorn	1	Cdg-Gen., Military Research and Development Center	C
16.	Gp Capt. Surasuk Marungruang	1	Chief of Staff Officers to Dep. Chief of Staff	C
17.	Gen. Ma Pho-ngam	1	Specialist to Supreme Cdr Headquarters	C
18.	Gen. Phuchong Ruttanawan	1	D-G, Office of Defence Plan and Military Strategy	C
		4	Dep. Cdr, Special Warfare Command	
19.	Major Gen. Songkitti Chakkabhatra	1	Dep. Cdg Gen., 4th Army Area Command	C
		2	Cdg Gen., 4th Army Area Cmd	
		3	Superintendent, Education Division, Chulachomklao Royal Military Academy	
		4	Special Advisor, MoD	
20.	Gen. Manus Paorik	2	(Major Gen.) Cdg-Gen. of 1st Cavalry Division	C
21.	Major Gen. Pornchai Karnlias	2	(Lt-Gen.) Chief of Staff for Development Unit	C
22.	Gen. Chaleomchai Wirunpetch	2	Chief of Staff, 4th Army Area	C
		4	Cdg Gen., 5th Infantry Div.	
23.	Major Gen. Jirasit Kasakomol	2	Cdg-Gen. 1st Infantry Div.	C
		3	Dep. Cdg-Gen., 1st Army Area Command	

Table 4.1: Rotation and appointment of military officers connected to Thaksin Shinawatra *(continued)*

Order	Name	App't order	Appointment	Relationship
24.	Major Gen. Anupong Paochinda	2	Cdg-Gen. 2nd Infantry Div.	C
		3	Cdg-Gen., 1st Infantry Div., King's Royal Guards	
		4	Dep. Cdr, 1st Army Area	
25.	Major Gen. Bhrinnt Suvanadat	2	Cdg-Gen. 11th Army District	C
		4	Cdg-Gen., 1st Infantry Div., King's Guards	
26.	Major Gen. Trairong Indharadat	2	Special Advisor to the PM	C
		3	Chief, Office of the PSec., MoD	
		4	Senior Expert to PSec., MoD	
27.	Major Gen. Chatchai Thawonbudtra	2	Aide-de-Camp to the PM	C
		3	Army Advisor	
28.	Gen. Sanit Prommas	2	Dep. Cdg-Gen., 1st Cavalry Division	C
		3	Cdg-Gen., 2nd Cavalry Div.	
29.	Admiral Werayut Uttamot	2	Chief of Staff, Royal Thai Navy Headquarters	C
		3	Dep. C in C, 3rd Fleet, Royal Thai Fleet	
		4	Dep. Chief of Staff and Cdr, Joint Staff College	
30.	Rear Admiral Rungrut Bunyaratapan	2	Superint., Naval War College	C
		4	Dep. C in C, 1st Fleet, Royal Thai Fleet	
31.	Rear Admiral Rapol Kamklay	2	D-G, Finance Department	C
		3	D-G, Naval Ordnance Dep't	
		4	Dir., Naval Intelligence	
32.	Rear Admiral Nikom Homjaroen	2	Dep. C in C, 3rd Fleet, Royal Thai Fleet	C
		3	C in C Naval Air Division, Royal Thai Fleet	

Table 4.1: Rotation and appointment of military officers connected to Thaksin Shinawatra *(continued)*

Order	Name	App't order	Appointment	Relation-ship
33.	Rear Admiral Chatchawan Simanondaprinnya	2	Chief of Staff, Coastal Defence Force	C
		3	Senior Expert, Thai Navy	
34.	Rear Admiral Chaiwat Bukkaratna	2	D-G, Naval Ordnance Department	C
		3	Asst C in C, Thai Navy Headquarters	
35.	Rear Admiral Pisit Glinfuange	2	C in C, Marine Corps Training Center, Royal Thai Marine Corps	C
		3	Senior Expert, Thai Navy	
36.	Captain Kosok Prakongsap	3	D-G, Air Combat Centre	C
37.	Group Captain Sakolchai Loedrit	3	Senior Engineer	C
38.	Group Captain Siripong Wanuntrakul	3	Chief of the Air Staff	C

Appointment order dates: 1 = Sep 2002, 2 = 18 Mar 2003, 3 = 29 Aug 2003, 4 = 25 Aug 2004.
Abbreviations: Asst = Assistant, C in C = Commander in Chief, Cdg = Commanding, Cdr = Commander, D-G = Director-General, Dep. = Deputy, Gen. = General, Lt = Lieutenant, Minister of Defence = MinD, Ministry of Defence = MoD, PSec. = Permanent Secretary
Relationships: A = Family, B = Family of Minister of Defence, C = Friend in the Armed Forces Academies Preparatory School, Class 10
Sources: The Armed Forces Academies Preparatory School Yearbook 1967 (Class 10), numerous issues of *Matichon Daily* and *Matichon Weekend*.

for prominent criminals. He once insisted in an interview that this did not make him a 'mafia' military officer, but rather a 'big hearted' soldier.[63] Chaisit certainly gained a reputation for hosting a large

number of charity dinners during his term at the Army Development Headquarters. Soon after becoming assistant army commander,
he made a bid to become chair of the executive committee of the
Royal Turf Club, a nomination supported by a number of influential
military officers. However, the Turf Club had long been dominated
by the former secretary-general to the Democrat Party, Sanan
Kachornprasart, who rallied his forces to ensure that the 'new blood'
team led by Chaisit was routed by 331 votes to 32.[64] Thaksin was
believed to have urged Chaisit to concentrate on his army career –
but the Royal Turf Club electoral feud was an interesting microcosm
of wider Thai politics, illustrating the tensions between a political
establishment closely associated with the Democrat Party and a
newly-arrived but increasingly powerful challenger.

When Chaisit assumed the top army post, Thaksin seized the
moment by promoting another 13 of his Class 10 classmates at the
same time. In just under a year, Thaksin had placed 35 of his
classmates in key military posts, so creating for himself a remarkable
base of loyal supporters, several of whom commanded key front-
line troops (see Table 4.1). These promotions were not confined to
the Army, but also included the Marines and the Air Force. The
result was a powerful new military clique based on Thaksin's Class
10 colleagues, a clique with considerable political influence. Class 10
graduates now headed a range of key command units, including
three in the Air Force, three in the Navy[65] and nine in the Army (see
Chart 4.1).[66] Whilst there were no Class 10 graduates in senior
positions at the Supreme Command following the 2002 and 2003
reshuffles, it was striking that ten Class 10 officers were well placed
to succeed a cohort of senior officers in the Supreme Command who
were due to retire in 2004 or 2005. These included Major General
Trairong Indharathat and Colonel Worawat Indharathat, close
military allies of Thaksin who had been collaborating with him
from an early stage (see Chart 4.3).

Thaksin faced little opposition from the other armed services
over the creation of a personal patronage network based on his army
classmates. The Air Force was sympathetic to Thaksin from the

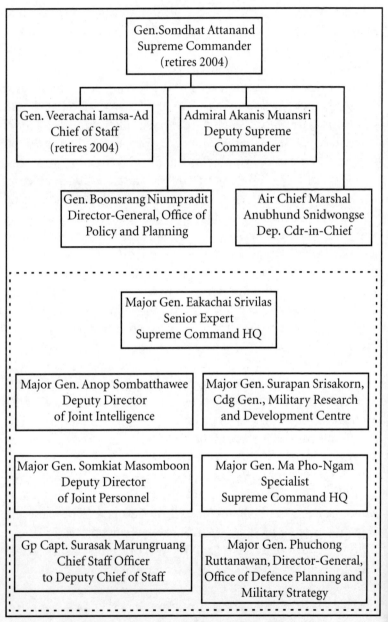

Chart 4.2: Office of the Supreme Commander

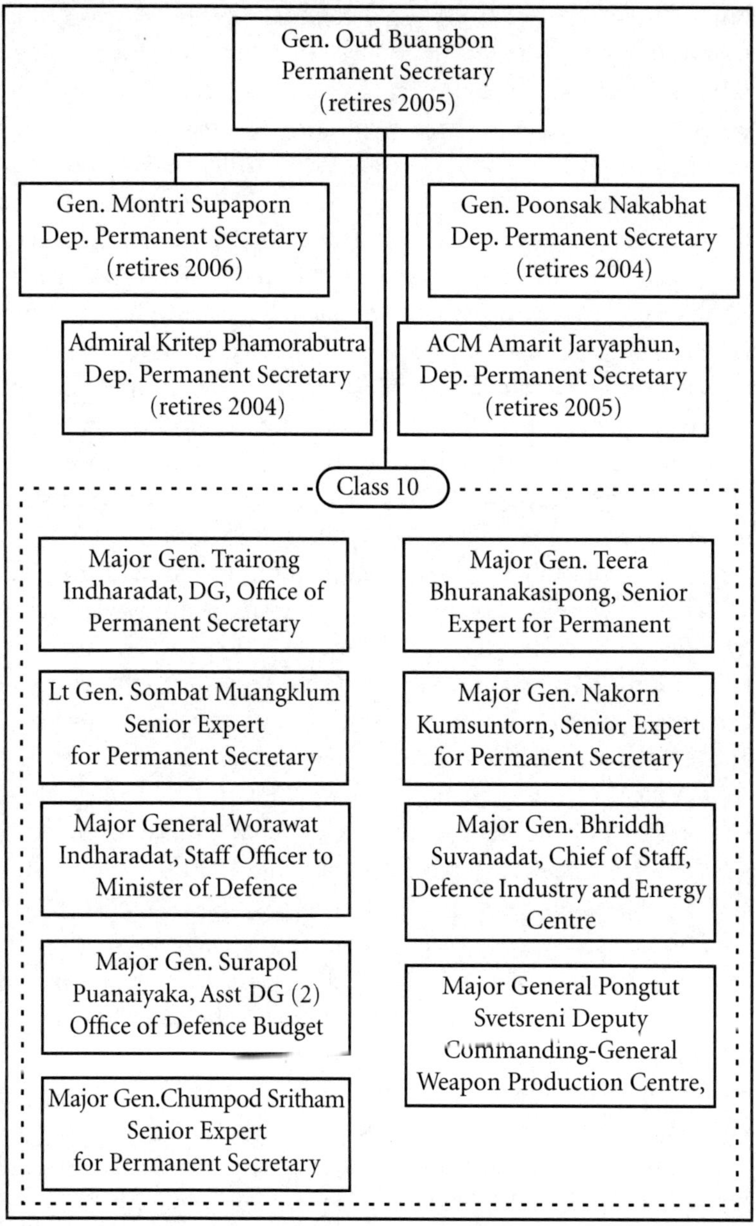

Gen. Oud Buangbon
Permanent Secretary
(retires 2005)

Gen. Montri Supaporn
Dep. Permanent Secretary
(retires 2006)

Gen. Poonsak Nakabhat
Dep. Permanent Secretary
(retires 2004)

Admiral Kritep Phamorabutra
Dep. Permanent Secretary
(retires 2004)

ACM Amarit Jaryaphun,
Dep. Permanent Secretary
(retires 2005)

Class 10

Major Gen. Trairong
Indharadat, DG, Office of
Permanent Secretary

Major Gen. Teera
Bhuranakasipong, Senior
Expert for Permanent

Lt Gen. Sombat Muangklum
Senior Expert
for Permanent Secretary

Major Gen. Nakorn
Kumsuntorn, Senior Expert
for Permanent Secretary

Major General Worawat
Indharadat, Staff Officer to
Minister of Defence

Major Gen. Bhriddh
Suvanadat, Chief of Staff,
Defence Industry and Energy
Centre

Major Gen. Surapol
Puanaiyaka, Asst DG (2)
Office of Defence Budget

Major General Pongtut
Svetsreni Deputy
Commanding-General
Weapon Production Centre,

Major Gen.Chumpod Sritham
Senior Expert
for Permanent Secretary

Chart 4.3: Office of the Permanent Secretary of the Ministry of Defence

outset, and Air Force Chief ACM Kongsak Wanthana was an old friend of Thaksin's sister, Yaowapha Wongsawat, who led a major faction within the Thai Rak Thai Party.[67] In late 2003, Kongsak, who was a widower, married a close friend and secretary of Thaksin's wife Pojaman.[68] Thaksin's special relationship with the Air Force was reflected in his regular use of their planes for both domestic and international travel. It was also illustrated by his headline-grabbing 30-minute flight in the navigator's seat of an F-16 in April 2003.[69] Chuan had repeatedly refused similar offers, believing that they were a ploy by the armed forces to ingratiate themselves with him. Yet Thaksin declared jokingly after the flight that he would ask the Air Force to make him a Wing Commander. Pictures of Thaksin in an F-16 pilot's uniform subsequently appeared on the cover of a 'War on Drugs' pop CD and in literature distributed to participants in the October 2003 Bangkok APEC meeting.[70] He also promised to look sympathetically at procurement requests by the Air Force.[71]

Thaksin's various manoeuvres successfully displaced Prem's elaborate military patronage network. In a break with precedent, Prem was not even consulted over Surayud's transfer to the Supreme Command. Whereas in the past prime ministers had been involved in the selection of Army Commanders but had generally left the appointment of subordinates to the top brass themselves, Thaksin selected not only the new Army Commander, but also his deputy. This was made possible by the appointment of Thaksin's loyal supporter Thammarak to the post of Defence Minister.

Prior to Surayud's transfer, Prem had been very unhappy with Thaksin's criticism of the Army chief's approach to issues on the Burmese border,[72] even summoning Thaksin to his Sao Thewes residence in June 2002 to give the prime minister a piece of his mind.[73] Prem's support for Surayud's hardline stance on the UWSA was seen as reflecting the King's own views, given his calls for the need to combat the drug threat.[74] When Thaksin responded by removing Surayud from his post, Prem grew increasingly unhappy, using his well-established channels to certain newspapers to make the public aware of his views. Prem now no longer hosted an annual New Year's celebration at his residence, at which he had previously welcomed large numbers of well-wishers including prominent military men, politicians and senior civil servants. Only a month after Surayud's retirement from military service in 2003, and in accordance with a royal command, Prem appointed him as the privy councillor in charge of security and development.[75] This was a clear signal that Surayud was looked upon with great favour in royal quarters, and could be interpreted as a deliberate rebuke to Thaksin.

OTHER TACTICS TO SECURE MILITARY SUPPORT

Thaksin used a variety of methods to secure support from the military. Early on in his term, he appointed no less than 53 Army generals to posts as advisor to the prime minister, based at Ban Phitsanulok.[76] Later he added a further 30 generals to this contingent. Thaksin was also inclined to look favourably on military requests for arms purchases, most of which had found little support from the Chuan government.[77] The prime minister even went on overseas trips for the purpose of exploring possible arms purchases, accompanied by senior officers from all three forces.[78] Thaksin also announced various budgetary increases for the armed forces, including an additional budget of 9.2 billion baht (or 215 million US dollars) for the military.[79] The prime minister announced on the aircraft carrier HMTS Chakrinarubet during his major inspection of the armed forces in 2003: 'His Majesty the King has told me to increase the military budget as soon as the government is able to...'. Thaksin continued, 'His Majesty the King said that the armed forces have been short of funds for several years, but the military needs to be efficiently maintained and in a state of preparedness for a combat at any time'.[80] Along with Thaksin's control of the promotions process and his creation of a network of supporters within the armed forces, his support for increased military spending could only help him to win friends and influence people in uniform. Thaksin was engaged in helping the military to move beyond the dark years that had followed Black May, supporting their rehabilitation and acknowledging the salience of their political and economic roles.

CONCLUSION

In an Army policy statement he gave on 10 October 2003, after his official assumption of the Commander in Chief post, General Chaisit Shinawatra declared:

> The policy of the army in my era is a combination of government policies and those of the past army chiefs, mixed with policies newly issued to match the situation. In the future, we will develop the army into an electronic force or 'e-Army' according to the government policy ... .[81]

He was also at pains to pledge the continued loyalty of the Army to the royal institution, saying:

> ... the Army will give the most importance to activities organized to honour His Majesty the King, Her Majesty the Queen, auspicious royal celebrations, and many other activities of members of the royal family. Also, the army will support all the projects initiated under His Majesty's ideas with all our capacity... .[82]

Chaisit then went on to insist that the military was not involved in politics, only collaborating with the government as one of the government's instruments.[83] During the first part of his term as Army chief, Chaisit has indeed pursued major initiatives advocated by the Thaksin government, notably by supporting the development of the army into an 'e-army', and by speedy moves to create a good relationship with Burma by joining hands in running 20 twin border village projects, modelled on the Yong Kha-Doi Tung development project.[84] Chaisit acted as intermediary during negotiations to resolve conflicts between the Burmese military government and the Karen minority by moderating two negotiations for a ceasefire between Gen Bo Mya of the KNU and General Khin Nyunt, the

Burmese prime minister.[85] However, Chaisit has placed the greatest emphasis on commercial initiatives related to the Army's economic activities.

The new policy of creating an 'e-army' created a pretext for a new focus on how to allocate the Army's major sources of revenue. It has become common practice for Army chiefs to select their closest aides to head the Army's television station, the important cash-cow Channel 5. Chaisit appointed General Preecha Premaswad, his classmate from the Armed Forces Preparatory School, to the post of Channel 5 director.[86] He subsequently ousted Pacific Intercommunications Corporation,[87] which had been in charge of supplying hourly news bulletin for all the 126 army-run stations, from 22 December 2003 onwards. Instead, Royal Thai Army Radio and Television Channel 5 were directed to set up a news centre to supply content for the hourly radio news bulletins.[88] In practice, however, Traffic Corner Holdings – which belonged to members of Thaksin's family[89] – replaced Pacific Intercommunications, taking charge of marketing management for hourly news bulletin broadcasts on all army-run radio stations, commencing from January 2004.[90]

Although it might be assumed that Chaisit's main priorities after taking up his post in October 2003 would centre around resolving Burmese border security issues and supporting the government's war on drugs, in practice his most pressing concerns related to the Army's business activities. His predecessor Somdhat and former Channel 5 director Lieutenant General Thira Bookphitak had planned to list the television station on the Stock Exchange of Thailand on 9 September 2003 – just before Somdhat was expected to leave the top Army post. Chaisit had become involved in this controversial issue around six months earlier, when it had emerged that Somdhat's plan involved the Army retaining only a minority 30 per cent of the 110 million shares in Channel 5, while another 40 per cent would be held by minor shareholders. Despite the fact that the flotation of shares on the Stock Exchange of Thailand had not yet taken place, clusters of shares seemed to have been allocated to certain well-connected groups of people, and there were rumours that sizeable sums of money had already changed hands. There were also no clear arrangements for resolving some dubious outstanding debts owed to Channel 5 by various private companies, which amounted to several million baht.[91]

When Chaisit assumed the post of Army chief, he created a new company, Tor Tor Bor 5 plc, in order to register on the Stock Exchange of Thailand. There were changes in the executive committee of both Royal Thai Army Radio and Television Channel 5, as well as changes among the board and management of all three subsidiary companies – Tor Tor Bor 5 Marketing, Tor Tor Bor 5 Radio and Tor Tor Bor Production and Entertainment.[92] But the plans did not go smoothly. In January 2004, Tor Tor Bor 5 plc withdrew its application to register on the stock market; the company subsequently had to reduce its capital to underwrite its losses, changed its name to RTA Entertainment and was awarded a 30-year concession by Channel 5 management to produce programming for the Channel. Programme development at RTA Entertainment was headed by Thaksin's nephew, Sompop Shinawatra. The deal aroused intense public criticism and was widely portrayed as a conflict of interest between Thaksin's family and the government.[93] Chaisit, who had pushed through the 30-year concession, quickly found himself at odds with the men he appointed as Director of Channel 5, and by 14 July had changed Director three times in less than six weeks.[94] On 24 June, Thaksin himself was forced to intervene, freezing Channel 5's plans and ordering an investigation into the controversies surrounding the station's finances.

This episode illustrates that the beneficiaries of the repoliticization of the Thai military under Thaksin are by no means confined to a small number of his close relatives. The allocation of economic benefits in Royal Thai Army Radio and the Royal Thai Army Television Channel 5, along with the prospective listing of RTA Entertainment on the Stock Exchange of Thailand, could lead to the transformation of the Army and its communications arms into a direct support device for the Thaksin government. At the same time, the pickings were so potentially rich, and the associated politics of benefit-sharing so tricky, that Thaksin's own cousin was unable to oversee the process smoothly. The result was a vivid illustration of the dangers of collusive relationships between the military and the government.

Radio programmes controlled by the military were increasingly being used to support Thai Rak Thai initiatives, such as a daily programme concerned with the One Tambon, One Product project, economic development and tourism, broadcast between 5 and 6 pm. Such crude use of the broadcast media to support government policies harked back to the propagandist approach of former military regimes. At the same time, Chaisit's interest in exploiting new sources of revenue for the Army's broadcasting operations was a blatant form of commercialization of military resources, made all the more complex because of the intimate ties between the military, the prime minister and the ruling party. Thaksin's policy meant that military concerns would now be floated on the stock market, becoming more or less indistinguishable from other business activities.

One argument for placing a man such as Chaisit in charge of the Army is that his presence should ensure that there is no prospect of a coup d'etat, or other form of threat by the military to civilian rule. Yet there are a variety of ways in which a newly-rehabilitated military can threaten or undermine the democratic process if it becomes too closely aligned with an individual prime minister or a particular political party. Thaksin's classmates are not an especially talented or impressive bunch of men; they owe their remarkable recent rise very largely to his personal patronage.[95] They are not even dignified by the claims to ideological coherence made for other factions such as Class 5 or the Young Turks.[96] Rather, they are an externally-created faction, shaped and moulded entirely because of Thaksin's rise to the premiership.

The close personal ties between Thaksin and the Army undermine principles of military professionalism and neutrality, a potentially dangerous state of affairs. What Thaksin's repoliticization of the armed forces clearly reveals is that they were never bypassed. Chai-Anan's picture of a tastefully sidelined military institution actually hinged upon the crucial refereeing role played by Prem, and only applied while civilian political leadership was relatively weak. Under Prem's tutelage, the military learned to adapt themselves to civilian rule during a period characterized by a vibrant civil society and growing demands for reform. Once those demands had been super-ficially assuaged by the 1997 constitution, and once Thaksin had suc-ceeded Prem as a 'surrogate strongman' of a very different species, reformist generals were quickly pushed aside and clientelist criteria began to shape the promotions structure of the military. The lesson of military promotions in the 1970s and the 1980s was a simple one: balancing factions, cliques and classes is crucial. Just as the 1977 coup (and the 1981 and 1985 coup attempts) reflected the strength of the Young Turks of Chulachomklao's Class 7, so the 1991 coup was a direct outcome of the excessive dominance of Class 5. By 2001, the Thai military had no strong factions that looked likely to assert their own influence in the political sphere, but Thaksin quickly changed the rules of the game, creating a new military clique that will have important ramifications for the future. While Chaisit is close to 60, the graduates of Class 10 of the Armed Services Academies Prepara-tory School are not due to retire until 2010.

Thaksin's decision to 'promote' Chaisit to the nominally superior post of Supreme Commander from 1 October 2004 apparently testified to his intense dissatisfaction with his cousin's performance as head of the Army. Chaisit's inept handling of the Channel 5 issue, com-bined with the Army's lamentable performance over political violence in the South, had combined to exasperate the prime minister. Chaisit was reported to have been taken aback at his abrupt elevation.[97] But by selecting General Pravit Wongsuwan to replace him, Thaksin was keeping his options open: Pravit, like Chaisit, would retire in 2005, allowing for yet another new appointment to the crucial Army com-mander post. Thaksin was now changing his Army commander more frequently than many of his cabinet colleagues.

Under Thaksin, the supposedly 'bypassed' Thai military – who had actually been woven by Prem into an ingenious web of patron-age, with support from the palace and the Democrats – emerged from the political closet. They were enlisted as overt supporters and beneficiaries of Thai Rak Thai and its associated economic interests. Remembering the mistakes of his role models Kukrit and Chatichai, Thaksin believed that the military should be co-opted rather than challenged. The problem was that such a blatant form of co-optation reversed the reformist direction that had characterized political change in Thailand since 1992. Instead of marking the triumph of Thailand's vibrant private sector over its moribund military and bureaucracy, Thaksin's rule celebrated the kind of distasteful structural corruption that had characterized earlier periods of Thai politics. In this respect, Thaksin seemed to be emulating Chatichai more than Sarit or Phibun; but in Thaksin's re-make of the Chatichai period, the military were invited to join the buffet, and so never staged their coup. Though attractive in the short term, ensuring the goodwill of the armed forces towards Thaksin, the long term consequences of reversing the hard-won, reluctant and tentative return of the Thai military to the barracks were potentially alarming.

NOTES

1   For serious discussions of Thaksin, see Ammar Siamwalla, 'Thaksin-omics', *Matichon*, 25 December 2002; Pasuk Pongphaichit and Chris Baker, *Thaksin: The Business of Politics in Thailand*, Chiang Mai, Silkworm, 2004; Pitch Phongsawat 'Senthang prachatippatai lae kanpraptua khong rat thai nai rabop Thaksin' [Democracy and the adaptation of the Thai state under the Thaksin system], *Fa diao kan*, 2, 1, 2004; Ukrist Pathmanand, 'The Thaksin Shinawatra group: a study of the relationship between money and politics in Thailand', *Copenhagen Journal of Asian Studies*, 13, 1998, pp. 60–81; Ukrist Pathamanand, 'From Shinawatra group of companies to the Thaksin Shinawatra government: The politics of money and power merge', paper presented at the International Conference on Crony Capitalism, Quezon City, Philippines, 17–18 January 2002; Ukrist Pathmanand, 'Sethasat kan-muang khong khlum thun torakomanakhom rang wikrit sethakit thai' [Political economy of telecom capital groups in post-crisis Thailand], unpublished research report for Professor Pasuk Phongpaichit's Thailand Research Fund project 'Khongsang lae phonrawat khong khlum thun

rang wikrit sethakit thai' [The structure and dynamics of capital in post-crisis Thailand], presented at Faculty of Economics, Chulalongkorn University, 29 January 2004; Sorakon Adulyanon, *Thaksin Shinawatra: asawin khloen luk thi sam* [Thaksin Shinawatra, Knight of the Third Wave], Bangkok, *Matichon*, 1993; Surathian Jakataranund, *Natee ti prian prawatisat* [A Minute that Changed History] Bangkok, *Matichon*; and Walaya (Phumtham Vetchayachai), *Thaksin Shinawatra: ta du dao thao tit din* [Thaksin Shinawatra: Eyes on the Stars, Feet on the Ground], Bangkok, *Matichon*, 1999; as well as numerous publications featuring Thaksin's interviews, speeches and accomplishments, such as Khomdueon Jaudjaratfah (pseudonym) *Khum kom khawi kit: Thaksin Shinawatra* [Sharp Words, Sharp Thoughts: Thaksin Shinawatra], Bangkok, Siang Dao.

2   Books recommended by Thaksin include Juan Enriquez's, *As the Future Catches You*, New York, Crown Publishing, 2001, and Hernando De Soto's *The Mystery of Capital*, New York, Basic Books, 2002. These two books appear to contain the seeds of some of Thaksin's policies, including his asset capitalization policy.

3   Pitak Inthrawityanunt was a co-founder of the Thai Rak Thai Party. He joined Thaksin's team after accompanying Bangkok Bank owner Chatri Sophonpanich on a pre-election visit to demonstrate support for Thaksin from powerful businessmen. Later on, Pitak was appointed a deputy prime minister in the first Thaksin government.

4   Perhaps surprisingly, Thaksin's other political role model was Chuan Leekpai, whom he claimed to admire for his simplicity, honesty, strong principles and down-to-earth approach. Chuan originally approached Thaksin to join the Democrats for the September 1992 election, but Thaksin resisted. See Walaya, *Thaksin Shinawatra*, pp. 162–163.

5   Senior Thai politicians are typically assigned police adjutants, nominally to provide security for them, but in practice to act as general factotums and facilitators.

6   Preeda still serves as an advisor to Thaksin. He has recently published a memoir combining reminiscences with moral lessons: Preeda Patthanathabut, *Guru kanmuang* [Political Mentor], Bangkok, Amarin, 2003.

7   Pasuk Phongpaichit and Chris Baker, *Thaksin: The Business of Politics in Thailand*, Chiang Mai, Silkworm, 2004, p. 38.

8   Walaya, *Thaksin Shinawatra*, p. 84.

9   The political experience Thaksin gained from Preeda may have influenced Thaksin's populist policies, given that Kukrit adopted a

similar approach to rural development and social welfare issues. See Walaya, *Thaksin Shinawatra*, p. 85.

10   Ukrist, 'From Shinawatra group of companies', p. 38.

11   Pimthai News Agency, 2 May 2004, 13 June 2003.

12   Later on, Thaksin announced that Thai Rak Thai would rule for 20 years, or until 2020. *Bangkok Post*, 2 November 2003.

13   Sorakon, *Thaksin Shinawatra*; Plai-Or Chananon, *Pho kha kap phattanakan rabop thunniyom nai phak nua pho so 2464–2532* [Traders and the development of the capitalist system in the North, 1921–80], Bangkok, CUSRI, 1987, pp. 53–54; Ukrist, 'The Thaksin Shinawatra Group', p. 67.

14   Walaya, *Thaksin Shinawatra*, p. 52.

15   Sorakon, *Thaksin Shinawatra*, p. 30, Ukrist, 'The Thaksin Shinawatra Group', p. 68.

16   The Thaicom 1 project had originally been approved by the Chatichai government, but the contract was never signed. The NPKC had the project reviewed, reducing the investment protection period from 25 years (as originally proposed by the Communications Ministry) to eight years, with a proposal for one additional free channel. Walaya, *Thaksin Shinawatra*, pp. 139–140.

17   For examples of an argument along these lines, see Suchit Bunbongkarn, 'The Thai military in the 1990s: a declining political force?', in Wolfgang S. Heinz, Werner Pfennig and V. T. King (eds), *The Military in Politics: Southeast Asian Experiences*, Hull, Centre for South-East Asian Studies, University of Hull, 1990, pp. 117–120.

18   See Michael Kelly Connors, 'Political reform and the state in Thailand', *Journal of Contemporary Asia*, 29, 2, 1999, p. 203.

19   Thirayuth Boonmi wrote: 'This will lead to the transfer of power and righteousness from the state to the society, from civil servants to business people, technocrats and the middle class. The society will change from a closed society to an open one, from conservatism to a more open-minded perspective, from nationalism to a wider accept-ance of internationalism and regionalism, from the centralization of power to the decentralization of power...', in *Jut plian haeng yuk samai* [Turning Point of the Era], Bangkok, Vinyuchon Publishing, 1994, pp. 40–41.

20   Chai-Anan Samudavanija, 'Old soldiers never die, they are just by-passed: the military, bureaucracy and globalisation', in Kevin Hewison (ed.) *Political Change in Thailand: Democracy and Participation*, London, Routledge, 1997, pp. 42–57.

21   Samuel Huntington, *The Third Wave: Democratisation in the Late Twentieth Century*, Norman, University of Oklahoma Press, 1991, p. 243.

22   James Ockey, 'Thailand: the struggle to redefine civil-military relations', in Mutiah Alagappa (ed.), *Coercion and Governance: The Declining Political Role of the Military in Asia*, Stanford, Stanford University Press, 2001.

23   John L. S. Girling, *Interpreting Development: Capitalism, Democracy and the Middle Class in Thailand*, Ithaca, NY, Cornell University Southeast Asia Program, 1996, p. 22.

24   Duncan McCargo, 'Security, development and political participation in Thailand: alternative currencies of legitimacy', *Contemporary Southeast Asia*, 24, 1, 2002.

25   Pasuk Phongpaichit, 'Civilising the state, civil society and politics in Thailand', *Watershed*, 5, 2, November 1999–February 2000, p. 24.

26   McCargo, 'Security, development and political participation', pp. 53–54.

27   Duncan McCargo, 'Democracy under stress in Thaksin's Thailand', *Journal of Democracy*, 13, 4, 2002, pp. 123–124.

28   Chai-Anan, 'Old soldiers never die', p. 56.

29   For a story about one technocrat agreeing to accept a cabinet post only after a personal approach from Prem, see Suparat Chuayaurachon, 'Ten technocrats accept Thai cabinet posts: officials', Agence France Press, 24 October 1997.

30   Chai-Anan, 'Old soldiers never die', pp. 55–56.

31   Connors, 'Political reform', pp. 202–203

32   Rodney Tasker and Gordon Fairclough, 'Star turn', *Far Eastern Economic Review*, 20 May 1993.

33   Suchit Bunbongkarn, *Thailand: State of the Nation*, Singapore, Institute of Southeast Asian Studies, 1996, pp. 64–65.

34   Surayud's promotion was surprising for three reasons. First, he was only 55, and so had five years left until retirement – which suggested a longer-than-usual spell in the top job. Second, he had not been occupying one of the top five posts from which the appointment was traditionally made (*Matichon Weekend*, 6 October 1998). Third, he had a problematic background because his father, former Phetburi MP Lieutenant Colonel Payom Chulanont, was an ex-committee member of the Communist Party of Thailand (*Matichon Weekend*, 8 December 1998).

35   *Bangkok Post*, 28, 29 July 1998.

36 *The Nation*, 27 January 2001.

37 *Bangkok Post*, 17 May 1999; *The Nation*, 27 January 2001.

38 Ockey, 'Thailand: the struggle'.

39 Duncan McCargo, 'Balancing the checks: Thailand's paralyzed politics post-1997', *Journal of East Asian Studies*, 3, 2003, p.145.

40 Rodney Tasker, 'General agreement', *Far Eastern Economic Review*, 1 October 1998.

41 Thitinan Pongsudhirak, 'Thailand: democratic authoritarianism', *Southeast Asian Affairs*, Singapore, Institute of Southeast Asian Studies, 2003, p. 283.

42 General Thammarak Isarangkura na Ayudhaya, former Internal Security Operations Commander, was a founding member of the Thai Rak Thai Party. General Thawal Sawaengphan was a former deputy army commander and a student of the Chulachomklao Royal Military Academy Class 7, who had also helped found Thai Rak Thai. General Chetta Thanajaro, former army commander, was once invited to join the Democrat party by Major General Sanan Kachornprasart, the then secretary-general of the party. However, Chetta turned down Sanan in favour of Thai Rak Thai. General Yuthasak Sasiprapha, former permanent secretary of defence, despite his close ties with Chart Pattana, eventually joined Thai Rak Thai at the behest of his younger brother, deputy supreme commander General Akaradej Sasiprapha, (*Matichon Weekend*, 22 January 2001).

43 Shawn W. Crispin and Rodney Tasker, 'Thai defence chiefs march out of step', *Far Eastern Economic Review*, 13 September 2001.

44 Thaksin was briefly deputy prime minister under Chavalit in 1997.

45 *The Nation*, 27 January 2001.

46 McCargo, 'Balancing the checks', p.145.

47 *Matichon Weekend*, 13 August 2001.

48 'Critics fear political interference in Army', *The Nation*, 6 August 2002.

49 *Matichon Weekend*, 13 August 2001.

50 *Matichon Weekend*, 29 October 2001.

51 Somdhat is married to Khunying Wichitra Attanand, while General Yuthasak is married to Khunying Oraphan, both daughters of Prapas (*Prachachat*, 12–14 August 2002).

52 Somdhat has been engaged in a range of business activities since 1972. The former owner of 16 companies, by 2003 he owned only six, mostly engaged in property management (*Prachachat*, 12–14 August 2002).

53   *The Nation*, 6 August 2002

54   Wassana Nanuam and Yuwadee Tunyasiri, 'Army to toe government line on Rangoon', *Bangkok Post*, 6 August 2002.

55   Jariya Hoffman, 'Reformist general departs', unpublished World Bank paper, 2 September 2002.

56   *Siam Rath Weekly*, 17–23 January 2003.

57   Chaisit was the assistant army commander in chief, second division, in charge of armed troops, logistics, purchasing and budgets. See *Matichon Weekend*, 21–27 October 2002.

58   Nophakhun Limsamaraphan, 'What's in a name?' *The Nation*, 24 August 2003.

59   '…he said in an interview that he was a rural officer, living in the South for ten years …', Bancha Tingsangwal 'Mai chai fah likit' [Not determined in heaven], *Nation Weekend*, 19 August 2002.

60   He was awarded an Army scholarship to attend a military academy in Virginia, USA. Nophakhun, 'What's in a name?'

61   His father is Senior Colonel Sak Shinawatra, a retired army technical officer. Cited in 'The golden age of the fourth Shinawatra generation', *Nation Weekend*, 19 August 2002. General Chaisit Shinawatra is one of five siblings, three of whom served in the military. They are: 1) Lieutenant Colonel Surachit Shinawatra (who died on a mission in Laos); 2) General Uthai Shinawatra, deputy permanent secretary of defence; 3) General Chaisit Shinawatra, Army Commander in Chief; 4) Captain Prawit Shinawatra, who resigned from the military to work as a captain for Thai Airways and 5) a sister who opened the silk shop Tor Shinawatra in the Sukhumvit area. Source: Piyawant Prayuksilp and Saowaluk Karnjanasali, 'Shinawatra mai mi khrai ngo' [There are no stupid Shinawatras], *Nation Weekend*, 28 October 2002.

62   'Unveiling Weena Shinawatra…', *Matichon Weekend*, 5–11 September 2003.

63   Wassana Nanuam, 'General has a point to prove', *Bangkok Post*, 24 October 2002.

64   *International Herald Tribune*, 31 October 2002.

65   These comprise the assistant commander in chief, Royal Thai Navy Headquarters (Rear Admiral Chaiwat Bukkaratna), commander in chief of the naval air division, Royal Thai Navy (Rear Admiral Nikom Homcharoen) and the deputy commander in chief of the Third Fleet, Royal Thai Navy (Admiral Werayut Uttamot).

66 These comprise the chief of staff for the Army Development Unit (Porn-chai Kranlert), First Army Region deputy commander (Jirasit Kesako-mol), commanding-general of the First Infantry Division, the Royal Guards (Anupong Phaochinda), commanding-general of the Second Cavalry Division (Sanit Phrommas), commanding-general of the First Cavalry Division (Manas Paorik) and commanding-general of the Eleventh Army Circle (Prin Suwannathat). In the air force, they comprise the Air Force chief of staff (Group Captain Siriphong Wanantrakul) and director-general of the Air Combat Centre (Captain Kosok Prakongsap).

67 A younger sister of Thaksin, deputy head of Thai Rak Thai, and wife of Somchai Wongsawat, permanent secretary of the justice ministry.

68 Salilawan Siriwong na Ayuthaya, personal secretary and close friend of Khunying Pojaman Shinawatra from their days at Saint Joseph's Convent School and during their time as international students in America, married ACM Kongsak on 6 November 2003, cited from *Matichon Weekend,* 14–20 November 2003.

69 *The Nation,* 24 April 2003.

70 Agence France Press, 15 May 2003; *The Nation,* 16 October 2003.

71 *The Nation,* 24 April 2003.

72 Wassana Nanuam, 'Prem vents displeasure on Thaksin', *Bangkok Post,* 6 July 2002.

73 On 5 June 2002 (*Matichon,* 7 June 2002).

74 Thitinan, 'Thailand', p. 283.

75 *Royal Gazette,* general announcement edition, Issue 120, Special Segment 134, 20 November 2003 and *Matichon Weekend* 12–18 December 2003. General Surayudh was later invited to be an advisor to the Royal Turf Club (*Phujatkan,* 22 January 2004), an especially significant signal in the light of Chaisit's failure to win election to the club committee.

76 In the Thai context, creating largely meaningless advisory positions is a standard means by which senior figures establish patronage networks and attempt to secure support.

77 ACM Pong Maneesilp, the then air force Commander in Chief sub-mitted a proposal to buy weapons for anti-terrorism activity (*Phujatkan,* 1 October 2001). The cabinet also gave the green light for the Army to buy two helicopters worth 970 million baht and for the Navy to buy a coastal inspection device from China (*Phim Thai,* 27 August 2003).

78 In mid-October 2002, PM Thaksin along with a team of military officers from the three forces and the supreme command travelled to

Russia to consider purchasing weapons as well as visiting a Russian satellite project (*Phim Thai*, 12 October 2002).

79 Jariya Hoffman, 'Reformist general departs'.

80 Wassana Nanuam, 'Defence gets B 3bn after King's request', *Bangkok Post*, 20 July 2003.

81 *Matichon Weekend*, 17–23 October 2003.

82 *Matichon Weekend*, 17–23 October 2003.

83 'We adhere to the no-interference-with-politics principle. At present, the Armed Forces don't interfere with politics, anyway. Yet, as the military and the armed forces are one of the government's instruments, we have to collaborate with the government. Nowadays, the military is already in order. Politics and government are two different things and you have to learn to distinguish them'. (*Matichon Weekend*, 17–23 October 2003.)

84 Wassana Nanuam and Subin Khuenkaew, 'Armies join forces to curb trafficking, assist villages', *Bangkok Post*, 17 December 2003.

85 *Matichon*, 23 February 2004.

86 During the time Gen Somdhat Attanand was the army chief, Lieutenant General Theera Bookphitak, a classmate of the Armed Forces Preparatory School Class 3, was appointed as director of Channel 5 (*Matichon Weekend*, 16–22 January 2004).

87 Pacific Intercommunications Corporation is owned by Piya Malakul na Ayudhaya. The company started operations when Piya's brother Pang Malakul na Ayudhaya, a classmate of General Chetta Thanajaro (then Army commander in Chief), was the director of the Army Television Channel 5. In addition, Pacific Intercommunications has produced programmes for over ten years for the Jor Sor 100 station, which is run by the Military Communications Division of the Supreme Command. (*Krungthep Thurakit*, 25 December 2003.)

88 *Matichon*, 23 December 2002.

89 Replacing Pacific Intercommunications with Traffic Corner reflected a familiar pattern, in which one well-connected private company was replaced by another when a new military commander assumed office. Just as there were plans to spin off companies from the Army's TV Channel 5 to register on the Stock Exchange, Traffic Corner Holdings was making similar preparations to launch itself on the Thai bourse.

90 *Krungthep Thurakit*, 25 December 2003. Chaisit also appointed several of his Class 5 classmates to take charge of the Army's other business

activities. He appointed Major General Wibul Raksaseri as the deputy director of the Royal Thai Army Radio and Television Station Channel 5, and Major General Yuthasak Raksri to look after the Army Golf Club (*Matichon Weekend,* 16–22 January 2004).

91 *Matichon Weekend,* 16–22 January 2004.

92 *Krungthep Thurakit,* 12 December 2003.

93 See Shawn Crispin, 'Battle stations', *Far Eastern Economic Review,* 8 July 2004.

94 Chaisit's appointments as Director of Channel 5 were Preecha Premasawat (October 2003), Sahachai Chuanchaisit (4 June), Surairit Chantaratip (11 June) and Chatree Phattanaphan (12 July 2004). *The Nation,* 14 July 2004.

95 PM Thaksin declared at a reunion dinner of his Armed Forces Academies Preparatory School Class 10 in May 2002: 'I can't understand this at all. Some have just come out of the shell and are already old, grey-haired and nearly bald …' (*Matichon Weekend*, 20–26 May 2002).

96 See Duncan McCargo, *Chamlong Srimuang and the New Thai Politics,* London, Hurst, 1997, pp. 19–24, 31–33.

97 *Bangkok Post*, 25 August 2004.

CHAPTER 5

Thaksin's Political Discourse

Like the many philosophers who said that if you want to be a good leader, you have to be a master of story-telling, so you have to tell the public that you are leading them to a better place. Otherwise, the resistance to change will be too much.

It is very difficult for Asian people, especially the Buddhists, to follow the vision because they are satisfied with their current life. They may complain a little bit but they are fine. – Thaksin Shinawatra, New Straits Times, 10 July 2003.

TO A MUCH GREATER EXTENT than any other figure in Thai politics, Thaksin Shinawatra has sought to promote his agenda and career through the assiduous use of marketing, a strong emphasis on language and systematic attempts to influence and control the country's media. This approach reflected insights he and his advisors had derived from examining the changing political climate in developed countries such as the United States and Britain, where there was growing evidence that voters could be swayed by the judicious choice of attractive language. Since the voting public frequently mistrusted politicians and were sceptical about their promises, the key to attracting important groups of 'swing' voters was to present oneself as a new kind of politician, an anti-politician politician.

The popular anonymously-published Joe Klein novel *Primary Colors*,[1] a thinly-disguised account of Bill Clinton's 1992 election campaign, had highlighted these themes: Jack Stanton, the Clinton character, is a master of beguiling buzz phrases, typically seeking to avoid fixed positions by emphasizing abstract emotions and values. In a book on Clinton, Klein identifies his most impressive speech as one in which he reduced his political agenda to series of abstractions: choice, opportunity, responsibility and community.[2] Similar ideas were adopted by Tony Blair in the 1997 British general election campaign, using the slogan 'New Labour, New Britain'.[3] This was a rebranded political party stripped of its old political language, presenting itself not in terms of traditional left-wing ideas, but as a vibrant alternative to the prevailing Conservative-dominated order. Jennifer Lees-Marshment describes how Labour engaged in extensive product design, product adjustment, implementation and communication strategies in the run-up to the 1997 general election.[4] Thai Rak Thai was the inheritor of this Clinton-Blair mantle of deft rebranding, the recreation of words and images.

Norman Fairclough,[5] in his book *New Labour, New Language*, argues that under Blair's leadership, Labour set about 'forging' a new politics, which actually required a new language in order to express its ideas, aspirations and goals; furthermore: 'New Labour is involved in a "reinvention of government" which in itself entails a greater salience for language'.[6] On Blair's rhetorical style, Fairclough unpacks a number of Blair personae that emerge from various speeches and interviews: 'Tony Blair does not always speak in the same way, but he has a distinctive repertoire of ways of speaking which he moves between in a recognisable way'.[7] One of these is the persona of Blair the 'normal person', who does not sound like a politician, and who indeed once wrote 'I don't actually feel much like a politician'.[8] Fairclough argues that it is undesirable constantly to craft language in order to win support, since this is no basis for the establishment of long-term trust, but leads ultimately to 'contempt for politics'.[9] This implies that a marketing-driven approach to politics is inherently dangerous and undesirable. This chapter approaches Thaksin from this perspective, asking whether the crafting of language he has practised is part of a marketing-driven approach.

The problem here is that Thaksin himself is not adept at using language in such creative ways. Thaksin Shinawatra is no Blair or

Clinton: he is not especially articulate, is not a good public speaker and lacks both stage presence and an easy television manner. He is not an especially good front man for his own marketing campaign; unlike the consummate professional politician Tony Blair, he is not really capable of reshaping his personality for political advantage. Unlike Bill Clinton, he would hardly relish the opportunity to improvise if his aides gave him the wrong text for an important political speech.[10] In the Thai context, Thaksin's political language operates quite differently from that of prominent Western politicians. Thaksin operates with a large team of staffers who prep him extensively, yet in the end often speaks off-the-cuff. This means that Thaksin's language is sometimes wobbly – leave him alone in a radio studio and he is quite likely to drift off-message, reverting to his 'real' self, ranting about his critics and sounding hopelessly shrill. In other words, there are two main modes of Thaksin's political language: scripted and unscripted. Whereas truly professional politicians such as Clinton are self-scripting, never exposing their real thoughts to the wider public, Thaksin struggles constantly to subordinate his real self to the higher demands of the marketing project. This tension in him is rather interesting, producing a constant disjuncture between official and unofficial forms of language. In his pre-political life as a wealthy business tycoon, he was completely at liberty to speak his mind; old habits die hard.

THAKSIN'S WEEKLY RADIO PROGRAMME

On 28 April, Thaksin began giving weekly radio broadcasts on Saturday mornings, in imitation of the American president. By November 2001, the programmes were being transmitted on at least 385 radio stations nationwide, from 8.00 am to 8.30am.[11] The programme was originally confined to stations operated by the Public Relations Department, but quickly spread to practically every station in the country.[12] This was the first time in Thai history that a prime minister had his own weekly radio programme. The radio medium was convenient both for the presenter – who could easily broadcast the programme from outside Bangkok or even outside Thailand – and for listeners, who could tune in at work or while commuting. As *The Nation* explained:

> The concept is simple: Thaksin chats casually about domestic or global events of the week. Government policies and performance are discussed, but not as a direct official report of achievements. The premier may put on a straight reporting style, go on the defensive or offensive, be sarcastic or ironical. He pleads for public support and understanding .... Program host Hiranyaprul opens the radio program but never knows beforehand what Thaksin plans to speak about and is not supposed either to ask questions or raise points during the show.

> Behind the scenes, a team of government spokesmen serve as the show's editorial staff. The team monitors incidents during the week and selects interesting items. The number of issues brought up is not fixed, ranging between 10 and 30 stories according to the situation each week.

> The administration plans four or five topics that will steer the direction of news interest, according to an informed source. Thaksin occasionally announces new policies, such as the construction of roads to boost employment, which sometimes backfires by stirring heated debate. Thaksin always chooses to act first rather than have his hand forced. He doesn't mind if his initiatives sometimes backfire because in most cases they are successful. In 'Prime Minister Thaksin talks to the people', he is able to direct people's attention and opinions, even though he may occasionally draw criticism.

> Thaksin prefers to change the situation rather than being forced to change by it. He is not pleased if the ploys initiated by him do not go as planned. In any case, it shows that the incumbent administration has a well-organized management and that its leader will not allow himself to be put on the defensive. The moral of the story is that the winner is the person who controls the game.[13]

Thaksin's radio programme aroused the interest of the Election Commission, which planned to monitor the broadcasts to ensure that he did not talk about Thai Rak Thai's policies or campaign for his candidates in the run-up to any elections.[14] Thaksin was, however, free to use the programme to talk about his work as prime minister. This distinction between Thaksin the politician and Thaksin the prime minister was clearly a difficult one to understand, let alone to police. Another controversial aspect of the programmes was their length – during 2002, Thaksin began to exceed the length of his half-hour slot by up to 15 minutes, thereby encroaching into the airtime of other scheduled broadcasters. One DJ, Nattakarn Panniam, threatened to take Thaksin to the Adminstrative Court; her show's private sponsors were unhappy at their promotional opportunities being curtailed.[15] Arguably, Thaksin's appropriation of time belonging to others illustrated his sense of superior entitlement to public and private resources. Eventually, the length of the broadcasts was extended to a whole hour.

The programmes addressed an extremely wide range of subjects, and were in any case rather miscellaneous. Rather than focusing each week on a particular theme, Thaksin would hop from one issue to another, expressing his views on whatever was topical – or simply whatever was bothering him. He frequently spent much of the broadcast listing the activities he had been engaged in over the previous week, telling stories about his life and work designed to demonstrate his dedication to the job of prime minister. Issues covered in 2003 included emotive discussions of the war on drugs (3 March), a report on the first joint Thai-Cambodian cabinet meeting (31 May), the arrest of a Jemaah Islamiah terrorist suspect in Thailand (16 August), praise for the creation of Thailand's first Islamic bank (2 September), his vision for 'One District, One Dream School' (7 October), his reasons for despatching Thai troops to Iraq (8 November) and the logic behind his latest cabinet reshuffle (15 November). Thaksin claimed that he normally made the broadcast wearing pyjamas, a relaxed approach which could help explain the combination of informality and carelessness that sometimes crept into his statements on air.[16] The importance of the broadcasts was illustrated by the fact that collections of transcripts were published in book form and were made available on the web within a couple of days of each programme going out.

The opposition Democrats had no equivalent means of expressing their views to the public, and were unable to secure a similar radio slot. In response, Democrat leader Chuan Leekpai launched a web-based 20 minute weekly programme, 'Chuan Online', at his website www.chuan.org in August 2002.[17] By making his broadcast on a Sunday, he was able to respond to Thaksin's programme the previous day. Though internet access remained relatively limited outside urban areas, the Chuan programme was followed closely by the media and helped the Democrats contribute to setting the news agenda for the week.

Thaksin's broadcasts offer some of the most interesting examples of his political language, and therefore deserve a degree of scrutiny. They represent a clear attempt by the prime minister to open a direct channel of communication with ordinary people, using a simple and intimate technology. For the rest of the week, most of his messages to the public would be channelled through news reports in ways he could not fully control, but the weekly broadcasts were his own special space, giving him the chance to explore some of his thoughts with the people and frequently to announce new plans and initiatives. Sopon Ongkara argued that this was his favourite method of communication:

> If he wants the people to hear his message, he prefers to let it be known heard – in one-way communication – on his radio chat programme every Saturday morning, He can say whatever he wants, all by himself in a studio, without nuisances or disruptive questions from anyone, least of all the tenacious Opposition.
>
> Predictably, on the Saturday morning following the House debate on the government's report on its performance, Dr Thaksin was very talkative on his radio show, making earnest pleas to his audience to understand and give him more time. It was an exceptional soft sell... [18]

Again emulating figures such as Blair, Thaksin sought to live up to his 'Think new, act new' slogan by constantly proposing new policies and ideas. His radio programme was one of his favourite places for announcing these. The weekend was typically a slow news period; his Saturday broadcast fed easily into the Sunday newspapers and often generated discussions that would spill over onto the Monday front pages. Hence the radio broadcast was a regular means by which he sought to set the news agenda for the week with issues of his own preference and choosing. At the same time, this approach was not without risks: the steady diet of new promises raised hopes that could not always be realized. The other danger was that he would himself drift 'off message', using broadcasts for negative rather than positive purposes. Suthichai Yoon argued that this was exactly what was happening:

> For the past few weeks, the prime minister is using more and more of the air-time to vent his frustration at his critics'. Instead of talking about vision and reporting on progress of his government's work in dealing with pressing economic and social problems, Thaksin tends to ramble and resorts to finger pointing.[19]

In one broadcast in late 2001, Thaksin challenged those in the media who had criticized him during an official trip to Japan, declaring: 'If you hate me, postpone the hate while I'm doing duties for my country'. In an editorial, *Thai Rath* newspaper reproached Thaksin for using the word 'hate' at least three times in his broadcast, arguing that Thaksin should not accuse academics or journalists who criticized the government's policies of hating him personally, or confuse their criticisms with 'scolding' and 'ridicule'.[20]

THEMES OF THAKSIN'S POLITICAL LANGUAGE

What are the themes of Thaksin's political language? It will be argued here that Thaksin's primary mode of address is didactic, like that adopted by the majority of Thai writers and public figures. The dominant themes of his public language are his own life and career (as moral exempla, rather like the life of the Buddha); the potted themes of his favourite management texts (airport bookstall readings on 'how to' improve efficiency, effectiveness and profits); a discourse of moderate nationalism; and a populist engagement with the concerns of ordinary people, articulated through references to a 'social contract' and associated policies. Combined with these broadly positive themes is a dissonant subtext: what appears to be a venomous loathing of his critics, a streak of anxiety, an undercurrent of insecurity that can border on the paranoid.

Didacticism

The pervasive nature of didacticism in Thai public discourse is difficult to understate. McCargo has argued that Thai newspaper columnists, whether popular or academic in style, frequently resort to didactic modes of discourse.[21] Thai writers, journalists and academics often seem almost incapable of eschewing the didactic mode, a mode they have learned from their own parents and teachers as well as from the incessant moralizing of the Buddhist fraternity. The same mode is also frequently favoured by politicians and other public figures. Most notably, it is the dominant mode of speech adopted by His Majesty the King.[22] This emphasis on didacticism has cultural underpinnings, reflecting deep respect for teachers, monks and superiors, and derives from an intensely hierarchical social structure. The Thai public has apparently long accepted the right of their leaders to lecture them; meetings in the Thai context are generally organized around one-way processes, in which senior people speak and their inferiors listen. Despite his claims to modernity, Thaksin was also completely immersed in this Thai approach to communication, which reflects an essentially paternalistic stance towards the public and the electorate. Indicative of his penchant for didacticism were his frequent claims that he would devote himself to teaching when he stepped down as prime minister – rather like his mentor Chamlong Srimuang, who founded a leadership school when he withdrew from full-time politics – and his spending a day teaching mathematics in a high school.

Thaksin's life as message

An important element of the Thai Rak Thai campaign was an emphasis on Thaksin as a self-made man, including the billboard slogan

'Let me use my life's knowledge and experience to solve the problems of the people'. Pasuk and Baker argue that Thaksin turned his life story into a *tamnan*, or political legend, which was only loosely based on real circumstances and events.[23] This legend was supported by carefully edited potted biographical sketches, including claims that he almost went bankrupt three times. As *The Nation* argued: 'Many are mesmerized by his vision and business success, as many Americans see Bill Gates as their model for success'.[24] In other words:

> If he can make so much money for himself, incant his sloganeers, think what he can do for you. No one, it seems, worries much that the main source of Mr Thaksin's wealth is precisely the sort of cosy arrangement that Thailand needs to get rid of.[25]

Thaksin's life story has been extensively chronicled by others. One interesting example was the book *Jak khon tua yai su jai duang noi* (From a big guy to a small heart), published in 2003, which dealt with Thaksin's ideas about educational reform and human resource development:

> The book opens with flashbacks to his childhood in a small Chiang Mai district. He recounts how he received his early education at a temple school behind a fresh [food] market. His school occupied a temple ground and classes were conducted in salas, or wooden structures set on poles and without walls. Despite coming from a remote area, his progress depended on education.[26]

Thaksin stressed the importance of internet skills, English and international culture in order to survive in the modern world, while education reform needed to create a society that generated its own intellectual capital.

Speaking to a Buddhist foundation in 1999, Thaksin talked about his understanding of the teachings of the great twentieth-century scholar-monk Buddhadasa. Then, true to form, he lapsed into reminiscence, explaining how after he finished his time as deputy prime minister in the Banharn government he found himself suffering for a year from a spiritual malaise. He was eventually able to shake off this sickness after being given a personal sermon by Phra Issaramunee, one of Buddhadasa's disciples. The lesson here was that even a wealthy and powerful man needed to remember the importance of adhering to morality and religious teachings.[27] Ironically, the monk concerned may not have heeded his own teachings: Phra Issaramunee left his temple in disgrace in 2001, after becoming 'embroiled in a messy sex and embezzlement scandal'.[28]

Thaksin appeared to have a good understanding of the importance of such narratives. He told a Malaysian interviewer:

> Like the many philosophers who said that if you want to be a good leader, you have to be a master of story-telling, so you have to tell the public that you are leading them to a better place. Otherwise, the resistance to change will be too much.
>
> It is very difficult for Asian people, especially the Buddhists, to follow the vision because they are satisfied with their current life. They may complain a little bit but they are fine.[29]

In other words, political messages had to be cloaked in didactic tales, which emphasized the moral exempla offered by leaders to the wider population. In the context of an essentially conservative society such as Thailand's, successful leadership was all about effective story-telling.

Management-speak

Thaksin's weakness for hanging on the utterances of selected international management gurus provided a counterbalance to his use of nationalist and personalized rhetoric. Both he and some of his most senior ministerial colleagues (notably Somkid Jatusripitak, Surakiart Sathirathai and Purachai Piumsombun) held American doctorates, and he was singularly inclined to see the latest business bible as a source of profoundly valuable insights. He took to recommending management books to his cabinet colleagues, and his selections were even given special billing in Central bookstore and the Bangkok bookstore chain Asia Books. The names of leading American universities such as Harvard were regularly intoned by Thaksin.

Thaksin's enthusiasm for receiving the latest wisdom from Harvard reached new heights when he proposed spending between 45 and 50 million baht to bring Harvard Business School professor Michael Porter to Thailand for a single day, to give a lecture to government and business leaders that would help them understand the challenges for Thailand to achieve global competitiveness.[30] The idea rebounded when Professor Porter's office denied that such an offer had been made, saying instead that the Thai government had offered less than half of this sum for him to carry out a six month research project on prospects for Thailand's economic recovery. The thrust of the idea testified to an interesting combination of boldness and generosity, a willingness to buy in good ideas and act accordingly. Yet it also reflected a deference to American interpretations and solutions that sat oddly with Thaksin's talk of local wisdom and self-help.

Porter visited Thailand in 2003, and spelled out the results of his rather costly researches into Thailand's competiveness. His report was not a hymn of praise for Thaksin's achievements; rather, he focused on the failures of the Thai government to address the core problem of productivity, stressing that despite positive overall growth rates, ordinary Thai people were not becoming more productive or better-off. Porter made various recommendations, including the need for greater competition among local companies, more transparent bidding processes and government moves to challenge vested interests.[31] He also stressed that economic policy should be de-centralized to the regional level. None of these recommendations sat easily with Thaksin's growth-centred and export-driven approach to economic recovery. Suthichai Yoon argued that: 'to prove that the government wasn't using the well-known Harvard professor only as part of its branding an marketing package', the government ought to commission a panel of local experts to work on his detailed analyses and recommendations.[32] It was ironic that Thaksin felt the need to commission a Western expert to tell Thais what most of them already knew, and even more ironic that he failed to act on the detailed advice of his hand-picked and highly paid consultant. Some critics suggested that Porter was destined to become one of Thaksin's 'monthly gurus', who would quickly pass from favour after tendering the 'wrong' advice.

Somkid Jatusripitak credited the American marketing guru Philip Kotler of Northwestern University – with whom he had co-authored two books – as a crucial influence on his own thinking It was typical of Thaksin to have as his close advisor someone who had collaborated intensively with a leading US author of business books. Kotler gave a seminar on political marketing in Thailand in 2001, but got into hot water with the audience when he seemed to suggest that the press should adopt a positive role in relation to government policies.[33]

Concerned with the slow pace of bureaucratic reform, Thaksin organized an intensive MBA-style training course for some 200 permanent secretaries, department heads, state enterprise bosses and provincial governors. Overseen by deputy prime minister Somkid Jatusripitak, the course represented what a government house source termed 'a top-down strategic approach to policy management'.[34] True to form, the government planned to invite various global gurus (some of whom never came) to address the trainees: including former Secretary of State Henry Kissinger, Dipak Jain (dean of the Kellogg Business School at Northwestern University) and Narayana Murthy (chairman of Infosy Co, an Indian-based software giant. Murthy had earlier spoken at a National Science and Technology Development Agency seminar, expounding upon lessons Thailand could draw from India's successful development of an IT industry.[35] Following the seminar he had a private meeting with Thaksin.

Straight out of management textbooks was Thaksin's radical proposal to move Thailand's clocks forward by one hour, to place the country in the same time zone as Singapore, Hong Kong and Malaysia. 'He was quoted as saying these three economies were in good health and the time adjustment will benefit the Thai stock market'.[36] This was an example of the kind of deadline-grabbing Thaksin proposal that went nowhere, a one-day wonder of an idea.

A typical Thaksin speech was one he gave to the Thailand chapter of the Young Presidents Organization (YPO), at Bangkok's Plaza Athenee Hotel on 19 August 2003.[37] He opened with a reference to a book he had recommended the previous week, *It's Alive*,[38] which emphasized the need for highly adaptive business enterprises. After a quick summary of the book's arguments, he moved on to a second management book, *Leading at the Speed of Growth*, which stressed that a leader had to change as his organization changed. Taking these management texts as cues, he referred to some recent developments in Thailand and in his own life – the IMF programme, his constitutional court case, the events of 11 September and the attendant difficulties he faced in dealing with the country's economic problems in his first year. He moved on to explain how the principles of rapid adaptation and responsive leadership had served him well in dealing with this situation. The key was successful delegation:

> I have no work. I have no ministries to supervise, and authority has been delegated to deputy prime ministers. Managers must delegate …

He stressed that human resources could only be developed if people read more:

> As far as I know, graduates with local bachelor's degrees who do not read will not get anywhere. They need to read all the time to become well rounded.

He concluded with a clear indication of his didactic impulses:

> I will stay another five years, two terms, as there will not be any challenge left for me. I will go and teach. There will be no poverty, no 'mafia' or societal ills.

The speech showed clear influences of management textbooks: a series of bullet points held together by a certain thematic thread, but essentially incoherent. Thaksin was attempting to include a range of buzz phrases, scoring political points and highlighting the most positive features of his own record, whilst ostensibly talking about issues such as adaptability. His own life and political persona were inextricable from the arguments he sought to advance; he could scarcely hold back from his favourite theme, his own personal triumphs and leadership abilities. It was the speech of a successful businessman who skims lots of management books, perhaps while taking planes (he mentioned in the speech that he had made more than 50 overseas trips since becoming prime minister). It was not the speech of a systematic thinker, nor of a professional politician: the tendency to boast was too pronounced.

Nationalism

Pasuk and Baker argue that Thaksin engages in a very muted nationalism, noting that Thai Rak Thai does not make much use of the conservative images of the Thai map and the national flag: 'Thaksin's party's slogan ends with "for every Thai", not "to cure the nation's problems" like Chat Thai'.[39] They also quote Thaksin himself as saying 'I am not calling for people to become nationalistic, but to have a sense of nationhood';[40] and note that he prefers to talk about *banmuang* (a loose term for people and society) rather than 'harder' terms such as *chat* (nation). His use of nationalist rhetoric chimed in with the popular feelings of resentment towards the West that had been generated by the 1997 economic crisis. Thais referred to this period as the 'IMF era', and were deeply critical of the perceived mismanagement of international financial institutions. Indeed, one survey showed that a majority of Thais believed that the economic crisis had been caused by the IMF.[41] At a time when the ruling Democrats were seen as a 'pro-IMF' party, adopting a kind of nationalist posture was electorally very expedient for Thai Rak Thai. Yet how deep did Thaksin's nationalist thinking run?

Discussions of Thai nationalism typically focus on conservative ideas of the Thai nation, articulated in various forms by Rama VI (who coined the phrase 'nation, religion, king'), Phibunsongkhram and Sarit Thanarat. Political parties with names such as Chart Thai, Prachakorn Thai and Chart Pattana played on such ideas; the first two parties dated back to the 1970s, while the last was actually a Chart Thai spin-off party. However the most important new parties of the 1980s and early 1990s omitted the words 'Chat' and 'Thai' from their titles. Although both were founded by retired generals,

Palang Dharma (moral force) and New Aspiration adopted a moral, aspirational stance as their core identity rather than a conservative, nationalist stance. Palang Dharma founder Chamlong Srimuang articulated ideas of localism and Thai-ness (*khwam pen thai*) in a low-key fashion, transmuting conservative, Cold War constructs of the nation into a moderate, alternative nationalism which tapped into a collective nostalgia for a simpler mode of rural life.[42] Like Thaksin, however, Chamlong was of Chinese descent; the irony underpinning his quest for Thai-ness was that he was himself culturally *lukjin*. Here is one key to unpacking Thaksin's nationalism, and the party name – meaning 'Thais love Thai' – shows that at one level, he did protesteth too much. Asserting his Thai-ness so boldly was an important manoeuvre to counter any ambiguity concerning his own ethnicity and identity.

Kasian Tejapira distinguishes between two modes of resurgent nationalism in post-crisis Thailand: what he terms the 'crony capitalist nationalism' of big business groups and the 'radical populist nationalism' of NGOs and social activists.[43] Arguably, the key to Thaksin's electoral success was his ability to tap into both strands of nationalist sentiment, though Kasian notes in a postscript that crony capitalist nationalism quickly gained the upper hand over the more radical variety once Thaksin gained power.[44] Jim Glassman argues that the Thaksin government's economic nationalism is 'a distinctly post-colonial and even "post-nationalist" phenomenon'. Essentially, he sees this nationalism as a ploy to divert attention from the real priorities of the Thai leadership:

> In particular, while TRT's dominant social supporters have maintained their international economic profile throughout the moment of Thai 'nationalism', the party's leadership has increasingly tried to truncate the political space available to popular organizations opposing its policies, particularly be adopting an anti-internationalist position as the measure of patriotism and social responsibility. Thus, TRT's scale politics reveal that it is 'nationalist' only in the sense that it is both limited and politically calculating.[45]

He goes on to argue that members of Thailand's economic elite – including agribusiness and banking magnates – had a strong vested interest in supporting certain statist measures that would protect their position in the difficult aftermath of the crisis. Similarly, nationalist rhetoric had a strong appeal to owners of small and medium-sized enterprises, who felt that the Democrat Party had been overly concerned with the needs of the finance and banking sectors. Some Thaksin advisors, notably the 'Octobrists' whose political roots lay in the 'anti-imperialist' struggles of the 1970s, were naturally sympathetic to nationalist ideas and rhetoric.[46] These ideas also had an appeal to villagers and workers who had been engaged in struggles against the policies of the Chuan government – notably the protest movement against the Pak Mun dam in the Northeastern province of Ubon. Yet by 2003, it was becoming increasingly obvious that Thaksin adopted a highly conservative view of such protests, and was increasingly reverting to the well-worn rhetoric of 'national security'. Brown and Hewison argue that 'the language of economic nationalism' provided an important cover for the conflicts of interests underpinning government policies.[47] Glassman is clear that Thaksin does not really want to advocate a closed-door economy; his economic gurus are all neo-liberals such as the Peruvian Hernando de Soto and the Harvard competitiveness expert Michael Porter. Glassman argues:

> With his position consolidated, Thaksin has moved to repress the most oppositional populist voices in this coalition, disciplining Thai society to work in support of the geographically expansionist neomercantilist project for which he and his elite are harnessing the Thai state.[48]

At the same time, Glassman insists that 'TRT nationalism, though in some ways weak, is very real'[49] – yet it would be a mistake to think such new forms of nationalism are not highly significant, though they may defy ready categorization.

One of Thaksin's proudest moments was his 'independence day' speech in August 2003, when he declared that Thailand had now repaid its debts to the IMF:

It overture was a patriotic song hailing the heroes of Ban Rajan who snatched up swords to defend the kingdom from Burmese invaders in the late 1700s, while a gigantic Thai flag served as a backdrop. Prime Minister Thaksin stood in front of the local and international press corps and announced proudly,: 'From now on, we are free of the IMF'. That almost drew tears from emotional fans on the front row who gave a standing ovation to show their support. Supporters were overwhelmed, and even critics of his populist tendencies conceded it was his best performance to date … .

Thaksin urged Thai people to fly the national flag as a symbol to show the Kingdom's freedom from the stand-by credit agency…

Thaksin said: 'Debt to the IMF was a pain for the nation, and I promise you that if I am still around, this debt to the IMF will be our last'.

The real message, therefore, is not about 'independence', but about 'how independence was achieved'. Thaksin on Thursday evening was telling the Thai public that if they trust their leader, all dangers will be overcome. That long dormant political line, made famous by former strongman and prime minister Field Marshal Plaek Pibulsongkram, has come back to life.[50]

This episode suggests that Pasuk and Baker's notion of Thaksin's nationalism as essentially moderate may need revision; as time passed and the premier gained in confidence, he appeared increasingly willing to engage in a much more strident conservative nationalist language and rhetoric, using symbols such as the national flag in a far cruder fashion than before. Political analyst Sunai Phasuk told Associated Press: 'He presents himself as the champion, the guardian of the country. That is his image'.[51] Thaksin staged a repeat performance in the year 2004, addressing a Bangkok stadium full of supporters 'decked out in the blue, white and red of the national flag'.[52] This time, he called on all Thais to fly the national flag at their homes and offices, on the auspicious occasion of the Queen's 72nd birthday.[53]

Nationalism is only one element in Thaksin's rhetoric, however; a further strand is the distinction between Asia and the West. Thaksin is often eager to include other Asians (notably the Chinese, Malaysians, Singaporeans and Indians) within his circle of reference, expanding 'we' beyond the borders of Thailand, to include other vibrant Asian economies with features worthy of emulation. Weaker Asian economies are in close proximity, but one step removed from Thailand itself. In meetings with Chinese leaders, Thaksin is believed to have called for Asians to play a more proactive economic role vis-à-vis the West. He made this argument explicitly in April 2002 in his speech to the Bo'ao Forum for Asia, a China-sponsored gathering Asian political and economic leaders:

> Thai Prime Minister Thaksin Shinawatra complained that Asian economies 'concentrate more on fighting each other in price wars than on forging Asian unity'. He said they should band together to make the Western-dominated world trade system a 'fair regime for all'. 'We must learn to rely on each other and reinforce … inter-Asian trade'.[54]

Ultimately, Thaksin has little interest in either nationalism or Asian regionalism. These ideas are simply devices he uses to articulate his political and economic ambitions, but they do not reflect any obvious coherence of thought.

Social contract

At times, Thaksin's language starts to resemble that of former Philippine president Joseph Estrada. Asked to withdraw from the 2001 elections because of the constitutional court case, Thaksin replied:

> My vision is not blurred. I can still aim my gun and pull the trigger. … Before I die I want to kill our enemies first, and these are poverty, drugs and corruption.[55]

At a closed seminar of concerned academics, activists and journalists held to discuss the Thaksin phenomenon in January 2004, it was argued that Thaksin was adopting a paternalistic approach to government:

> Citizens become clients who are made to queue up to receive
> handouts from Thaksin. The majority of villagers eligible for
> Village Development Funds believe their approved loans came
> out of Thakin's own pocket instead of the government's
> coffers.[56]

This blurring of the distinction between the government, the state and the person of the prime minister was epitomized by a television commercial to promote the government's poverty registration programme. The commercial showed a poor family listening to the radio and hearing the voice of Thaksin telling them that he would be able to clear their debts. The commercial was criticized by some observers as pure propaganda, which had no place in a democratic society.[57] However, the creator of the advertisement explained that 'his creative concept was to use the transistor radio as a medium between the prime minister and the public because he was inspired by the popularity of the prime minister's weekly radio programme every Saturday'. Ideas such as the 'social contract' were examples of 'creative concepts' developed by Thaksin's marketing department for promotional purposes. They had nothing to do with his real approach to governing Thailand.

Marketing

Somkid Jatsuripitak, Thaksin's first finance minister, played a key role in drafting the party's policy platform and developing electoral strategies.[58] Through marketing and surveys, he and his team worked out how to respond to the wishes of rural voters. Researchers had travelled to villages all over Thailand to establish the concerns of the electorate.[59] Thai Rak Thai's marketing strategy was strongly influenced by the experience of British political parties, 'the archetypal practitioners of political marketing'.[60]

Jennifer Lees-Marshment, a British academic specialist on political marketing, dispensed with using traditional political science approaches to classifying political parties. Instead, she adapted the language and perspective of management studies to divide parties into three types or orientations: product-oriented, sales-oriented and market-oriented.[61] Product-oriented parties resembled those described by Panebianco as 'mass bureaucratic', with a focus on membership and party organization. Sales-oriented parties were typically parties whose product was in decline, 'trying to persuade voters that the party they had once identified with was still the one they should vote for'.[62] By contrast, a market-oriented party was one that designed its behaviour to reflect voter preferences, first using market intelligence to identify the demands of the electorate.[63] This was a description that precisely fitted Thai Rak Thai. She argued that many businesses moved through these three phases at different stages in their development, but that in the British context a market orientation now had the best chance of ensuring that a party could gain and retain power. At the same time, parties in power had to struggle to ensure that they remained market-oriented, since 'If a party wins power with a market-oriented product, over time it may remain convinced of its worth, and be unwilling to see it changed'.[64] In other words, a market-oriented party had to be constantly studying changing market conditions and be ready to adapt its policies and presentation accordingly.

Krairit Boonyakiat, head of Biophile Corportation, argued that Thai Rak Thai had created a textbook marketing campaign using a five-point strategy referred to as AIDAS: 'awareness, interest, design, action and satisfaction'. The first stage involved promoting brand awareness and associating the party name with populist policy ideas such as the debt moratorium, Village Development Fund and 30-baht healthcare scheme. These policies were used to attract the interest of potential voters. A design was then introduced to firm up that interest, using a colourful logo and images of the party leader. 'Action' came with the election itself and the opportunity to cast votes for the new party, while satisfaction would come later once the policies took effect. The party also carefully segmented its marketing, targeting practical programmes at rural voters, but emphasizing Thaksin's leadership qualities for the urban electorate:

> Other parties also tried to bank on advertising and PR. But their tools were not good enough. They might have had the

money, but they did not know how to spend it. Thai Rak Thai had both the money and the tactics. The image of the product was also good. Its PR style was hard-hitting.[65]

Krairit argued that Thai Rak Thai had created one of the best marketing campaigns seen in Thailand in recent years. The only drawback with such a campaign was that its very success raised enormous expectations, and delivering 'satisfaction' would require successful follow-up, otherwise a 'harsh backlash' could follow.

Ogilvy and Mather's Witawat Jayapani argued that consistency had been the key to Thai Rak Thai's success, creating a 'brand personality' for both party and leader. Advertising agency SC Matchbox, a Shin Corp subsidiary, had played a key role in creating the brand. At its heart was the 'think new, act new' campaign which reflected the idea of a new generation of leadership. Another key element was Thai Rak Thai's success in differentiating itself from other parties, along with using communications 'in an integrated and complete fashion, out-performing and out-financing all the other parties'. Offers such as the 30-baht healthcare scheme were highly effective. 'In effect, the message sent out was that if you voted for me, you would get these rewards. It was a sales promotion'.

The general manager of Amway (Thailand), Preecha Prakobit, argued that Thai Rak Thai worked quite differently from its own direct sales methods. Whereas Amway began by using personal contacts to develop sales, only later employing mass media, Thai Rak Thai emulated the local direct sales company Mistine by promoting expensive media campaigns before sending out direct sales personnel to the local level. Preecha observed that Thai Rak Thai put considerable efforts into person-to-person communications and gained benefits from activities such as sponsoring community football matches.

Although political marketing often gets a bad press, Lees-Marshment insisted that it should not be confused with populism:

> [P]olitical marketing is often seen as aiding populism, but
> Smith and Saunders (1990: 298) argue that the perspective

of populism is short-term and is in fact rooted in the selling era. If a party kept switching issues or offered inconsistent or impracticable product designs (Smith and Saunders (1990: 299) give the example of reduced taxation and increased public spending and thus 'voodoo economics') it would destroy the party's credibility.[66]

This opens up an interesting set of questions in relation to Thaksin and Thai Rak Thai: did the party adopt a sales orientation in the countryside, emphasizing the populist programme, and a marketing orientation in urban areas? Was there actually a contradiction between two major elements of the Thai Rak Thai approach? A further issue also emerges from this analysis:

> The rise of a market-oriented party nonetheless raises important normative questions, because the basic idea of a market orientation is to follow, rather than lead, voter demands. It implies that conviction politics is over.[67]

Such an argument implies that Thaksin's approach to politics contains a fundamental contradiction: is it driven by the market and crafted by focus groups, or is it about strong visionary leadership? Clearly, Thai Rak Thai would like to have it both ways. Arguably, Thaksin is not simply a market leader, but also a political salesman. Lees-Marshment recognizes that her arguments apply with more force to Britain than to other countries, and that market-oriented parties may be less appropriate in different kinds of society. She cites the example of Silvio Berlusconi's *Forza Italia*, which she argues combined elements of marketing, sales and product orientation.[68]

Writing in *Krungthep Thurakit*, Attachak Satayanurak argued that the populism of Thai Rak Thai reflected a strategy to dominate the political process:

> In the beginning, make people so thrilled by the policy that they believe that the party works for the impoverished or majority of the nation. From there, try to make the society feel that there are enemies trying to undermine the country

and that they or their colleagues are the only ones defending the country from those enemies. Eventually he (the prime minister) and his colleagues become the individuals who speak and act on the behalf of the people and the nation.

The populist dictatorship will generate disputes and the other side of the disputes will be blamed as the enemy of the nation and society. This condition gives populist dictatorship the legitimacy to crush the enemy for the sake of safeguarding the nation, with the consent of people who believe they will benefit from the state in future.[69]

Thai Rak Thai's populist policies were the subject of both domestic and international criticism, and Thaksin came under considerable scrutiny from the regional press in the run up to the election, when both the *Straits Times* and the *Asian Wall Street Journal* questioned both his policies and his fitness for office.[70] The *Journal* compared him to the grasshopper in Aesop's fable – playing all summer and then starving, in contrast to 'worker ant' Chuan Leekpai of the Democrats. Thai Rak Thai responded by implying that the newspaper was biased in favour of the Democrats, a charge the *Journal* strongly rejected.[71]

THAKSIN AND THE MEDIA

The Thai media is typically quick to applaud new political parties and initiatives, and Thaksin benefited from a long press honeymoon which lasted from the founding of the party in 1998 until well into his first year of office. By regional standards, Thailand has a remarkably free print media, though electronic media have long been subject to government control and interference. At the same time, the Thai press is highly partisan, and some elements of the press are only too willing to do the bidding of wealthy powerholders. As McCargo has noted, it would be dangerous to assume that a relatively outspoken and vigorous Thai media can be equated with an effective and critical media.[72] As a media magnate himself, Thaksin was well placed to cultivate good relations with reporters. In his earlier political roles, he had been well known for hosting dinners and parties for the media. During his time as foreign minister in the first Chuan government, he was briefly embroiled in controversy following a party at which he gave out free mobile phones to reporters covering the foreign desk beat. After complaints to the Reporters' Association of Thailand, all the phones were returned. Thaksin's Shinawatra Group also gave out free gold necklaces hidden in pieces of cake at a business reporters' party in December 1995.[73] While Thaksin used similar 'carrot' approaches to curry favour with the media after the founding of Thai Rak Thai, he also used a range of 'sticks' to discourage critical reporting and dissent. As Kavi Chongkittakorn put it:

> Thaksin's spin team, with part of its staff mapping out strategies in Government House, designs news and plans newspaper headlines. Filers and tips are placed to key reporters; the day's events and message are crafted in a way that is new to Thailand.[74]

Thai Rak Thai was believed to use a 'media monitoring centre' in the office of the government spokesman to rate newspapers columns and articles as 'supportive', 'critical' or 'misleading' according to their level of support for the government – and marking hostile columns with a 'bomb' symbol.[75] The energies devoted by Thaksin and his advisory team to media 'spin' and management reflected the importance he attached to effective communication with the voters, which he placed at the heart of his priorities.

A clear indication of Thaksin's real attitude to the media emerged just before the 2001 elections, when Shin Corp purchased a controlling interest in iTV, an 'independent' television station with a reputation for strong and critical news coverage. More than 20 of the more outspoken iTV journalists were immediately fired; there was a general perception that scrutiny of Thai Rak Thai was subsequently toned down. Thaksin adopted a strategy of forming financial and other connections with leading daily newspapers, most of which were notably muted in their criticisms. Exceptions included the Nation Group – with both English and Thai language dailies, as well as broadcasting interests – which adopted a consistently sceptical view of the prime minister and his party, and the small, combative daily *Thai Post*. In 2002 it emerged that the Anti Money Laundering Organization had been investigating the financial affairs of the out-spoken Nation Group editor-in-chief Suthichai Yoon and other senior executives of the company. While the government strongly denied that these investigations were politically motivated – and swiftly dropped the proceedings – the moves seemed like a crude attempt to intimidate critical voices. *Nation* editor Pana Janviroj argued that such investigations could not have been instigated without orders from above.[76] Ironically, AMLO was one of the new bodies introduced after 1997 in order to clean up Thai public life.

In August 2001, the Special Branch issued a warning letter to the business daily *Krungthep Thurakit* (part of the Nation Group), accusing the newspaper of irresponsible behaviour and of acting in a way that could have affected international confidence in Thaksin and might create disorder in the nation.[77] The crime committed by the newspaper was publishing a translated version of a Reuters report, saying that the prime minister might be banned from politics for 16 months if found guilty of assets concealment by the Constitution Court. The action testified to a degree of anxiety – bordering on paranoia – about the assets case. In the few weeks prior to the assets hearings, the Thai Broadcasting Journalists' Association documented no less than 14 cases of government interference in the news content of state-owned broadcasting outlets.[78] Chulalongkorn University academic Wilasinee Phipitkul commented on the fact that virtually all media reports of the assets trial were the same, apparently all derived from supporters of the prime minister.[79] Around the same time, the government spokesman announced that journalists would only be able to talk to government ministers with formal appoint-ments, and that their interviews would be taped to make sure reports were accurate.[80] Neither of these measures lasted long.

At the beginning of 2002, Thaksin declared that he would limit the interviews he gave to the media to one or two structured occasions each week, rather than responding to questions whenever ambushed by reporters.[81] The decision reflected his growing awareness that he was prone to making serious gaffes in off-the-cuff remarks, as reflected in the nickname 'Misguided billionaire', which he was given by a group of Government House reporters on 1 January 2002. At the same time, press criticism of Thaksin over issues such as interfering in the state-owned media or his sarcastic jibes at academics did not arise because of such faux pas – they reflected real concerns about his policies and attitudes. Thaksin was just as likely to put his foot in it in the privacy of his radio studio as when he was waylaid by a pack of reporters.

Opposition politicians seized upon issues such as the AMLO investigation into Nation Group executives as evidence of Thaksin's growing preoccupation with maintaining absolute power.[82] However, his party spokesman, Suranan Vejjajiva, argued that Thaksin – who had only recently entered politics following a private sector career – was simply being misunderstood:

> When he works, he thinks more in terms of efficiency, in terms of getting things done. ... He's trying to say, 'Don't criticize me yet. Let me finish my work.' But some members of the media are not giving him a chance. And he finds that frustrating because he comes from a world where there was not much criticism.

Suranan went on to assert that Thaksin simply 'needs to explain himself more clearly'. The Thai Journalists' Association begged to differ, declaring 2001 'The Year of Media Intimidation'. In March 2002, 374 academics and over a thousand journalists signed petitions criticizing the government's attitude towards the media. The petition by journalists was the largest of its kind since 1973.

By late 2003, freedom of expression was clearly facing a range of threats in Thaksin's Thailand. On 1 January 2003, Nation Group reporters at Government House dubbed Thaksin an untouchable 'demigod' presiding over an 'illusory' government. The appelation reflected Thaksin's growing reputation for making headlines by denouncing his critics.[83] In a statement published at the end of 2003, the Thai Journalists' Association described 2003 as a year in which they had been reined in: 'The interference in the work of the Thai media has grown more complicated and subtle and is continuing to eat into the mechanism of the media'. Kavi Chongkittakorn, a senior editor at the Nation group, argued that having failed to reform itself, the Thai media was now being 'tamed and co-opted' by the Thaksin government. He declared that '[News] publishers are now the biggest prostitutes in town'.[84] Alongside this co-optation process, dissenting voices were being silenced. The critical Philippine academic Waldon Bello, a long-time Thai resident affiliated with Chulalongkorn University, was unable to obtain a visa to enter the country at the time of the October 2003 APEC meeting. Supinya Klangnarong, secretary-general of the Campaign for Media Reform and a leading campaigner for free speech, was sued for civil libel by Shin Corporation over comments in *Thai Post* newspaper in July 2003 in which she claimed that the company had benefited from government policies. Shin Corporation also sued three editors of *Thai Post* over claims that Thai Rak Thai policies had aimed at boosting Shin Corporation's businesses.[85]

The Committee for the Protection of Journalists also noted that television news anchors had uncritically repeated the government line throughout the 2003 'war on drugs', 'repeatedly announcing without scepticism that the [more than 2000] deaths were the result of gang feuds'.[86] Meanwhile, critical voices claiming that the deaths resulted from extra-judicial killings went unreported or were banished to inside pages; nor was there any substantive investigative coverage of the issue.

Ubonrat Siriyuvasak noted that after Thaksin came to power,

> all independent political talk-show hosts on television and radio ... have had their contracts cancelled and their programmes removed from the airwaves.
>
> With iTV under Shin Corp's wing, Thaksin now controls all television networks, including the state-controlled channels 3, 5, 7, 9 and 11, as well as nationwide radio stations operated by government agencies ... .
>
> Saturating the air waves with one-way communication is turning state-controlled media into propaganda machines,

enabling the government to sell its populist policies to the masses in an effective manner, as well as creating a good public image for the government.[87]

Thaksin's Deputy Interior Minister Pracha Maleenont came from the family which had long controlled the popular Channel 3. When a Channel 3 Government House reporter, Kasemsan na Ayutthaya, produced some critical coverage of Thai Rak Thai, the station removed him and his crew from their beat, on the basis that they had been 'disrespectful to the prime minister and his aides'.[88] From late 2003, Thaksin's Army Commander cousin Chaisit Shinawatra oversaw Channel 5 and dozens of radio frequencies owned by the army. The gradual disappearance of critical voices from the airwaves was a slow but inexorable process that occasionally made headlines. Early on, the popular presenters Fongsaman Chamonchan and Suriyong Huntasan were removed from the Public Relations' Department radio programme 'Bantung Satanakan', apparently because they were seen as unsympathetic to Thai Rak Thai.[89]

Another good example was a spat between the government and Independent News Network (INN), which operated Ruam Duay Chuay Kan (Uniting to Help Each Other), a 24-hour phone-in news programme on 96 FM that served as an information lifeline for taxi drivers and other Bangkokians. INN found itself in hot water after broadcasting an interview in which former Interior Minister Purachai Piumsomboon criticized Thaksin for removing him from his post as justice minister. The programme was abruptly taken off the air on 1 March 2003, provoking considerable public disquiet. In the event, normal service was restored three days later – but the episode was an important reminder that control of radio frequencies remained firmly in the hands of the military, which leased the airspace to programmers at its own pleasure and discretion. Thaksin himself denied that the Army's failure immediately to renew INN's lease was at all related to the Purachai interview controversy.[90] To critical observers, however, this was a further example of the way in which a prime minister claiming to 'think new, act new' continued to adopt a very old and conservative approach to broadcast media. As Thepchai Yong pointed out, the original reasons for allocating radio frequencies to the military reflected the needs of the Cold War, and had long since been replaced by a web of clandestine financial deals and personal contacts.[91] Despite his often-declared interest in introducing private sector efficiencies to areas previously dominated by the state, the Thaksin government had made little progress in reforming the anachronistic spoils system allowing the military to control radio broadcasting.

Thaksin demonstrated a deeply-held view that the press was in a conspiracy against him and ought to assume a different and more positive role:

> Thaksin's attitude toward the media seemed to be summed up in remarks he made to the press corps in May, following a visit to Europe to promote Thai trade relations. 'You media people have to believe me', he said. 'Today, serving your country is more important than sending your news dispatches daily to your editors. Think before you do anything that damages the country'.[92]

Ironically, this was an argument that many earlier Thai politicians had found persuasive, largely because of the tradition of a highly critical print media that typically berated all governments for their failings.[93]

In January 2004, the media subcommittee of the National Human Rights Commission produced a report on the progress of media reform in 2003. While the report noted some minor steps forward – particularly the Administrative Court ruling that the methods used to selected members of the National Broadcasting Commission and the National Telecommunications Commission were invalid – the main findings were a depressing catalogue of government moves to undermine media independence. A prime example was the purchase of large numbers of shares in the Nation Multimedia Group by investors linked to Suriya Jungrungpreangkit, the Transport minister and secretary-general of Thai Rak Thai. Since the Nation Group had been particularly willing to criticize the ruling party and prime minister, this was a disturbing trend.[94] The Committee to Protect Journalists claimed that Suriya's relatives had purchased around 20 per cent of the company – more than twice as large a holding as the next two leading shareholders They quoted Supinya Klangnarong of the Campaign for Media Reform as saying 'This purchase is linked with political clout and that's what makes us really worried'.[95] In similar fashion, newspapers that were seen as oppositional found themselves deprived of government-funded advertising. *The Nation* claimed that 'if any newspaper should dare to report negatively on the government, Matchbox Co, the advertising arm of Shinawatra Corporation, will withdraw its advertisements without explanation'.[96] The Thai Journalists' Association complained directly about these sorts of intervention in a statement marking World Press Freedom Day on 3 May 2004:

> It is known to the public that the Thai government and members of the Cabinet are interfering in the media by using economic bargaining through government agencies' advertising budget and stock acquisition, therefore, there is growing concern about the editorial independence being threatened by the political forces.[97]

In February 2004, the editor of the *Bangkok Post* was forced to resign, a development widely linked to government pressure.[98] This emphasis on targeting the English-language press reflected the preoccupation of the Thaksin government with presenting a positive image to the outside world.

The beginning of 2004, however, saw a discernible shift in the climate of metropolitan opinion concerning Thaksin's performance, and a resulting increase in media pressure. Episodes such as the government's repeated but completely implausible denials over the existence of bird flu in Thailand's chicken population and growing political and security problems in the deep South strained his ability to spin events in a positive light. As Suthichai Yoon noted, Thaksin had enjoyed a three year media honeymoon on the back of economic recovery.[99] Suthichai summarized Thaksin's attitudes to the media in five principles. The first four principles were: treat the media as an enemy, deny everything negative, 'use angry language to threaten critics and scare off detractors', and avoid all discussions of perceptions, feelings and ethical standards. The fifth and final principle was:

> Do the same thing over and over again, but expect different results. Every time a crisis breaks out, go on TV and the radio and say: 'I know every detail of this issue. It will be solved in two weeks'.[100]

In other words, it was a strategy based on 'bluffing a way through' any given crisis. When this strategy failed, Thaksin tried another approach: the massive diversionary tactic. The bid to purchase Liverpool Football Club in May 2004 was a classic example of such a tactic, reflecting the advice given in Robert Greene's book *48 Laws of Power*, one of Somkid's favourites:

> Draw attention to yourself by creating an unforgettable, even controversial image. Court scandal. Do anything to make yourself seem larger than life and shine more brightly than those around you.[101]

By generating a huge debate about whether it was appropriate for Thaksin or Thailand to buy a major stake in a British football club, the prime minister succeeded in displacing violence in the South and a parliamentary no-confidence debate from the front pages of the newspapers, and replacing substantive issues with an essentially spurious issue of his own devising. The Liverpool story was just the latest example of such tactics. At a seminar organized by the Thai Broadcast Journalists Association in November 2003, Thakerng Somsap complained that Thaksin systematically diverted attention away from corruption issues and towards the war on drugs and on influential people. He even suggested that the prime minister had delayed his cabinet reshuffle for two weeks in order to capitalize on reports about an alleged murder.[102] There was a pattern here of government attempts to determine the news agenda, closely emulating the tactics of media masters Tony Blair and Bill Clinton.

THAKSIN AND THE INTERNATIONAL MEDIA

Thaksin Shinawatra's unease with the international media became evident long before he actually entered Government House. The feud really began with the publication of a short piece in *Time* magazine by Robert Horn.[103] The article discussed some of Thaksin's previous political debacles, including his two unsuccessful spells as deputy prime minister, and observed that despite his claim to be a leader for the digital age, he was allied with some old-style 'analogue' politicians. At the same time, the headline reflected a view that Thaksin was putting the past behind him and mounting a strong bid for the prermiership. The article was translated into Thai by *Matichon*, and produced critical responses from Thai Rak Thai figures, notably from party spokesman Suranan Vejjajiva. Suranan criticized the article for containing factual inaccuracies, but never produced any convincing examples of these. He also criticized the 'foreign intellectuals' quoted in the article, saying, for example, that Duncan McCargo was an admirer of Chamlong Srimuang – and so might blame Thaksin for destroying the Palang Dharma Party – but 'Thais knew better'. Pongthep Tepkarnchana, deputy secretary-general of Thai Rak Thai, similarly criticized foreign intellectuals for their inability to understand Thailand properly.[104] Thaksin himself complained that the Thai press focused on the phrase 'analogue knight' (*asawin analog*), which never appeared in the original *Time* article, but became a kind of local media shorthand for a set of criticisms about him. Simply put, the controversy over the *Time* article was not really about the substance of the original article, but reflected the way in which the Horn piece allowed local media to revisit longstanding criticisms of Thaksin.[105]

Relations with the international media grew more strained after Thaksin took office, especially in relation to the widely-read weekly regional newsmagazine *Far Eastern Economic Review*. Unlike most other Bangkok-based foreign correspondents, *Review* correspondents were Thailand specialists with longstanding networks of contacts; most of them also spoke Thai. But a short 175 word article published by the *Review* in January 2002 generated uproar.[106] The piece touched upon tensions between the palace and Government House and alluded to the royal family's business activities. The offending issue of the magazine was banned in Thailand, swiftly disappearing from news-stalls and Thai Airways flights. On 23 February the two Bangkok correspondents of the magazine – Shawn Crispin and Rodney Tasker – had their visas suspended; moves were then made to deport them as a threat to national security. This was an extraordinary development: no foreign journalist had been expelled from the Thailand since the authoritarian dark days of the 1977 Thanin government. Only following a letter of apology from the *Review*'s publishers did an immigration panel reverse an earlier decision to deport the two foreign correspondents. The magazine never retracted the substance of the story. While Thaksin and his ministers repeatedly insisted that the moves against the two correspondents were not politically motivated, few believed them. Informed sources suggest that the decision not to expel the pair followed a specific request from the palace. In a separate development, the 2–8 March 2002 issue of *The Economist* – containing a 15-page special feature section on Thailand – was withdrawn from circulation, following concerns that it made inappropriate references to the monarchy.

Capitalizing on the nationalist mood of the moment, Thaksin declared that if journalists came to destroy Thailand he would consider them *persona non grata*, whatever their race or nationality.[107] The irony here was striking: Thaksin, the Western-educated, globalizing telecommunications magnate had adopted a hard-line reactionary approach to the international media. A few weeks later, the prime minister seemed to have mellowed slightly, telling *Review* reporters in a fence-mending interview that his enemies were plotting to topple him by stirring up trouble in the eyes of the public.[108] This talk of dirty tricks and a media conspiracy was distressingly familiar and echoed similar claims by his much less sophisticated predecessors

Banharn Silpa-archa and Chavalit Yongchaiyudh. On the one hand, Thaksin and those around him were highly attentive to the advice, analyses and commentaries of foreigners – primarily Americans – yet on the other hand they developed an antagonistic relationship with the international media.

THAKSIN AND HIS CRITICS

2003 began with a blistering attack on Thaksin by Thirayuth Boonmi, his most persistent critic. A former student leader from the 1970s, Thirayuth had pursued an unconventional academic career following his appointment as a sociology lecturer at Thammasat University. An intriguing combination of public intellectual and newsmaker, he used newspaper columns and a stream of slim paperbacks on catchy themes to promote critical views of Thai society and politics. No one could accuse Thirayuth of harbouring a particular animus against Thaksin; in the past, he had been extremely critical of Chuan Leek-pai and other politicians. Where Thirayuth outshone other Thai social critics was in his remarkable boldness, his willingness to speak his own version of truth directly unto power. While most journalists and academics initally held back from head-to-head confrontation with Thaksin, Thirayuth taunted the businessman-turned-prime minister remorselessly from the outset. At the same time, Thirayuth was an academic loner, a skilled maker of enemies. Thaksin had little to fear from such attacks; yet by dignifying his criticisms with detailed and sometimes venomous responses, the prime minister actually turned Thirayuth into a much bigger problem than was necessary.

Thai Rak Thai went to considerable lengths to counter Thirayuth's analysis of Thaksin. *The Nation* published a 1,000 word rebuttal by Suranan Vejjjiva of Thirayuth's latest criticisms of the prime minister.[109] Suranan countered that Thirayuth himself was abusing the media:

> Thirayuth's work could have been accorded with more serious consideration if he hadn't tried too hard with his gimmicks to attract public attention through coinage of

words like 'Thaksinisation' and 'Thaksinocracy'. As such, his analysis cannot be called a piece of academic work because it is clearly biased against Prime Minister Thaksin Shinawatra. Thirayuth has chosen wrongly to 'sell' his analysis to a mass audience and to manipulate the mass media, most of whom decided to go along with sensationalism, leading to a distortion of facts. It's a pity that members of the public do not benefit as much as they should from the analysis.[110]

The problem with this kind of response – whether from Thaksin himself or from one of his lieutenants – was that it seemed to dignify the prime minister's critics, creating the impression that he had been really riled by the statements of a single university lecturer. Surely a man of Thaksin's immense power and status ought to have been above such petty considerations? When Thirayuth launched an even more venomous diatribe against Thaksin in July 2004, calling him a 'monstrous baby' surrounded by 'Thaksinocronies',[111] Thaksin managed to contain himself, saying that he appreciated the fact that Thirayuth only criticized him once a year.

In January 2004, a group of academics and critics gathered over a weekend in Chiang Mai to discuss critical perspectives on the government's performance. Thaksin's emphasis on controlling the media was one of the topics under discussion, along with the government's populist programmes, conflicts of interest and cronyism.[112] However, the closed-door meeting soon made headline news and papers circulated among participants were summarized in detail in *Matichon* newspaper. Some participants were concerned that there might be reprisals as a result.

The January gathering was a taste of things to come, however. In April 2004, senator, broadcaster and former Thammasat University economist, Chermsak Pinthong, published an edited collection entitled *Ru Tan Thaksin* [Staying One Step Ahead of Thaksin].[113] Contributors included some very well-known names: Kasem Srisamphan, Thirayuth Boonmi, Ubonrat Siriyuvasak, Pasuk Pongphaichit, Chermasak Pinthong, Somkiat Tangkitvanich, Sulak Sivaraksa and Prawase Wasi. The book sold 45,000 copies in its first two weeks, demon-

strating the demand for critical perspectives on Thaksin as an anti-
dote to the hagiographic volumes that had been filling bookstore
shelves and windows. The inclusion of Sulak and Prawase, two of
Thailand's most famous public intellectuals, was highly significant –
not least because both had expressed support for Thaksin around
the time of the 2001 election. As Sulak put it in his contribution:

> Prime Minister Thaksin Shinawatra, whom this writer and
> other well-meaning members of civil society supported when
> he first came to office because his policies appeared to be
> pro-poor, has shown himself to be a conceited, intolerant,
> dictatorial ruler, who has no respect for democratic values,
> good governance, or the rule of law.
>
> Thaksin lost no time in showing his true colours. He
> made enemies of anyone with dissenting views, particularly
> academics, intellectuals, non-governmental organisations
> and civil society.[114]

The book was edited by elected senator, prominent broadcaster and
former Thammasat University economist Chermsak Pinthong, who
had been banished from the airwaves by forces loyal to Thaksin and
his party. *Staying One Step Ahead of Thaksin* was marketed as a
'citizen's handbook' to shed light on the prime minister's policies and
methods. Asked to explain the popularity of the book, Chermsak
responded:

> 'The enjoyment of this book is not unlike the pleasure one
> derives from watching a classic Thai soap opera on TV. The
> fact that one already has intimate and detailed knowledge of
> every twist and turn of the whole plot does not distract one
> from the sort of emotional involvement and personal
> identification with the protagonist.'
>
> 'For example, in Baan Sai Thong (an all-time favourite
> romance of Thai women) everybody knows how the pro-
> tagonist is taken in by an aristocratic household as a lowly
> dependent but eventually works her way up to become the
> undisputed owner of the huge estate', Chermsak explains
> with a strong hint of irony.[115]

A second volume of critical articles on Thaksin, also edited by Chermsak, was launched in August 2004. *Ru Than Thaksin 2* included 16 contributors, notably the leading economist, Ammar Siamwalla, Thammasat political scientists, Seksan Prasertkul and Kasian Tejapira, and the distinguished retired diplomat, Asada Chainam.[116] As 2004 wore on, Thaksin's critics became increasingly vocal, incensed by a variety of issues ranging from the Liverpool Football Club debacle to the shenanigans at Channel 5 and the EGAT privatization controversy – not to mention the political violence in the South and the re-emergence of bird flu. Thaksin's honeymoon was over; and spats between politicians and critical academics and commentators were nothing new in Thailand. What was striking, however, was the extreme venom of the exchanges, which had become highly personalized. Thailand's public intellectuals felt that the government was treating them with barely-disguised contempt, while Thaksin seemed completely incapable of tolerating any form of critical scrutiny.

CONCLUSION

Thaksin was in certain respects a new sort of Thai politician, with a completely new understanding of marketing, media and language. In this respect, his approach to politics owed far more to consummate professional politicians such as Blair and Clinton than to any of his Thai predecessors. He sought to tell stories to the Thai electorate, spinning forth new initiatives on a weekly basis. Yet the irony was that Thaksin Shinawatra was no Tony Blair: he lacked the easy command of language that is the hallmark of the natural politician. Herein lay Thaksin's problem. The relentless use of language by someone who struggles constantly with his own lack of fluency all too easily produces a shrill tone, a hectoring didacticism. And instead of engaging in a dialogical relationship with the language of others – the languages of political opponents, of rivals, critics, journalists and pundits – this mode of language degenerates rapidly into monologue. Monologue of this kind requires a monopoly of the means of communication, since to ensure that it is always heard, other voices must be turned down or simply silenced. Lack of fluency in a weak individual breeds nervousness and hesitancy, but in a strong and powerful individual such as Thaksin, it can produce an overconfident raising of the voice.

Since the growth of critical voices during 2004, Thaksin's radio programmes have changed their tone. He is less prone to responding to critics or extemporizing on hobbyhorse issues. He appears instead to be sticking more closely to a structured script that concentrates on what he and his government have been doing 'for the people'. Towards the end, he starts to seem hurried, apologizing that although he still has many issues to talk about, he will have to drop some of them. For a while, he began using the broadcasts to respond directly to public petitions complaining of wrongdoing.

Thaksin has grasped the central problem of contemporary politics – the need to communicate directly and personally with citizens and voters. His weekly radio programme is an impressive testament to this understanding. But in an open society, that communication needs to involve listening as well as speaking: political discourse must form part of a dialogue, however unsatisfactory, between the ruled and their rulers.[117] Once dialogue (or at least the illusion of dialogue) ends, the democratic spell is broken. Thai prime ministers do not need to engage in dialogue with the electorate – they can operate perfectly well through backroom deals, money politics and a range of other tactics and strategies. Even if dialogue falters between Thaksin and the citizens of Thailand, he may be able to remain in power for some considerable time. But it would be a shame if he allowed the dialogue he appeared to establish with the people during his early time in office to break down, and to be replaced by a dull and dangerous sermonizing. To pursue the analogy with marketing, Thaksin needs to ensure that he responds to the changing demands of consumers and respects their concerns about the direction of Thai Rak Thai. Should he fail to do so, Thai Rak Thai could revert to the more familiar product or sales oriented mode of political party. Thaksin is then likely to experience a gradual but inexorable loss of support, as Thailand's notoriously fickle voters become bored with his image and his promises.

NOTES

1   It later emerged that the author was political journalist Joe Klein.

2   Joe Klein, *The Natural*, London, Hodder and Stoughton, 2002, p. 39.

3   Jennifer Lees-Marshment, *Political Marketing*, Manchester, Manchester University Press, 2001, p.186.

4   Lees-Marshment, *Political Marketing*, pp.181–210.

5   Fairclough is a leading proponent of a sociolinguistic approach known as critical discourse analysis, which focuses on the way in which language is used and discursive strategies constructed. Savitri Gadavanij has applied such an approach to the study of Thai political language; examining the case of parliamentary no-confidence debates in the second half of the 1990s, she argues that the language used in these debates is carefully constructed to bridge the discrepancy between the formal and hidden agendas of the speakers. See Savitri Gadavanij, 'Discursive strategies for political survival: a critical discourse analysis of Thai no-confidence debates', unpublished PhD thesis, University of Leeds, 2003.

6   Norman Fairclough, *New Labour, New Language*, London, Routledge, 2000, p. 5.

7   Fairclough, *New Labour*, p. 96.

8   Cited in Fairclough, *New Labour*, p. 98.

9   Fairclough, *New Labour*, p. 160.

10 Klein describes an episode where Clinton had to ad-lib part of a major speech when the wrong text was loaded into a teleprompter, an experience Clinton claimed to have enjoyed. Klein, *The Natural*, pp. 83–84.

11 Amronrat Sa-ardsorn, 'Weekly radio address: PM grabs people's ear', *The Nation*, 5 November 2001.

12 As Thepchai Yong puts it: 'of course, nobody cares to tell us whether it is being done voluntarily or on somebody's order'. 'Media reform is looking increasingly remote', *The Nation*, 23 December 2003.

13 *The Nation*, 5 November 2001.

14 *The Nation*, 5 February 2002.

15 Associated Press, 19 May 2002.

16 *The Nation*, 2 January 2004.

17 *The Nation*, 23 August 2002.

18 Sophon Ongkara, 'Why is Thaksin hiding from the House?' *The Nation*, 3 March 2002.

19 Sutichai Yoon, 'Hard Talk', *The Nation*, 27 November 2001.

20 Quoted in *Bangkok Post*, 2 December 2001.

21 Duncan McCargo, *Politics and the Press in Thailand: Media Machinations*, London, Routledge, 2000, p. 136 [also Bangkok, Garuda Press, 2002, p. 194].

22 The King himself referred to the prime minister as 'Teacher Thaksin' in his 2003 birthday speech. For an interesting discussion see Michael Kelly Connors, 'Thaksin's Thailand – to have and to hold: Thai politics in 2003–2004'. Paper presented at the Thailand Update Conference, Macquarie University, 20–21 April 2004. http://www.latrobe.edu.au/socsci/staff/connor-thaksin.rtf

23 Pasuk Phongpaichit and Chris Baker, *Thaksin: The Business of Politics in Thailand*, Chiang Mai, Silkworm, p. 25. Again, there are similarities with Chamlong Srimuang, who published a bestselling autobiography that played up certain incidents in his childhood and passed rapidly over some awkward episodes. See Duncan McCargo, *Chamlong Srimuang and the New Thai Politics*, London, Hurst, 1997, pp. 218–222..

24 *The Nation*, 8 January 2001.

25 *The Economist*, leader, 13 January 2001.

26 *The Nation*, 8 August 2003.

27 Chang Noi, 'One handful of leaves: a lesson', *The Nation*, 7 July 2003.

28 *Financial Times*, 16 October 2001.

29 *New Straits Times*, 10 July 2003.

30 *Business Day*, 23 July 2001.

31 *The Nation*, 11 May 2003.

32 *The Nation*, 5 June 2003.

33 Michael H. Nelson, 'Thailand's house elections of 6 January 2001: Thaksin's landslide victory and lucky escape, in Michael H. Nelson (ed.) *Thailand's New Politics: KPI Yearbook 2001*, Bangkok, White Lotus 2002, pp. 409–410.

34 *The Nation*, 2 July 2003.

35 *The Nation*, 23 June 2003.

36 *Investors' Digest* (Malaysia), 16 February 2002.

37 *The Nation*, 21 August 2003.

38 Christopher Meyer and Stan Davies, *It's Alive: The Coming Convergence of Information, Biology and Business*, London, Thomson Learning, 2003.

39 Pasuk Phongpaichit and Chris Baker, '*The Only Good Populist is a Rich Populist*', Thaksin Shinawatra and Thauland's Democracy, Southeast Asia Research Centre Working Papers Series No. 36, Hong Kong, Southeast Asia Research Centre, City University of Hong Kong, 2002, p. 11.

40 *The Nation*, 10 January 2002.

41 See Duncan McCargo, 'Populism and reformism in contemporary Thailand, *South East Asia Research*, 9, 1, 2001, pp. 89–107.

42 McCargo, *Chamlong Srimuang*, pp. 198–204.

43 Kasian Tejapira, 'Post-crisis economic impasse and political recovery in Thailand: the resurgence of economic nationalism', *Critical Asian Studies*, 34, 3, 2002, pp. 333–335.

44 Kasian 'Post-crisis economic impasse', pp. 339–341.

45 Jim Glassman, 'Economic nationalism in a post-nationalist era: the political economy of economic policy in post-crisis Thailand', *Critical Asian Studies*, 36, 1, 2004, p. 40.

46 Glassman, 'Economic nationalism', pp. 50–51.

47 Andrew Brown and Kevin Hewison, *Labour and Politics in Thaksin's Thailand*, Southeast Asia Research Centre Working Papers Series No. 62, Hong Kong, Southeast Asia Research Centre, City University of Hong Kong, 2004, p. 9.

48 Glassman, 'Economic nationalism', pp. 59–60

49 Glassman, 'Economic nationalism', p. 61.

50 Jeerawat Na Thalang, 'PM bangs the war drums of TRT's triumph', *The Nation*, 2 August 2003.

51 *Associated Press*, 9 June 2003.

52 Joe Cochrane, 'Business: the Bold Coast', *Newsweek*, 12 January 2004.

53 Thai Press Reports, 5 January 2004.

54 Associated Press, 12 April 2002.

55 *Newsweek*, 15 January 2001.

56 *The Nation*, 20 January 2004.

57 *The Nation*, 23 January 2004

58 *The Nation*, 11 January 2001.

59 *Australian Financial Review*, 31 January 2001.

60 *The Nation*, 10 February 2003.

61 Lees-Marshment, *Political Marketing*, pp. 45–48.

62 Lees Marshment, *Political Marketing*, p. 46.

63 *The Nation*, 10 February 2003.

64 Lees-Marshment, *Political Marketing*, p. 47.

65 *The Nation*, 11 January 2001.

66 Lees-Marshment, *Political Marketing*, p. 223.

67 Lees-Marshment, *Political Marketing*, p. 223.

68 Lees-Marshment, *Political Marketing*, p. 221.

69 *Krungthep Thurakit*, 20 December 2002.

70 *The Nation*, 30 December 2000.

71 *The Nation*, 4 January 2001.

72 McCargo, *Politics and the Press*, p. 176 [252].

73 McCargo, *Politics and the Press*, pp. 70–71 [100].

74 *The Nation*, 20 August 2001.

75 *The Nation*, 3 December 2001.

76 *Washington Post*, 23 March 2002.

77 Associated Press, 7 August 2001.

78 *The Nation*, 20 August 2001.

79 *The Nation*, 20 August 2001.

80 Associated Press, 7 August 2001.

81 *The Nation*, 8 January 2002.

82 *Washington Post*, 23 March 2002.

83 *Korea Herald*, 6 January 2003.

84 *The Nation*, 28 October 2003.

85 For details see www.cpj.org.

86 See www.cpj.org.

87 From Ubonrat Siriyuvasak, 'Anokhot sua seri nai rabop Thaksin' [Future of the free media under the Thaksin system] in Chermsak Pinthong (ed.), *Ru Tan Thaksin* [Staying One Step Ahead of Thaksin], Bangkok, Kho Khit Duay Ton, 2004, pp. 169–183. Translation from *The Nation*, 24 April 2004.

88 *The Nation*, 20 August 2001.

89 *The Nation*, 20 August 2001.

90 *The Nation*, 4 March 2003.

91 *The Nation*, 4 March 2003.

92 See details at www.cpj.org.

93 Editorial, *The Nation*, 8 December 2003.

94 *The Nation*, 29 January 2004.

95 Quoted at www.cpj.org.

96 *The Nation*, 20 August 2001.

97 For full text see www.tja.org.

98 For details, see *The Nation*, 22 February 2004.

99 *The Nation*, 1 April 2004.

100 *The Nation*, 1 April 2004.

101 Quoted in *The Nation*, 28 April 2004.

102 *Bangkok Post*, 2 November 2003.

103 Robert Horn, 'This time he's serious', *Time*, 6 March 2000.

104 *Naeo Na*, 2 March 2000.

105 For a fuller discussion of this issue, see Duncan McCargo, *Media and Politics in Pacific Asia*, London, Routledge, 2003, pp. 142–45.

106 'Right royal headache', *Far Eastern Economic Review*, 10 January 2002.

107 *The Nation*, 28 February 2002.

108 Michael Vatikiotis and Rodney Tasker, 'Prickly premier', *Far Eastern Economic Review*, 11 April 2002.

109 *The Nation*, 17 January 2003.

110 *The Nation*, 17 January 2003.

111 *The Nation*, 28 July 2004.

112 *The Nation*, 20 January 2004.

113 Chermsak Pinthong (ed.), *Ru Tan Thaksin* [Staying One Step Ahead of Thaksin], Bangkok, Kho Khit Duay Ton, 2004.

114 Quoted in *The Nation*, 23 April 2004.

115 Quoted in *The Nation*, 3 April 2004.

116 Chermsak Pinthong (ed.), *Ru Tan Thaksin 2* [Staying One Step Ahead of Thaksin 2], Bangkok, Kho Khit Duay Ton 2004. .

117 Klein notes that Clinton was endlessly interested in listening to ordinary people's stories and concerns, often over-running his schedule as a result. *The Natural*, pp. 195–196.

CHAPTER 6

Thaksin's New Political
Economy Networks

The videotape stunned a nation. A senior intelligence chief was seen handing over $15,000 in cash to an opposition politician, in an attempt to ensure that a certain candidate became the president of parliament. The political fallout culminated in the head of the government fleeing the country, later resigning by fax.

A MAJOR SCANDAL WHICH BROKE in Peru in September 2000 revealed that President Alberto Fujimori's intelligence advisor and confidante Vladimiro Montesino had created an elaborate benefit-sharing network, which incorporated bankers, journalists and the leaders of opposition parties.[1] Crucial exchanges between these actors were captured on the 'Vladivideos', a series of recordings of secret meetings held at the headquarters of the National Intelligence Secretariat. Luis Moreno Ocampo argued that only by using the idea of power networks was it possible to understand how favours and resources are really allocated in a political system such as Peru's, characterized by a small elite with complex interlocking interests. Montesino acquired personal control over a range of government agencies, staffing them with longstanding friends and old classmates. Ocampo cites a study by Jean Cartier Bresson, who cautions that mutually beneficial relationships between political interest groups and other well-connected bodies can undermine democratic norms and principles: behind a façade of constitutional democracy, real power may lie in the hands of well-networked elites.[2] Bresson defined such networks as follows:

> In our approach, a corruption network is structured in a
> clandestine manner by mobilizing multiple 'resources' such
> as financial interests, obedience to hierarchy, solidarity,
> family, friends (ethnic or tribal, religious, political, regional,
> sectorial, corporative…), violence. Its objectives, which are
> no less multiple, range from covering up illegal activities –
> small or large – to the rerouting of competition practised by a
> legal market. The objectives include the funding of political
> parties. The enlarged reproduction of corrupt exchanges can
> be explained by a complex network of interpersonal relation-
> ships and associations.[3]

Similar arguments may be advanced in relation to Southeast
Asian countries. This is especially true of the Philippines, a country
with a long tradition of democratic procedures and practices – yet
where remarkable inequalities of wealth distribution mean that the
state remains weak, and political and economic power has been
captured by a small number of wealthy families. Alfred McCoy has
described this system as 'an anarchy of families'.[4] These elite families
have been able to control whole sectors of the economy, including
the sugar industry, mining, logging, and banking. Paul Hutchcroft
has argued that family ownership of Philippine banks is so strong
that it has become difficult to determine whether some banks are
run as real businesses or simply as family piggy banks.[5] Hutchcroft
argues that this lax approach to banking undermines the whole
economy of the Philippines. The blurred distinction between private
interests and the public interest helps create the phenomenon of
'booty capitalism',[6] an extractive system based on crude rent-seeking
and the use of violence to guarantee profits.[7]

Thailand is supposed to be far removed from this kind of Latin
American-style political economy. It has been characterized by over
four decades of impressive economic growth – apart from a two year
dip after mid-1997. It has a vibrant civil society and an outspoken
media that help curtail abuses of power; and the liberal 1997 constitution is full of safeguards to ensure that the elected government
is accountable to the public, and behaves in a transparent manner.

Thailand has never before been characterized by the kind of dynastic politics that have blighted the Philippines, India or Bangladesh, and no major Thai leader has sought to become prime minister. Until Thaksin.

The existence of a powerful oligarchy in the Philippines and an elaborate presidential power network in Peru illustrate the extent to which even in an apparently democratic regime, flagrant abuses of power are all too possible. By using the concept of power networks, it is possible to explore the real dynamics of money, politics and influence in democratic countries such as Thailand. Focusing on networks helps analysts to move beyond generalizations about leadership, political change and reform, and engage in a close scrutiny of how power is actually exercised.

BACKGROUND: THAILAND'S POLITICAL ECONOMY

Thailand has long enjoyed a relatively open political system compared with other Southeast Asian countries, an openness fuelled by rapid economic development since the 1960s. John Girling explains these trends as follows. In the 1980s Thailand demonstrated a different tendency from most other countries within the region by virtue of its shift from authoritarianism to democracy. Indeed, Thailand provided a 'classic' correspondence between development and democracy, the economic turning point being the changed role of the state under Field Marshal Sarit Thanarat from one of support of economic nationalism and public corporations to providing essential infrastructural services for the benefit of private enterprise. The economic boom of the 1960s in Thailand swelled the demand for well-trained administrators, leading to an expansion of universities and thus in the number of students. These were the students who, in 1973, spearheaded the 'constitutional' demands of civil society against the authoritarian regime headed by Sarit's military successors. Therefore, even though the democratic period lasted for a very short period due to the brutal suppression that took place in 1976, the less confident and more factionalised military leaders could not return to the old days of the 'bureaucratic polity'. By 1980, business leaders played a prominent part in a 'bureaucratic-parliamentary compromise'.[8]

During the 1990s considerable changes took place in Thailand, both in terms of political structures and the emergence of linkages between different sources of economic and political power. Hewison argued that Thailand had reached a turning point where new modes of power were generating pressures for social and political reform, although the objectives of these reform processes were highly contested.[9] Whereas Hewison emphasized the expansion and dominance of major business groups, Anek Laothammatas and Thirayuth Boonmi stressed the role of the middle class.[10] It is argued here that the formation of new power networks has been a central feature of only two recent periods of Thai political history, corresponding with two important premierships: the Prem period (1980–88) and the Thaksin period (2001–present).

During other periods, priorities were different. Chatichai Choonavan concentrated on securing a support base from provincial politicians such as Narong Wongwan, Montri Pongpanich, Banharn Silpaarcha, and Suwat Liptapallop – along with some new business groups, such as that of Pairoj Piamphongsarn. Yet this support base proved completely unreliable, grounded in ad hoc alliances rather than lasting networks. These provincial politicians proved willing to offer their support to the highest bidder, pledging loyalty to a succession of governments which rewarded them with lucrative ministerial posts. These included the Suchinda government, the first and second Chuan governments, the Banharn government, and the Chavalit government. Major businesses emulated the example of provincial politicians, by creating multiple connections with a range of senior politicians, switching loyalty in the pursuit of short-term economic advantage. None of these party leaders were able to establish a sufficiently strong network of links for provincial politicians or business leaders to provide them with an enduring political base.

The military remained significant political players, but had been floundering since the upheavals of October 1973, which ended the relatively unified force that existed under the authoritarian regimes of Sarit-Thanom-Prapas. Now the military was divided into cliques based on their year of graduation from the Chulachomklao Military Academy, thus creating what has come to be termed 'classmate politics'.[11] As such, the military lacked the coherence to shape dominant political networks, and personal relationships between particular politicians and particular military officers or cliques became the norm. Chulachomklao's Class 7, for example, formed part of Prem's support base; later on, Major-General Manoon Roopka-chorn supported Chatichai, and General Viroj Saengsanit was a close ally of Banharn.

By contrast, Prem and Thaksin proved capable of forging power networks centred upon themselves – though these networks had quite different origins, structures and impacts. Prem founded a patron-client network of linkages between high-ranking military officers, large business conglomerates, politicians from major parties and influential members of the media during his eight-year term as prime minister, some of which still persist. This network was based largely on his personal *barami* (loosely translatable as 'charisma'), the military and political authority he secured through a series of top jobs (he was successively and at one point simultaneously Army Commander-in-Chief, Minister of Defence and Prime Minister), the then-prevailing 'semi-democratic' system which privileged the power of government officials over elected politicians and the relative institutional weakness of the military. As a leader who proved acceptable to both the military and to civilian politicians, Prem was able to make himself the centre of an elaborate nexus of power.

By contrast, Thaksin's network was of much more recent origin. His early ventures into politics – one short spell as foreign minister, and two as a deputy prime minister – were not especially successful. But immediately following his 2001 election victory, Thaksin was able to create and consolidate a remarkably extensive network of power and influence, one which came quickly to eclipse that of Prem.

Thaksin's network embraced several large business conglomerates, political parties, the National Assembly, the military and the police, all intricately linked to Thaksin and certain members of his family. How this power network has been formed, the nature of its role and functions and its likely impacts on the future direction of Thailand's political economy will be examined here.

THE POLITICAL AND ECONOMIC BASIS OF THAKSIN'S POWER NETWORK

Prem's power network was based on a traditional form of Thai political power, the military. The 1978 constitution stipulated that the prime minister had to be supported by parliament, but did not have to be a member of parliament: these provisions formed the basis of a hybrid system under which a military man could head the government, working with a cabinet that mixed elected politicians with unelected technocrats. Prem's ability to combine both military and political portfolios illustrated the extent to which he was the consummate hybrid figure. While Prem did have close ties with certain business groups – reflecting favours done in the past – they did not comprise a major network.[12] Prem's connections with political parties were also more in the nature of personal ties than large-scale structural connections; Prem did not have his own political party or faction. Standing somewhat apart from the political fray, his considerable personal authority partly derived from the sense that he was not personally entangled in party politics. Prem's basic stance was highly conservative, reflecting his military background. It is striking, for example, that he never made an official visit to any of Thailand's socialist neighbours during his eight years as prime minister. During his premiership, economic policy was driven largely by technocrats and civil servants, especially those associated with the National Economic and Social Development Board. In other words, his power network derived from the conventional political structures then prevailing under Thailand's heavily bureaucratic regime.

By contrast, Thaksin's power network is based upon a new kind of political and economic structure, one based upon the growth of the new business conglomerates that began to assume increasingly open roles within Thailand's political order during the 1990s.[13]

The crucial turning point was the transformation of Thai society produced by two major events of 1997: the economic crisis, and the new constitution. The crisis led to the restructuring of all the major business conglomerates, many of which emerged with sizeable debts. This resulted in a significant transformation of capital in major business groups, ranging from leading commercial banks to industrial and retail giants. A number of domestic conglomerates were bankrupted or were taken over by multinational corporations or foreign companies.[14] Faced with a struggle for survival, some debt-ridden conglomerates sought direct access to political power as a means of defending their business interests.

At the same time, the 1997 constitution gave an unprecedented boost to the power of the executive branch, and especially to the office of prime minister.[15] In particular, a prime minister could only face a parliamentary no-confidence debate if the opposition could muster two-fifths of the lower house in support of their motion,[16] while rules to reduce the scope for party-swapping by MPs were calculated to create more stable government coalitions.[17] A new provision requiring all MPs to hold at least a bachelor's degree, combined with the introduction of a party list system for 20 per cent of parliamentary seats, meant that the composition of the National Assembly tended to favour urbanized elites over other social classes. At the same time, a number of independent agencies were created to scrutinize the workings of the executive, including the National Counter Corruption Commission, the Constitutional Court and the National Broadcasting Commission. A new 'impeachment' provision was also introduced under which public office-holders could be called to account through a petition of at least 50,000 voters. Despite these checks and balances, the package of reforms introduced by the 1997 Constitution amounted overall to a blueprint for strong prime ministerial authority.

The economic crisis and new constitution of 1997 created the conditions for an alliance comprising politicians with strong financial backing, along with large business conglomerates, to assume leading roles in politics without having to depend on traditional power groups such as the military and the civilian bureaucracy. As the head of a business conglomerate which had emerged relatively unscathed from the economic crisis, Thaksin Shinawatra was well-placed to take advantage of the new political environment created by the 1997 constitution. Whereas Prem had created a highly effective network which relied primarily on connections rather than cash, Thaksin had all the financial resources required to buy friends and influence people. These resources increased dramatically within a short space of time. Prior to becoming Foreign Minister in 1995, Thaksin put his own fortune at 70 billion baht.[18] By 2003, his family-owned companies were valued on the Stock Exchange of Thailand at over 425 billion baht and amounted to almost 9 per cent of all the stocks trading on the Thai stock market.[19] In other words, the family wealth of the Shinawatras had increased more than sixfold in less than a decade. A combination of expanded business activity and rising share values meant that this wealth was constantly increasing, and Thaksin's family branched out into ever more businesses, including private hospitals,[20] an airline[21] and various new ventures started by his siblings.[22] This exceptionally robust financial base allowed Thaksin to provide considerable incentives to encourage others to participate in his new networks.

NEW POLICIES AND MAJOR CAPITAL NETWORKS

During the early period following the foundation of Thai Rak Thai, Thaksin attempted to differentiate his party's policies from those of the Democrats, who had been primarily focused on addressing the problems of the country's financial institutions. Whereas Democrat Finance Minister Tarrin had been accused of adopting a 'banker's perspective' on economic recovery, Thaksin proposed an alternative way forward using 'populist' policies aimed at relieving the financial burdens of low income groups.[23] Thaksin also positioned Thai Rak Thai as the party of small and medium scale domestic business, arguing that fostering these businesses was essential in order to ensure that Thailand remained globally competitive. His nationalistic advocacy of a mix of local expertise and high technology struck a popular chord with many Thais.[24]

While these policies were widely noted, less visible was the way in which Thaksin sought to involve a number of major business conglomerates in Thai Rak Thai's political project, bringing them into his inner circle. The relationship between Thaksin's populist policies and big business requires some scrutiny.

POPULIST POLICIES?

Thai Rak Thai's 'think new, act new' programme of policies, widely touted at the time of the 2001 general election, was based on a number of key ideas designed to appeal to rural voters.[25] These policies were propagated through an unrelenting public relations campaign and garnered overwhelming support for the government and the prime minister himself. The policies were widely interpreted as being populist,[26] or a blatant political strategy by a group of politicians bent on winning the 2001 election by capitalizing on the Democrat Party's alleged failures. These failures were parodied as the futile efforts of a handful of bank executives struggling to control the devastating economic crisis of 1997, mainly by introducing reforms dictated by the International Monetary Fund. A closer analysis of the dynamics of power, however, will show that the populist policies of Thai Rak Thai were carefully designed as a political strategy to consolidate support at the grassroots level while also protecting and expanding the economic control and political influence of those allied with Thaksin Shinawatra.

At the grassroots level, these policies involved the granting of a three-year debt moratorium for farmers, the establishment of one-million-baht community development funds in every village, the creation of the 'One village, one product' project and the creation of a 'people's bank'. Thaksin and his associates reinvented the Government Savings Bank, a savings institution originally established in 1913 and revamped in 1947 to serve people from low-income groups. Under a new name and using a new way of managing loans, the government implemented micro credit schemes offering 100,000-baht loans to small-scale businesses, to enable vendors and shopkeepers in urban and rural areas to borrow funds for business purposes.[27]

At the middle level, Thaksin and his advisors proposed a policy to develop small and medium-sized enterprises (SMEs). This was important both as a short-term response to the economic crisis, as well as to forge a long-term strategy for the country in terms of creating and maintaining a production base, creating employment and income support and promoting exports. Thaksin and his advisors argued that small and medium-sized enterprises are the key to building economic growth and stability in the future. An important plank of this policy was supporting bank lending to SMEs. In fact, Thai Rak Thai's 'populist' policies were not part of the party's formal political agenda from the outset, but emerged during the campaign, culminating in the 2001 general elections. Some elements did not at first appear in any party documents, but were added in response to perceived demand from the rural electorate. Many of these policies had actually been borrowed from measures to boost the economy previously advocated or undertaken by the Democrats.[28] While the populist policies were targeted at securing political support from the rural sector, the major beneficiaries of Thaksin's rise to power were actually large corporate groups.

MAJOR CORPORATE GROUPS AND THAI RAK THAI

Thaksin registered Thai Rak Thai on 14 July 1998, declaring that this was the first political party established under the new constitution and one that would serve and work for the benefit of Thai society.[29] The party was created by using funds derived from Thaksin himself and from his business associates. Speaking to a Thai Rak Thai convention in 2000, Thaksin declared:

I have asked for permission from my wife and children. I asked permission to use the family's wealth for political work. How then could I use their money to defame them? So, please don't fear my wealth. Please pursue the result and see whether I'm lying and how my behaviour is.[30]

Shortly after his overwhelming victory in the 2001 general election, he declared:

I have obtained enough already from this country. For fifty years from now, in case I could live to my one-hundredth year, I dedicate myself, my brains, and all my strength and time for the nation. Therefore, I am willing to use the personal funds I have accumulated to make this a political party that people could have some hope in. Before the political reform process was complete, I was ready, having several friends who made use of their personal wealth without ever troubling their families to come and help make this party a clean party that doesn't resort to corruption...[31]

As Thaksin announced to his party members, the funds to create Thai Rak Thai came from his own pocket and from those of his friends. In other words, the formation of Thai Rak Thai represented a pooling of resources by various giant business concerns. Thaksin's premiership was created and supported by a number of big corporate groups and represented the greatest concentration of economic and political power seen in Thailand since the end of the absolute monarchy in 1932. These big corporate groups formed the apex of the socio-political strategic pyramid generally known as the Thai Rak Thai inner circle, but which could also be termed a cronyist network.

Not surprisingly, telecoms giants are at the core of this pyramid, which embraces both Shin Corp – the largest of the telecoms giants and owner of the biggest mobile phone service – and Telecom Asia, the CP company which owns the largest landline telephone service. It also includes TT&T-Jasmine, one of the former Big Four Telecom groups, which now supports Shin Corp in both the political and

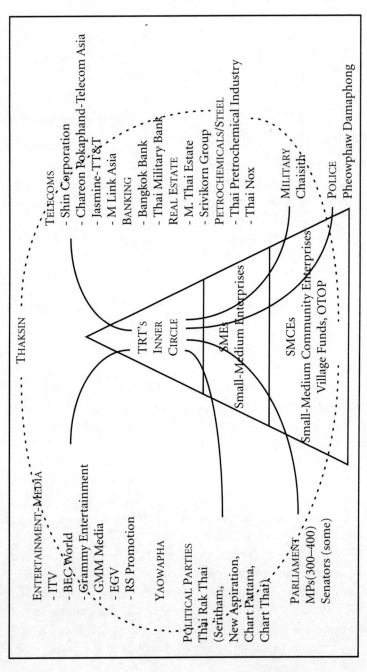

Chart 6.1: Thailand's new political power network since 1997

telecoms arena; its owner, Adisai Bodharamik, serves as commerce minister in the Thaksin government. Another member of the club is M-Link, a newcomer in the telecommunications industry that has recently registered on the Stock Exchange of Thailand. It is a joint venture between Thaksin's sister Yaowapha, and Suriya Jungrungruangkit, Secretary General of Thai Rak Thai and Minister of Communications.[32]

The base of the pyramid also includes Bangkok Bank, Thailand's largest commercial bank, and the Thai Military Bank, a medium sized bank in which Thaksin's family members are major shareholders.[33] These two commercial banks benefited tremendously from the Thaksin government's decision to stop pressuring banks to increase their level of capitalization. This had been one of the major policies of the Chuan administration, in compliance with proposals made by the International Monetary Fund. Instead, Thai Military Bank is currently receiving special privileges from the government's debt-supporting measures, through the establishment of the Vayupak Fund.[34]

A further component of the corporate alliance supporting the Thaksin administration derives from the petrochemical, steel and real estate sectors: TPI, a petrochemical firm with debts of more that 100,000 million baht, and Thai Knox Steel, a steel producer whose debts are around 10,000 million baht.[35] Both received special privileges from the Thaksin government. They are also closely associated with the inner circles of Thaksin's cronies; Thai Knox Steel owner Prayudh Mahakijsiri is a deputy leader of Thai Rak Thai and a party list MP – as well as the owner of a golf course frequented by Thaksin.

Other key elements are the deep ties between the Thaksin administration and the real estate sector. The real estate sector has previously played little direct role in politics, unlike the construction business, which has a long history of support for political parties in the rural areas. However, in recent years, real estate has assumed growing political significance. The M. Thai Estate group is a real estate group whose founder, Suchai Viramethikul, was a Sino-Thai (Techiew) businessman and owner of a torch factory in Samut

Sakhon. For over two decades he acquired property and gained the acquaintance of several leading Sino-Thai businessmen. He rose to prominence at the end of 1980 when he advised Hong Kong investors to purchase a large piece of property on Wireless Road from the Chartered Bank[36] and set up a leading real estate company by the name of M. Thai Estate.[37] Later on the company became more visibly involved in politics when his son, Dr Virachai Viramethikul, one of the founders of Thai Rak Thai, became an MP, was appointed an advisor to the Minister of Foreign Affairs and became chair of finance and banking committee of the House of Representatives.[38]

The Srivikorn Group[39] is another real estate group that has assumed a high profile through its support for Thai Rak Thai and Thaksin. Previously, Chalermbhand Srivikorn had been a key Democrat supporter in Bangkok, but had lost out to the party's southern wing and then abandoned politics in the early 1990s. In early 2000, Pimol Srivikorn was appointed as secretary to finance minister Somkid Jatusripitak. His mother, Khunying Sasima Srivikorn, was also made a board member of Thai Airways. Both M. Thai Estate and Srivikorn Group were expected to transfer their non-performing loans to the soon-to-be-established Thai Asset Management Corporation (TAMC).

Apart from the support he derives from mainstream business sectors, Thaksin enjoys a close relationship with the media and entertainment sectors, which provide him with considerable intellectual and cultural support that helps legitimate his premiership. In the past, the entertainment business was largely divorced from the political realm. The leading figure in the business, Grammy Enter--tainment owner and founder Paiboon Damrongchaikul, has been a member of Thaksin's private clique for the past ten years. This clique has regular gatherings every two months. During the period prior to the August 2001 asset concealment verdict, Paiboon provided Thaksin with moral support. Shortly afterwards, in November 2001, Grammy announced that it would start to levy copyright fees every time one of its songs was played in pubs, restaurants and other entertainment venues.[40] The announcement generated immense conflict between Grammy and its competitors, yet the Commerce Ministry – under Thai Rak Thai control – made no public reaction to it.[41]

Thai Rak Thai also enjoys strong ties to BEC World, the company which owns the mass-market Channel 3 television station. One of its former directors, Pracha Maleenont, ranked tenth on the Thai Rak Thai party list, was given the portfolio of Deputy Minister of Transport and Communications, overseeing management of Thai Airways. He was later transferred to the post of deputy interior minister, retaining considerable clout within the party. Thaksin has more recently developed close ties with other entertainment giants such as RS Promotions. Meanwhile, various entertainment companies were listed on the stock market, including iTV (owned by Thaksin's family), GMM-Media (a new Grammy company) and RS Promotion. All experienced burgeoning share prices which generated considerable benefits for their owners. At the same time, these groups provided a degree of backing for Thaksin's government. The reporting on iTV became markedly less critical than before;[42] and Grammy Entertainment asked its artists to contribute to key government projects such as the drug prevention program, the promotion of tourism and a project to compose a national song for the Prime Minister's campaign to pay respect to the Thai flag. Thaksin was able to rely on most media and entertainment companies to support the government through sponsoring charity events such as New Year celebrations held in all major towns across the country, and the 2003 APEC summit held in Bangkok.[43]

In late 2003, the relationship between the government, the media and the quest for popularity was graphically illustrated when iTV sold a substantial amount of equity to popular television host Traiphop Limpraphat and the Kantana Group,[44] as part of plans to increase the entertainment content of the station. The arrival of Traiphop, who has 20 years of experience hosting leading shows with ratings of up to 15 million viewers on Channel 3, was bound to prove an immense boost to iTV's popularity. Traiphop is widely believed to have made a fortune from the deal. The move also had wider political significance – as a Southerner from Surat Thani, Traiphop hailed from a major base of the Democrat Party.[45] The nation's favourite TV personality was set to become the jewel in the crown of a station in which Thaksin's family held a major stake – and a general election was approaching.

Overall, this web of connections amounts to the greatest assemblage of large business groups by a ruling Thai party. Whereas in the past these large capital groups stayed behind the scenes and lent their indirect support to political parties or the government, under Thaksin the leading capital groups in telecommunications, banks, petro-chemical industry, steel, property development and entertainment business sectors have become a significant force, openly playing a supporting role to the government and Thai Rak Thai. Major groups in this network have supplied co-founders of the party, have representatives on the party list, have provided people to assume executive roles in the party (including deputy leaders) and have even seen their representatives serve as ministers in Thaksin's administration. These groups have also made financial donations to the party. While some of these donations may seem relatively small, they indicate to the wider world the moral and political support Thaksin enjoys from favoured elements in the Thai business community.[46]

In addition, most leading businessmen in Thailand publicly praised Thaksin and his government throughout his first term as prime minister. Prominent figures such as Dhanin Chiaravanond, founder of the Charoen Pokphand group, and Chatri Sophonpanich of Bangkok Bank, have consistently expressed their admiration and support for Thaksin's performance as prime minister.[47]

Whereas people like Boonyasith Chokwattana[48] regularly express their views on political issues, people were more surprised when the normally tight-lipped Charoen Siriwadhanabhakdi, owner of the largest brewery business conglomerate and the New Imperial hotel group, also emerged as a supporter of the government. Charoen gradually shifted his support from the Democrat Party from late 2003 onwards.[49] He also planned a co-investment with Thaksin in the English football club Fulham, later changing tack to launch a bid to acquire a 25 per cent stake in Liverpool Football Club worth 3.5 billion baht.[50] This alliance reflected Thaksin's desire to bring into the Thai Rak Thai fold companies that had previously supported a range of political parties, a desire reflected in the pressure he brought to bear on alcoholic beverage companies and the manufacturers of the Red Bull stamina drink.[51]

THAKSIN AND THE MILITARY

Thaksin found his first foray into politics under the Palang Dharma banner a frustrating experience. He suffered the humiliation of a campaign to unseat him from his post as foreign minister by some members of his own party, who argued that as the owner of government concessions, he was constitutionally barred from serving in the cabinet.[52] After Thaksin assumed the leadership of Palang Dharma in 1995, a combination of infighting and declining electoral support saw the party virtually collapse. Thaksin became convinced that in itself, a political party did not offer a sufficiently firm base from which to pursue his ambitions. He therefore decided to dissolve Palang Dharma, create a new party of his own and make himself prime minister.[53] The lessons he had learned from the failure of his entanglement with Palang Dharma led him to seek an alternative power base within the military.[54] The essence of his plan involved taking personal control of the promotions process, installing his cousin Chaisit as Army Commander in Chief and placing a large number of his friends and former classmates from the Armed Forces Preparatory School Class 10 in key command positions.

Thaksin is in the fortunate position of not currently needing to rely on military support for himself or his government. However, the recent change in the Army's tough stance towards Burma has certainly proved very useful to him, and he is also doubtless gratified by consistent support from Army-controlled radio stations for Thai Rak Thai projects such as the 'One tambon, one product' scheme. But his real interest in the military is long-term. While Chaisit can help ensure Thaksin's control over the armed forces for the present,

Chaisit has no personal base in the Army's core fighting forces, the infantry, artillery and cavalry. Furthermore, Chaisit's accelerated promotion has undermined his standing with fellow officers, and his outspoken style has been known to arouse enmity. Crucially, Chaisit has not been successful in dealing with growing political violence in the southern border provinces, including the embarrassing theft of weapons from a military camp in January 2004, followed on 28 April by more than a hundred bloody deaths.[55] Thaksin can only wait for the time when his Class 10 classmates will assume the maximum control over key military forces, gradually nudging out Prem's associates and proteges, so that he can create a really solid political base immune from the vagaries of electoral politics and fluctuations in political popularity. This political base may become truly dependable in about 2008, around the time when Thaksin ought to consider stepping down from the premiership.

THAKSIN AND THE POLICE

Whereas for Thaksin the military forms an important part of his power base, an insurance policy against the uncertainties of Thai politics, the police function primarily as an instrument of important Thai Rak Thai agendas: the war on drugs, the suppression of organized crime and a crackdown on illegal forms of financial activity. Political interventions in the police are nothing new. In the past, politicians regularly interfered in the promotions process and made use of the police for essentially political ends, such as suppressing demonstrations.[56] The September 2003 police promotions list saw a number of officers who had close ties with Thaksin or his family (some of whom were Thaksin's classmates from the Armed Forces Academies Preparatory School Class 10, or were his classmates from the Police Cadet Academy Class 26) placed in charge of key units in the Police Department. These included the Crime Suppression Division, the Economic Crime Investigation Division, Central Investigation Bureau, the Highway Police Bureau, the Narcotics Suppression Bureau and the Metropolitan Police (Table 6.1). But Thaksin went far beyond these traditional modes of politicizing police activity, also using the police as a direct instrument of key government policies and thereby boosting his own popularity and that of his administration.

Among Thaksin's most important policy initiatives as prime minister were his anti-drugs policy and his policy of suppressing so-called 'dark influences'.[57] In pursuing these policies, he has been extremely reliant on an inner circle of senior police officers who have worked on their implementation. Not only have these policies won him considerable admiration from many Thais – they have also served as a significant means to weaken the influence of 'godfathers', provincial political power brokers who derive their wealth from illegal activities. In this way, Thaksin's policies aimed at undermining the financial base of political rivals both inside and outside Thai Rak Thai.[58]

On 4 December 2002, His Majesty the King gave a royal birthday speech that highlighted the growing drug problem and suggested that all Thais should collaborate in a war on drugs. The speech gave Thaksin the green light for a programme of draconian action. In response, Thaksin – widely believed to have his own private concerns about the drug problem – established an Anti-Narcotics Committee chaired by deputy PM Chavalit Yongchaiyudh. The committee set out a goal of winning the war on drugs by August 2004. However, Thaksin set a more ambitious and completely unrealistic goal of eradicating all illegal drug use in Thailand within a matter of months. He authorized narcotics suppression officers and the police to take all necessary steps to win this war, declaring that provincial governors and senior civil servants would be transferred if they failed to deliver results in the areas under their jurisdiction.[59]

The first phase of the war on drugs, emphasizing the stamping out of the *ya ba* (methamphetamine) trade, ran from February to April 2003 and was declared a complete success by the government in May 2003. The next phase in the war was a campaign against 'dark influences', aimed at eliminating all drugs from Thailand by 2 December 2003. This campaign involved weakening the influence of local godfathers who controlled drug trafficking, as well as various other kinds of racketeering. Fifteen crimes associated with 'dark influences' were named, including gambling, smuggling, illegal logging and human trafficking.[60]

In developing his campaigns against narcotics and illegal business, Thaksin was able to draw upon the expertise of a number of military officers well-versed in these issues. The leading figure in this group was Major General Trairong Indharathat, formerly a Class 10 classmate of Thaksin from the Armed Forces Academies Preparatory School, a tank commander and the owner of various businesses, including a stable of top racehorses,[61] and a security business for entertainment venues in the Sukhumvit area. Trairong had assisted Thaksin during his time with Palang Dharma, providing security for the party's politicians.[62] After Thaksin became prime minister, Trairong was appointed the prime minister's personal security advisor, escorting him in and out of Government House.[63] During this period he was assigned to handle tricky public order problems such as demonstrations by the Assembly of the Poor, and the organized crime gangs involved in tearing down some bars in the Sukhumvit area. Later on, Thaksin rewarded him for his military service by appointing him Chief of the Office of the Permanent Secretary at the Ministry of Defence.[64] Another important military officer who advised Thaksin on his public order campaigns was General Thammarak Isarangkura na Ayudhaya, whose family had long been politically active in the Northeast.[65] Despite being a newcomer to electoral politics, he was able to lead over 40 Isan Thai Rak Thai candidates to victory in the 2001 general election. Thammarak was a highly experienced intelligence officer, and had known Thaksin since his days as Chief of the Intelligence Unit in 1988.[66] Thammarak was a major channel through which Thaksin acquired inside information about issues relating to narcotics and dark influences. Based on this information, Thaksin was able to deploy his close friends in the police to take the appropriate action.

Thaksin employed a group of trusted police officers to handle the problem of 'dark influences'. One prominent member of this

Table 6.1: Police Reshuffle, September 2003

Order	Rank and Name	New Assignment	Relations
1	PLG Paisarn Thangjaitong	Assistant Cms-General (Crime Suppression 41)	PAC 22
2	PMG Kosin Hinto	Cdr, CSD 195	#
3	PG Suchat Kanchanaviset	Cdr, CIB	PAC 26
4	PLG Wongkot Maneerin	Cms, CIB	Class 10
5	PMG Suchat Muankeaw	Cdr, Highway Police	Class 10
6	PMG Wacharapol Prasanrachakit	Cms, NSB Police	
7	PMG Thanee Somboonsub	Cms, MetroP Bureau	
8	PMG Pisut Pumpichet	Cdr, MetroP Div'n 1	PAC 27
9	PMG Sumeth Ruangsawas	Cdr, MetroP Div'n 7	PAC 28/†
10	PLG Jongrak Jutanont	Cms, PP Region 2	
11	PLG Amnuay Disthkawee	Cms, PP Region 3	
12	PLG Achirawit Supanpesat	Cms, PP Region 4	
13	PLG Amarin Niemskul	Cms, PP Region 6	
14	PLG Somsak Bhuphasuwan	Cms, PP Region 8	
15	PLG Prung Boonpadung	Cms, PP Region 9	

Abbreviations:: PG = Police General, PLG = Police Lieutenant General, PMG = Police Major General, Cdr = Commander, Cms = Commissioner CIB = Central Investigation Bureau, MetroP = Metropolitan Police, PP Region = Provincial Police Region, PAC = Police Academy Class, Class 10 = Armed Forces Academies Preparatory School Class 10
Notes: # Relationship with Shinawatra family
  † Also Thaksin's personal police aide
Source: Bangkok Post, 10 September 2003.

group was Police Major General Surasit Sangkapong. About a year after he becoming prime minister, Thaksin transferred Surasit from Commander of the Highway Police to Commissioner of the Crime

Suppression Division.[67] One of Thaksin's classmates from the Police Cadet Academy Class 26, Surasit has played a central role in the government's anti-drugs campaign. This campaign was widely criticized for the large number of extra-judicial killings it generated, involving the violent deaths of both dealers and manufacturers, as well as numerous mysterious 'silent killings' (*kha tat ton*).[68] In addition, he was assigned to tackle the illegal numbers racket, before the government proposed legalizing the practice in early August 2003. Surasit was assigned to handle several sensitive cases involving dark influences. These included: the arrest of murder suspect Duangchalerm Yubamrung, the son of prominent politician Chalerm Yubamrung; the arrest and prosecution of Somchai Kunplome (an eastern seaboard organized crime boss, and father to Chart Thai party's Tourism and Sports Minister Sontaya Kunplome); and the case of Major General Khattiya Sawasdipol, who accused Police General Sant Sarutanont of unusual wealth.

The highly capable Surasit was also assigned another important task – raising money for the government outside the parameters of the state budget, funds that could be used to support Thai Rak Thai's populist policies. This accounts for Thaksin's appointment of Surasit as Director General of the Government Lottery Office in September 2003. He was replaced as Crime Suppression Division Commander by Police Major General Kosin Hintho. Kosin graduated from Class 28 of the Police Cadet Academy – two years after Thaksin – but owed his proximity to the Shinawatra family to an incident when he had swiftly apprehended a man who stole Thaksin's mother-in-law's handbag.

Two more of Thaksin's classmates from the Police Cadet Academy who were promoted were Police Major General Suchart Muankaeo, who assumed the Highway Police Division Commissioner post, and Police Major General Suchart Kanchanawises, appointed head of the Economic Crime Investigation Division. Another non-classmate, but only a year junior to Thaksin at the Police Cadet Academy, was Police Major General Pisut Poompichet, promoted to Metropolitan Police Division 1 Commander. Pisut had impressed Thaksin since his days as the head of the Economic Crime Investigation Division, especially because of his investigations into a rubber scandal involving a key member of the opposition Democrat Party, and charges of car smuggling against Dr Poosana Preemanote, a former Minister in the Prime Minister's Office.[69]

Another classmate of Thaksin from the Armed Forces Academies Preparatory School, Police Major General Wongkot Maneerin, was transferred from the post of Commissioner of the Police Cadet Academy to serve as Commissioner of the Central Investigation Bureau. This promotion of a close Thaksin friend had long been predicted: Wongkot is the husband of Thai Rak Thai party treasurer Sirikorn Maneerin. Sirikorn survived numerous ministerial reshuffles, lasting three years as Deputy Education Minister before being transferred to the post of Deputy Health Minister in February 2004.

Thaksin allies were also appointed to senior posts overseeing the provincial police. The 19 Isan police forces were supervised by Police Lieutenant General Amnuay Disthkawee and Police Lieutenant General Achirawit Supanpesat, commissioners of Region 3 and Region 4 respectively. Police Lieutenant General Amarin Niamsakul, the police inspector who had headed massage parlour bribery allegations, took command of Region 6, overseeing the lower North and upper Central Plains. Amnuay and Achirawit were both members of Class 21 and enjoyed close personal ties with Police General Pote Boonyachinda, a former police chief. Thaksin had been close to Pote since his telecom company first began doing business with the police force.[70]

At the same time, Thaksin's aspirations to use the police as an instrument of his own power and a means of pursuing his policies are not based solely upon his classmates from the Police Cadet Academy. They are also interwoven with the role of Police Lieutenant General Priewphan Damaphong, the brother of his wife Pojaman. Both Pojaman and Priewphan are themselves the children of a former deputy police chief. Only 53 in 2004,[71] Priewphan had already held a series of plum jobs in the police force.[72] As soon as Thaksin became prime minister, Priewphan was elevated to assistant police chief. He also played a crucial role in the narcotics suppression campaign, and was appointed as a specialist at the Anti-Money Laundering Office,[73] another important outfit employed by the government to scrutinize potential opponents. Priewphan is widely expected to become Thailand's police chief in due course, and to play an important role in implementing Thaksin's policies, as well as serving as a reliable source of revenue.

NEW POLICE FUNCTIONS UNDER THAKSIN

'I know a lot about the underground lottery.' Police Major General Surasit Sangapong, after officially taking up the post ofDirector-General of the Government Lottery Office.[74]

Thaksin's decision to choose Surasit, with his impressive record in cracking down on the underground lottery, to serve as the Director-General of the Government Lottery Office (GLO), did not mean that he expected Surasit to head a new lottery sales campaign. Rather, recognizing the Government Lottery Office as a major source of income generation, Thaksin wanted to use the GLO as an ATM machine, from which government could withdraw cash to fund activities outside the normal state budget.

In August 2003, the government issued 2-figure and 3-figure lottery tickets and increased the amount of the first prize to 100 million baht in order to boost ticket sales.[75] However, sales rates did not meet the government's expectations because of competition from the underground lottery. Underground lotteries typically use the same winning numbers as the government lottery, but give out a higher proportion of their takings as prizes, making them more attractive to small gamblers. For this reason, Thaksin and Surasit have been making considerable efforts to curb the activities of underground lottery operators.[76]

Money generated through the GLO is not subject to parliamentary scrutiny and can be used for charitable purposes, scholarships and other social welfare projects. The GLO can thus serve as a cash cow to fund 'populist' spending designed to favour an incumbent party and administration, without the government facing queries or challenges from the opposition. For example, the government has pledged to free Bangkok's motorcycle-taxi drivers from the control of local gangsters, who charge them fees to ply their trade within certain zones of the city. These gangsters typically provide motor-cycle-taxi drivers within their spheres of control with a particular design of jacket. Under Thaksin, the GLO issued jackets to motorcycle-taxi drivers to replace those of the gangsters, thereby symbolizing the determination of the government to follow through on its promises. In this respect, Thaksin was using GLO funds to boost the popularity of Thai Rak Thai in readiness for the next election campaign.[77] Apart from the purchase of jackets for motorcycle-taxi drivers, the government has allocated some GLO revenues for scholar-ship grants for poor children.[78] These scholarships have been awarded at presentation ceremonies held at Government House and presided over by the prime minister. On various occasions GLO funds have been used in an apparent bid to support government policies to combat dark influences, drugs, and underground lotteries. For example, in March the Metropolitan Police Commander was presented with five million baht by the GLO in order to purchase equipment for the crackdown on influential people in general and illegal lottery proprietors in particular.[79]

CONCLUSION: THE SCOPE AND LIMITS OF THAKSIN'S NETWORK

The extent, power, influence and profitability of Thaksin's networks cannot be understated: Thaksin has the most successful business network in Thailand. Companies belonging to the Shin Corp con-glomerate boast sales of hundreds of billions of baht – with all five subsidiary companies registered in the Stock Exchange culminating in a combined market value of nearly 500 billion baht.[80] Moreover, whenever Thaksin feels the need to spend, money is readily available both from his original base and from the constantly increasing funds his conglomerate can always raise on the Stock Exchange. These funds can be used to pay for elections and to control the behaviour of Thai Rak Thai MPs and the party's coalition partners.

At the same time, his power network also includes two important institutions which have been traditionally linked to politics, the military and the police. Thaksin has made the military his long-term political base, largely by promoting his relatives and classmates from the Armed Forces Academies Preparatory School Class 10. He has also won strongly from a lot of high-ranking officers, both through forging close personal ties with senior commanders in all three forces and through his generous support for weapons procurement requests.

The police have never recovered the political influence they had in the 1950s, before Police General Phao Sriyanon was conclusively defeated by Sarit. Thaksin is the first former policeman ever to become prime minister of Thailand; he is also the first ever civilian prime minister to revive the political significance of the police. He has created his own cadre of senior police officers, mostly his own classmates from the Police Cadet Academy, and used them to support the government's policies of cracking down upon drugs and dark influences. He relies on the police as sources of information, and especially as enforcers of his operations against organized crime, operations that frequently target crucial members or supporters of rival political cliques and parties. These operations serve to boost his own political standing and popularity. He has also placed the Government Lottery Office under the direct control of a loyal senior policeman, whom he has tasked with raising funds to support populist programmes.

At the same time, it is clear that this elaborate network is entirely dependent upon – and subordinated to – Thaksin's personal power and authority. The network has no prospect of becoming institutionalized, since it relates entirely to a single individual and is based largely on patronage. Whenever Thaksin's political power comes to an end, the network he has created will either completely collapse or assume an entirely new form. While the network assigns crucial roles to various of his relatives – Yaowapha within Thai Rak Thai and the parliament, Chaisit within the army and Priewphan within the police – all of these roles are supporting acts. Thaksin does not share power with these relatives; he assigns them power, which they simply exercise on his behalf.

The extent to which Thai Rak Thai is the embodiment of a single individual became apparent during the controversial run-up to the Constitutional Court's August 2001 verdict on his assets case. There was considerable public discussion about what would happen if Thaksin were obliged to step down from the premiership by a five-year ban on his holding political office. Then Interior Minister Purachai Piumsombun and Finance Minister Somkid Jatusripitak were widely touted as possible stand-ins for Thaksin, but neither had the public profile to assume the post. None of Thaksin's siblings was in the frame. Only Yaowapha was heavily involved in Thai Rak Thai, leading a faction of Northern MPs, but she had limited personal authority; the MPs only really followed her because of her direct line to the prime minister. Thaksin's other siblings – Yaowares Shinawatra, Payap Shinawatra, Monthatip Kowitcharoenkul and Yinglak Amornchat – had no substantial political role, instead concentrating on running their own businesses.[81]

Who else then could command enough charisma and power to win acceptance from the network apart from Thaksin? The only obvious candidate is his wife and trusted confidante, Khunying Pojaman Shinawatra, who has been the main support for his political career and the largest donor to Thai Rak Thai.[82] It is also said that she regularly attends a secret committee to review the cabinet agenda and discuss significant political economic issues. Yet although Pojaman has been Thaksin's crucial ally in both his personal and business life, does she have the ability and political savvy to win acceptance both from Thaksin's network and from wider Thai society?[83] It is one thing to support Thaksin and quite another to step into his shoes. Were Pojaman ever to become party leader or even prime minister, Thai politics would be transformed into Philippine-style family politics. This would undoubtedly produce strong criticism from those who are already uneasy about actual or potential conflicts of interests between the businesses of Shin Corp and the political power of Thaksin himself. For all Thaksin's talk of retiring at 60, and of Thai Rak Thai's remaining in office for 20 years, it is hard to see how the party could rule Thailand without him at its helm.

Thaksin's immense wealth has been central to his political rise. From the late 1980s onwards, Thai politics has been increasingly shaped by the power of money, especially at election times. Vote-buying has displaced the patron–client system as the principal determinant of electoral outcomes in rural areas, at all levels of the political system.[84] All Thai parties have affiliations with big business, and business leaders see access to political office as a means of boosting their business activities.[85] The 2001 general election allegedly saw the highest ever use of money in a Thai election, involving sums totalling over seven billion baht. Under these conditions, no political rivals are in a position to compete effectively with Thaksin and Thai Rak Thai.

In theory, Thailand's politics could be transformed by the emergence of truly representative political parties – but (as discussed in Chapter 3) the mass party remains an illusion in the Thai context. Thai Rak Thai remains a personalized rather than an institutionalized entity, and its millions of members are little more than a fiction, contrived to vacuum in financial support from the Election Commission.

Internally, Thai Rak Thai lacks powerful and effective structures. Purachai Piumsombun, the party's first secretary general (1998–2001), played little real role and was not widely accepted by party members. Most MPs remain closely aligned with personalized factions. The party's second secretary general, Suriya Jungrungreangkit, had no role in creating Thai Rak Thai: he assumed the post because of Purachai's resignation and a desire to become part of Thaksin's inner circle through his connection with Yaowapha, a co-investor in M-Link.[86] There are arguably only two substantial figures who work for the Thai Rak Thai Party itself – as distinct from working for Thaksin personally, or in a government post. One is deputy secretary general Pumetham; the other is party spokesman Suranan Vejjajiva, whose role is limited to responding to media stories which threaten to undermine Thaksin's popularity. Thai Rak Thai as an organization only springs temporarily to life for specific events and activities, such as preparing for by-elections, surveying voters and organizing meetings. Between 1999 and 2003, the party had only ten actual branches.[87]

Rather than developing Thai Rak Thai into a strong political institution, Thaksin has preferred to use traditional political strategies, expanding the party by absorbing other parties and political factions – in other words, by buying up discredited provincial politicans. In this respect, Thaksin has adopted much the same strategy as Banharn or Chavalit, except that his landslide election victory and his formidable financial resources give him the upper hand when dealing with political barons and faction leaders. Nevertheless, there are constant tensions between the old political barons and Thaksin's inner circle, particularly because Thaksin's various plans to create an UMNO-style super party threatened to curtail the barons' room for manoeuvre.[88] Discord within Thai Rak Thai grew more obvious during 2004, as the general election grew nearer. Plagued with political problems such as the unrest in the South and the emergence (and subsequent recurrence) of bird flu, Thaksin faced demands from faction bosses for more attractive posts, or increased financial subventions. Nevertheless, he held the trump card of an early dissolution of parliament, which effectively prevented troublesome MPs from jumping ship.

Thailand is neither Peru nor the Philippines. Yet under Thaksin, big business has directly seized political power, politics has become far more personalized than at any time since the Sarit era, and the prime minister has created an extraordinary power network that embraces the private sector, the media, the military, the police and a remarkable range of actors. To understand how Thaksin operates, it is important not to focus over-much on particular sectors of the political system or the economy. As Bresson argues, networks such as Thaksin's 'scramble boundaries' and lead to the deconstruction of conventional categories such as the public and the private.[89]

Accordingly, analyses need to grasp the extent to which his administration has successfully woven a wide variety of sectors into a complex web of connections controlled and manipulated by a single individual. Thaksin has done a remarkable job of displacing Prem's old power networks with new networks calculated to serve his own interests, becoming Thailand's new surrogate strongman in a remarkably short space of time. Thaksin's achievement is formidable, but it is also replete with dangers for the stability and integrity of both the economy and the political order.

NOTES

1   Luis Moreno Ocampo, 'Corruption and democracy: the Peruvian case of Montesinos', *ReVista*, Fall 2002. http://drclas.fas.harvard.edu/publications/revista/democracy/ocampo.html

2   Jean Cartier-Bresson, 'Corruption networks, transaction security and illegal social exchange', *Political Studies*, 45, 1997, pp. 463–476.

3   Bresson, 'Corruption networks', p. 469.

4   Alfred W. McCoy, 'An anarchy of families: the historiography of state and family in the Philippines', in Alfred W. McCoy (ed.) *An Anarchy of Families: State and Family in the Philippines*, Quezon City, Ateneo de Manila University Press, 1993.

5   Paul D. Hutchcroft, 'The political foundation of booty capitalism in the Philippines', Paper delivered at the annual meeting of the American Political Science Association, Chicago, September 1992, p. 6.

6   Hutchcroft explains that booty capitalism is a subdivision of rent capitalism, both of which are related to politics. The term is used to describe the theft of state resources by various interest groups and businesses outside the government. Paul D. Hutchcroft, *Booty Capitalism: The Politics of Banking in the Philippines*, Ithaca, NY and London, Cornell University Press, 1998, pp. 20–21.

7   Hutchcroft, *Booty Capitalism*, p. 21.

8   John Girling, 'Development and democracy in Southeast Asia', *The Pacific Review*, 1, 4, 1988, pp. 334–335.

9   Kevin Hewison, 'Of regimes, states and pluralities: Thai politics enters the 1990s', in Kevin Hewison, Richard Robison and Garry Rodan (eds) *Southeast Asia in the 1990s: Authoritarianism, Democracy and Capitalism*, Sydney, Allen & Unwin 1993, p. 181.

10 Anek Loathamatas, *Business Associations and the New Political Economy of Thailand: From Bureaucratic Polity to Liberal Corporatism*, Boulder CO, Westview Press, 1992; Thirayuth Boonmi, *Jut plian haeng yuk samai* [Turning Point of the Era], Bangkok, Vinyuchon Publishing, 1994.

11 Chai-Anan Samudavanija, *The Thai Young Turks*, Singapore, Institute of Southeast Asian Studies, 1982.

12 Prem had a close relationship with the owner of the Bangkok Bank and served as president of the New Imperial Hotel conglomerate, the owner of which was a beer baron who had been granted a concession from the government. In April 1996, Prem was appointed president of the advisory committee of Charoen Pokphand Group. Chai-Anan Samudavanija, 'Old soldiers never die, they are just bypassed: the military, bureaucracy and globalisation', in Kevin Hewison (ed.) *Political Change in Thailand: Democracy and Participation*, London, Routledge, 1997, p. 55.

13 While the first cabinets under the 1978 constitution included numerous military officers and technocrats, by October 1990 Chatichai's cabinet included 21 provincial businessmen.

14 Kevin Hewison, 'Thailand's capitalism: development through boom and bust', in Garry Rodan et al (eds), *The Political Economy of South-East Asia: Conflicts, Crises and Change*, Melbourne, Oxford University Press, p. 92.

15 See Rangsan Thanapornpan, 'The Political Economy of the 1997 Constitution', Research report submitted to the Thailand Research Fund, 2003.

16 *Constitution of the Kingdom of Thailand, BE 2540 (1997)*, Bangkok, Office of the Council of State, 1997, pp. 66–67, Article 185.

17 Duncan McCargo, 'Introduction: understanding political reform in Thailand', in Duncan McCargo (ed.), *Reforming Thai Politics*, Copenhagen, Nordic Institute of Asian Studies, 2002, pp. 1–18.

18 Pasuk Phongpaichit and Chris Baker, *Thailand's Boom!*, Chiang Mai, Silkworm, 1996, p. 29.

19 *The Nation*, 20 January 2004.

20 The Shinawatra family began by owning the Rama IX and Vibhavadi hospitals. More recently, Wichai Taengtong, a lawyer and close friend of the Shinawatra family, has become the major shareholder of the Paolo Hospital Group and the Phyathai Hospital Group. Some analysts

view him as a surrogate stakeholder for the Shinawatra family. See *Krungthep Thurakit*, 13 October 2003.

21 Air Asia Aviation (AAA) is worth 400 million baht and was founded with a 50 per cent Shin Corp holding. Air Asia (a subsidiary company of Malaysia's Air Asia Sdn Bhd) retains a 49 per cent stake, and Thai investors the remaining 1 per cent. *Siam Rath Weekend*, 21–27 November 2003, pp. 26–37.

22 These include M-Link, a mobile phone sales company formerly owned by Yaowapha before the shares were transferred to her sister Monthatip Kowitcharoenkul and registered on the Stock Exchange in March 2002. Another of Yaowapha's businesses was transferred to her daughters Chayapa and Cholnipa Wongsawat, who took up 38 per cent stakes in Traffic Corner Holdings, worth 420 million baht (*Prachachart Thurakit*, 15 March 2004, *Matichon Weekend*, 19 March 2004). This company previously produced folk music radio programmes and owned the *Bangkok Today* newspaper. More recently, it has been commissioned to produce hourly news bulletins for all army-run radio stations, and expanded its business co-producing several entertainment programmes with Channel 3, as well as publishing numerous entertainment magazines (*Krungthep Thurakit*, 13 March 2004; *Matichon Weekend*, 19 March 2004).

23 *Far Eastern Economic Review*, 17 June 1999.

24 *The Nation*, 25 October 1999.

25 For details of Thai Rak Thai's priority policies, see www.thairakthai.or.th. For the Policy of the Government delivered to the National Assembly, see Government Spokesman Affairs, the Office of the Prime Minister, at www.thaigov.go.th.

26 When General Chavalit Yongchaiyudh's New Aspiration Party assumed power in 1997, the party's support base and its emphasis on rural development, especially in the Northeast, was also interpreted as populist.

27 See People's Bank Project, Ministry of Finance www.mof.go.th.

28 Ammar Siamwalla, *Thaksinomics*, Bangkok, Thailand Development Research Institute, 2003.

29 *Bangkok Post*, 15 July 1998.

30 Thaksin Shinawatra's address to the Annual General Meeting of the Thai Rak Thai Party, Thammasat University, Rangsit, 26 March 2000.

31 Thaksin Shinawatra's address to the Annual General Meeting of the Thai Rak Thai Party, Thammasat University, Rangsit, 22 April 2001.

32 Its founder is Yaowapha Wongsawat, younger sister of Thaksin and wife of Somchai Wongsawat, Permanent Secretary of the Ministry of Justice. She is currently a deputy party leader and party list MP of the Thai Rak Thai Party. Monthatip Kowitcharoenkul, another of Thaksin's sisters, is a new shareholder who is also a major shareholder of the Thai Rungruang Company. See M-Link (Public Company) Annual Data Report, the Stock Exchange of Thailand.

33 Panthongthae Shinawatra was once a major shareholder. More recently his uncle Banpoj Damapong and his sister Phaethongtharn became the major shareholders.

34 *Krungthep Thurakit*, 25 June 2003.

35 Thai Knox Steel, owned by Prayudh Mahakijsiri, was the first company that the Krung Thai Bank assisted by waiving bad debts. In the case of TPI, the Thaksin government intervened over its debt restructuring problem to the extent that protests were received from its foreign creditors, including representations from the International Finance Corporation (IFC), a World Bank agency, and the US Ambassador to Thailand. Eventually the bankruptcy court determined that the Ministry of Finance should take over the administration of the company, a decision that caused great dissatisfaction among its foreign creditors. See 'Unreformed, unrefined, unrepentant', *The Economist*, 21 June 2003.

36 Suchai Viramethikul is a Sino-Thai (Techiew) businessman closely related to a large number of prominent figures, including a senior M. Thai Industry official who is the brother-in-law of Chatri Sophonpanich of Bangkok Bank, and Dr. Virachai Viramethikul, the youngest son-in-law of Dhanin Chiaravanond. He also has close associates among the clique of Field Marshall Prapas Charusathien. Suchai encouraged investors from Hong Kong to purchase a major piece of property in the Wireless Road area, which later became the site for All Seasons Place.

37 Srivikorn Group is a real estate concern registered on the Stock Exchange of Thailand. The group's large real estate development company is the All Seasons Property Company, a joint venture with a Hong Kong based company. It was set up in 1989 with registered capital of 1,000 million baht and is preparing to enter the Stock Exchange of Thailand. File of All Seasons Property Company, Department of Commercial Registration, Ministry of Commerce.

38 Dr Virachai Viramethikul is the youngest son-in-law of Dhanin Chiaravanond, head of the CP group. He sits on the board of M.Thai

Estate and is president of T. M. International Bank in Shanghai, a business owned by the Viramethikul family. He is also a founding member of Thai Rak Thai, and number 48 on the party list. See www.thairakthai.or.th.

39 Ukrist Pathmanand, 'Phuprakopkan asungharimmasap khanat yai 1960–1990: Khlum Srivikorn' [Giant real estate entrepreneur 1960–1990: Srivikorn Group], *Social Science Review*, 18, 1, 1996, pp. 40–65. A real estate development company owned by the Srivikorn family is the Golden Land Property Development Company, with registered funds of 625 million baht, a joint venture with a Hong Kong based real estate development company by the name of New World Development. See Golden Land Property Development Company file, Department of Commercial Registration, Ministry of Commerce.

40 From 1 November 2001, Grammy Entertainment announced it would be sending out its staff to collect fees for songs performed as part of karaoke entertainments. The fees would be levied according to the type of service rendered. See interview with Grammy chairman Apirak Kesayothin, *Phujatkan*, 8 November 2001.

41 The minister, Dr Adisai Bodaramik, is number 5 on the Thai Rak Thai party list. Dr Suvarn Valaisathien, Thaksin's legal expert specializing in revenue and accounting, is his deputy.

42 Shin initally purchased 40 per cent of iTV shares from Siam Commercial Bank. Later on, Shin purchased further shares and became the major stockholder, before registering the company on the Stock Exchange. See iTV (Public Company) documents, Stock Exchange of Thailand.

43 Prior to the 2001 election, some iTV reporters accused Thai Rak Thai's staff of interfering with the station's election coverage. The 23 reporters who made these allegations were fired after the takeover by Shin (*The Nation*, 27 September 2003). In September 2003, another batch of iTV reporters was fired (*The Nation*, 11 September 2003). Early in 2004, the *Bangkok Post* editor-in-chief, Veera Prateepchaikul, was transferred to another post. It was widely rumoured that his removal was due to the paper's refusal to toe the government line (*Matichon Weekend*, 20 February 2004). In addition *Siam Rath Weekend* editor-in-chief Rungruang Preechakul was pressured to resign because he had been too critical of the government. Pravit Rojanaphruk, 'Editor quits over censorship', *The Nation*, 25 February 2004.

44 iTV's raised equity capital resulted in an increase in the company's registered capital from 6,300 million baht to 7,800 million baht, with

this equity ratio: Shin Corp 43 per cent, Traiphop 10 per cent and Kantana 10 per cent. *Matichon,* 22 December 2003.

45 Nophakhun Limsamarnphun, 'The billion-baht TV-show host', *The Nation,* 21 December 2003.

46 The Offfice of the Election Commission of Thailand reported that in the year 2000, all telecommunications companies apart from Shin Satellite, Shin Corporation and AIS, and all Charoen Pokphand companies, gave financial support to the Democrat Party. However, in later years all telecommunications conglomerates and Charoen Pokphand Groups restricted their donations to Thai Rak Thai. Niphon Puapongsakorn, 'Kanphukkhat kap rabop thunniyom Thai' [Monopolies and Thai capitalism], in Chermsak Pinthong (ed.) *Ru than Thaksin* [Staying One Step Ahead of Thaksin], Bangkok, Kho Khit Duay Ton Books, pp. 115–116.

47 Thaksin once went to the headquarters of Bangkok Bank to campaign for votes and the president of the board, Chatri Sophonpanich,was seen welcoming Thaksin and declaring his support. This was widely publicized by the media afterwards.

48 Boonyasith was appointed an advisor to Finance Minister Somkid Jatusripitak. Dr Som, who is Somkid's brother, served as a financial advisor to Boonyasith's Sahapattanapibul Group prior to the economic crisis.

49 During October 2003, the Thaksin government initiated a policy banning alcoholic drinks advertisements on television and radio until a 10 pm watershed. Even though the policy was not targeted at Charoen's brewery business conglomerate, it still affected the income of the brewery business, which is the highest-earning component of the conglomerate. See *Matichon Weekend,* 31 October–6 November 2003.

50 Reported in the English newspapers *Daily Express* and *The Guardian,* quoted in *The Nation,* 17 March 2004, and *Krungthep Thurakit,* 16 March 2004.

51 Red Bull owner Chaleao Yoowittaya was close to Major General Sanan Kachornprasart and had been a longstanding backer of the Democrats. At one time he gave them monthly financial support of 100,000 baht through his son, Saravudh Yoowittaya, before cutting this to 50,000 baht in late 2003. *Matichon Weekend,* 31 October–6 November 2003.

52 The opposition to Thaksin was led by Palang Dharma's Squadron Leader Prasong Soonsiri, who had been embittered because Chamlong ousted him from the post of foreign minister to make way for Thaksin. Walaya, *Thaksin Shinawatra,* p. 166.

53 Former student leader Surathian Jakataranund is the manager of SC Estate, a property company owned by Thaksin's family. Surathian is one of Thaksin's political intimates, but always remains behind the scenes. In a 2004 book, he claims that Thaksin felt he had been unfairly criticized for having abandoned Palang Dharma and for having made easy profits from monopolistic businesses. He once told his close political associates while awaiting the verdict of the Constitutional Court in 2001 that he was ready to continue fighting, even if that meant enduring a five-year ban on holding political office. See Surathian Jakataranund, *Nathi thi prian prawatisat* [A Minute that Changed History], Bangkok, Matichon, 2004, pp. 31–32.

54 Thaksin's military network is described in detail in chapter 4.

55 In March 2004, Thaksin made another cabinet reshuffle in an attempt to solve the unrest in the South, transferring both interior minister Wan Muhammad Nor Matha and Defence Minister Gen Thammarak to Deputy Prime Minister posts, and removing them from oversight of the Southern security problem. Chaisit, however, remained untouched. *Phujatkan*, 12 March 2004.

56 See Sirivudh Hongpanich, 'The Police and Thai Politics,' unpublished MA thesis, Faculty of Political Science, Chulalongkorn University, 1976, and Yasuhiro Mizutani, 'The Development of the Modern Police Institution in Thailand: From the 1930s to the 1950s', unpublished paper, Graduate School of Asian and African Studies, Kyoto University, 2004, pp. 1–2.

57 For a discussion of defining terms such as 'godfather' in the Thai context, see Sombat Chantornvong, 'Local godfathers in Thai politics', in Ruth McVey (ed.), *Money and Power in Provincial Thailand*, Copenhagen, Nordic Institute of Asian Studies, 2000, pp. 54–58.

58 Moves to undermine godfathers and provincial politicians were highly effective in curtailing the influence of certain factions within Thai Rak Thai, especially that of Sanoh Thienthong's Wang Namyen faction. Once their financial bases were reduced, these local politicians were forced for rely heavily on funds from the party itself, which served to tighten internal party discipline.

59 *Thailand Country Report*, London, The Economist Intelligence Unit, February 2003, pp. 14–15.

60 *The Nation*, 21 May 2003.

61 The Assavayothin stable owns farms in Pakchong, Nakhon Ratchasima, Chiang Mai and Ayutthaya. Khao Sot Publishing's News Information Centre, *Khao Sot* newspaper.

62 Khao Sot Publishing's News Information Centre, *Khao Sot* newspaper.

63 List of advisors to the Prime Minister, compiled from information supplied by the Public Relations Department's news agency.

64 His brother, Colonel Worawat Indharathat, was promoted to become Chief-of-Staff to the Defence Minister (see Chart 4.2).

65 His father, Seri Isarangkura na Ayudhaya, was Buriram's mayor and nine term MP, *Siam Rath*, 31 March 2002.

66 He was the commanding officer of the Intelligence Unit in 1988, and was always strongly backed by the then Army chief Chavalit. *Matichon Weekend*, 5 February 1989; see also www.kalahome.com/history2.htm. He knew Thaksin during his time as intelligence chief and was later invited to become a founding member of Thai Rak Thai.

67 *The Nation*, 29 September 2003.

68 The figures for deaths in the war on drugs are contested. According to figures issued by the Interior Ministry, from 1 February to 8 August 2003, 48,362 drug dealers were arrested and a further 59 were extra-judicially killed. Overall, a total of 48,421 drug dealers and manufacturers were put out of action, while another 1,688 dealers and manufacturers were 'silently killed'. See Somkit Lerdpaithun, 'Rathaban Thaksin kap kan (mai) patibat tam jetana khong ratthathammanun' [The Thaksin government and its [not] acting in line with the intentions of the constitution], in Chermsak Pinthong (ed.) *Ru than Thaksin* [Staying One Step Ahead of Thaksin], Bangkok, Kho Khit Duay Ton Books, p. 155. Amnesty International, citing Thai police sources, stated in its 2004 annual report that 2,245 people had been killed in Thailand's war on drugs. See http://web.amnesty.org/report2004/tha-summary-eng. In his 2003 birthday speech, the King asked the national police chief to explain how some 2,500 deaths had occurred (*The Nation*, 6 December 2003).

69 Manop Thip-Osod, 'Hello, hello, hello. Who's in charge then?' *Bangkok Post*, 10 September 2003.

70 Manop, 'Hello, hello, hello'.

71 Born on 22 November 1948, he obtained an LLB from Thammasat University and an MSc in criminology from Eastern Kentucky University, USA, the same programme and university as Thaksin attended.

72 He served successively as a Crime Prevention and Suppression Police Inspector, Nang Leung police station (1980), Crime Suppression Division Commissioner (1995), Commissioner of the Police Immigration Office 2 (1995), Assistant Commissioner of the Central Investigation

Bureau (1996) and Deputy Commissioner of the Central Investigation Bureau (1998).

73 Approved by the House of Representatives on 26 February 2004. *Krungthep Thurakit*, 27 February 2004.

74 *The Nation*, 29 September 2003.

75 Wichit Chaitrong, 'State lottery: top prize upped to Bt 100 m', *The Nation*, 23 March 2003.

76 *The Nation*, 29 September 2003, and 23 March 2004.

77 *The Nation*, 29 September 2003

78 Wichit, 'State lottery'.

79 *Matichon*,13 March 2004.

80 *The Nation*, 20 January 2004.

81 Yaowares is the sister closest in age to Thaksin (she is three years younger), and used to have a food supplement business. She is currently President of the National Council of Women. Payap Shinawatra, Monthatip Kowitcharoenkul and Yaowapha Shinawatra run M-Link together. See share-holders list of M-Link in www.mlink.co.th/investor.asp. Only Thaksin's youngest sister, Yinglak Amornchat, works with a Shin Corp company, as a director of Advanced Info Service. (Athiwat Sappaitoon, *Kruap-khrua Shinawatra* [The Shinawatra Family], Bangkok, Wannasan Books, 2003)

82 Khunying Pojaman donated 240 million baht to Thai Rak Thai in 2000, 180 million baht in 2001 and 6.4 million baht in 2003 (as of March). Source: The Election Commission of Thailand.

83 Surathian, one of Thaksin's and Pojaman's intimates, explains that the couple are a perfect match: Thaksin is swift, audacious and usually pressures others to work, while Pojaman exudes delicacy and employs her gentle determination to persuade others to do her favours. Surathian, *A Minute*, pp. 21–25.

84 For details see William A. Callahan and Duncan McCargo, 'Vote-buying in Thailand's Northeast: the case of the July 1995 general election', *Asian Survey*, 36, 4, 1996, pp. 376–392; Surin Maisrikrod and Duncan McCargo, 'Electoral politics: commercialization and exclusion', in Kevin Hewison (ed.) *Political Change in Thailand: Democracy and Participation*, London, Routledge, 1997, pp. 132–148.

85 Daniel Arghiros, *Democracy, Development and Decentralization in Provincial Thailand*, Richmond, Curzon, 2001, p. 16.

86 M-Link was registered on the Stock Exchange in March 2003, after Suriya became the secretary general of Thai Rak Thai.

87 See http://www.ect.go.th.

88 Faction leader Sanoh Thienthing opposed the merger, arguing that it would lead to suspicions of benefit-sharing and centralization of power. He suggested that Thai Rak Thai would have no difficulty in winning re-election if the voters approved of the party's record (*Phujatkan*, 21 April 2004). Of course, Sanoh's own position was weakened every time Thaksin brought additional factions into Thai Rak Thai.

89 Bresson, 'Corruption networks', p. 470.

Conclusion: The Thaksinization of Thailand and Future of Thai Politics

THE MAIN CHAPTERS OF THIS BOOK have illustrated how Thaksin Shinawatra succeeded in assuming dominant positions in several different areas of activity. First, capitalizing on the economic crisis of 1997, he was able to transform his Shin Corp business empire. Shin Corp went from being just one of four large Thai telecom companies to a position of clear market leadership. Unlike its rivals, Shin Corp proved able to diversify successfully into other Asian markets, making it a truly regional business. Second, Thakin proved able to create new political party that quickly eclipsed all other Thai parties. Thai Rak Thai absorbed other factions and parties, and soon became the dominant force in the Thai political order. Third, Thaksin was not only concerned with parliamentary power: he also moved to create a strong group of allies within the military, based around members of his family and former classmates from the cadet school he had attended. By securing military support, he clearly hoped to take out an insurance policy that could protect him from the vagaries of electoral politics. Fourth, Thaksin put more effort than any previous Thai prime minister into establishing channels of communication with voters. His weekly radio address formed the core of these efforts, but they also extended to systematic attempts to ensure favourable coverage through a wide range of media outlets. Fifth, Thaksin sought to link his business, party, military, media and other connections together in an elaborate web of connections that amounted to a new kind of political economy network. By 2004, Thailand was well on the way to Thaksinization – there were few spheres in which the influence of the prime minister, his family businesses and his political party could not be felt.

A number of developments around the middle of 2004 were indicative of the trends facing Thaksin's government. His earlier talk of SMEs was displaced by the rhetoric of 'SML' – small, medium and large. Any size would do – this was a government with something for everyone, with no focus other than aggrandizing its own position. In an extraordinary scene in August, Thaksin unveiled a statue of Chatichai Choonavan in Korat, watched over by the prominent monk Luang Pho Khun. During the ceremony, the monk gave a *de facto* blessing to the union of the Chart Pattana and Thai Rak Thai parties, reflecting longstanding bargaining between Thaksin and Chart Pattana leader Suwat Liptapanlop. Despite his rhetoric about visionary leadership, Thaksin was bringing in ever more old-style politicians to swell the ranks of Thai Rak Thai.

The day before, the National Human Rights Commission had published a damning report on the government's record, especially concerning the bloody war on drugs. Thaksin's response had been to blast the Commission, denouncing it for airing Thailand's dirty linen in front of the international community, and asking why this independent agency was behaving like an opposition party. The irony was that he was meanwhile engaged in a process of neutralizing the opposition Democrats, whose MPs were defecting in a steady trickle to Thai Rak Thai. Indeed, a significant contingent had joined the newly revamped Mahachon Party, which had been taken over by former Democrat secretary-general Sanan Kachornprasart. It was an open secret that sources close to Thai Rak Thai were providing Mahachon with financial support. Thai Rak Thai was gradually con-solidating its hold over political power, despite the public perception – at least among the Bangkok middle classes – that the party was 'on the downslope' (*ka long*). A remarkable irony was that for all Thaksin's formidable power, Thai Rak Thai did not dare put forward its own candidate for the August 2004 gubernatorial election. For the party, non-participation appeared wiser than certain defeat. In the event, the youthful Democrat candidate Apirak Kosayodhin won a decisive victory in the August 2004 Bangkok governor election, trouncing a rival who had been tacitly backed by Thaksin.[1] The rising price of oil was another factor placing the government under pressure, since it was dictated by international developments beyond Thailand's control. Thaksin could control budgets, individuals and certain modes of information, but he did not have ultimate jurisdiction over the truth.

What of the future? In a perceptive review of the events of 2003, Thitinan Pongsudhirak proposed two alternative scenarios: Thailand Incorporated and Thaksin Incorporated.[2] We have adapted these to form the basis of four alternatives, including two further possibilities: Thailand Disincorporated, and Thaksin Disincorporated. Yet these four alternatives are not watertight and discrete; there are various areas of potential overlap between them.

THAILAND INCORPORATED

This scenario is essentially the Thaksin dream, the future as the prime minister and his advisors like to portray it. In this scenario, everybody wins from the policies of the Thai Rak Thai government. Thailand becomes something more resembling an East Asian developmental state, in which carefully selected sectors of the economy – SMEs, tourism, agribusiness, car manufacture – are nurtured by the government to achieve a high level of competitive advantage. At the same time, the main emphasis is on boosting domestic consumption rather than over-relying on export markets. Thailand's development has distinctly nationalist overtones, with an emphasis on self-reliance and a marked preference for Asian rather than Western inward investment. The closest analogy would be Mahathir's 1980s 'Look East' policy. This kind of economic model would be predicated on a one-party dominant political order, which would allow the state to resist capture or excessive bargaining by vested interests. Close collaboration between the private and public sectors would work in the overall interests of the country. Naturally, there were trade-offs: dissident voices in the media, academia and the social activist sector would be toned down and the opposition parties would be reduced to 'loyal' tokenism.

THAKSIN INCORPORATED

This scenario represents the view of many Thaksin critics. It sees the policies of the Thai Rak Thai administration as a cynical attempt by Thaksin to assume dominance in a wide range of sectors – the subject of much of this book. In this scenario, Thaksin uses his administration to advance the interests of his family businesses and those of his relatives and associates. Only a small group of people benefit substantially from his rule; the 'populist' policies turn out to be little more than an electoral ploy, though they do offer marginal benefits which continue to buy some support in rural areas. In this scenario, Thaksin is able gradually to entrench his power base to the point where he becomes both politically and economically unassailable. Thaksin or his proxies head the Thai government for three, four or even five parliamentary terms by casting themselves as the only serious political choice.

THAILAND DISINCORPORATED

In this scenario, Thaksin's government begins to collapse because of the economic contradictions it has created. Excessive personal debt will create an unsustainable burden, such that a relatively small downturn in the economy will have catastrophic results for many ordinary Thais. Thaksin will find that global economic realities, ranging from oil prices to investment decisions, have a profound impact on the performance of the Thai economy. The government will try to prop up its support base with very expensive populist programmes that have little impact. Eventually, a crisis of confidence in the Thai economy will occur, and the multi-faceted fallout will sweep Thaksin from power. Thailand will be left in a different situation from the post-1997 scenario, but nevertheless in a calamitous condition, generating new demands for political reforms that will prevent the very rich from seizing control of the government.

THAKSIN DISINCORPORATED

This scenario does not require an economic collapse to topple Thaksin, but envisages him facing a monumental political crisis. Prawase Wasi once remarked that political reform was needed because in the future, the present King would not be on the throne and institutional mechanisms were needed to ensure political stability.[3] Given that the post-1997 institutional mechanisms have already become essentially dysfunctional, Prawase's warning still rings very true. Thaksin's increasingly rapacious interventionism – such as recent attempts to politicize the process of monastic promotions – has the capacity to antagonize ultra-conservative forces in Thai society. At the same time, those sectors of the business community who believe they are losing out to economic interests aligned with Thaksin may eventually seek to oust him. He could ultimately face May 1992-style protests that would make his premiership completely untenable. Such protests could occur if Thaksin becomes profoundly alienated from the urban electorate, who are numerically small but of immense political significance. This is the most dangerous of the four scenarios, in that the possibility of serious violence would be extremely real.

Thaksin Shinawatra is not an ideas man. He is a brilliantly successful opportunist, who is gradually taking control of the state and economy of Thailand. His core project is the replacement of the old power group – a network based around the palace, Prem, elements of the Democrat Party, members of prominent establishment families and senior bureaucrats – with his own network of intimates and associates. This enterprise involves defusing political reform and neutralizing the competing players and institutions embodied in the 1997 constitution. In doing so, he has rescripted that constitution, ironically without changing a single word of it: the people's constitution has become the leader's constitution. The liberal project of the 1990s lies in tatters, replaced by the most authoritarian government Thailand has seen for more than 30 years. Thaksin is already the most powerful Thai prime minister for decades. Nevertheless, there are numerous realities that Thaksin and those around him cannot control. Sooner or later those realities may begin once again to reshape Thailand's profoundly malleable political order.

NOTES

1   'Apirak in landslide win', *The Nation*, 30 August 2004.

2   Thitinan Pongsudhirak, 'Thailand: democratic authoritarianism', *Southeast Asian Affairs 2003*, Singapore, Institute of Southeast Asian Studies, 2003, pp. 287–289.

3   For a discussion of Prawase's remarkable comments on political reform and the royal succession in a November 1995 speech, see Duncan McCargo, 'Populism and reformism in contemporary Thailand', *South East Asia Research*, 2000, 9, 1, pp. 94–98.

Bibliography

Ammar Siamwalla, *Thailand's Boom and Bust*, Bangkok, Thailand Development Research Institute, 1997.

——, 'Thaksinomics', *Matichon*, 25 December 2002.

——, *Thaksinomics*, Bangkok, Thailand Development Research Institute, 2003.

Amronrat Sa-ardsorn, 'Weekly radio address: PM grabs people's ear', *The Nation*, 5 November 2001.

Anek Laothamatas, *Business Associations and the New Political Economy of Thailand: From Bureaucratic Polity to Liberal Corporatism*, Boulder, CO, Westview Press, 1992.

——, 'A tale of two democracies: conflicting perceptions of elections and democracy in Thailand', in Robert H. Taylor (ed.), *The Politics of Elections in Southeast Asia*, New York, Cambridge University Press, 1996, pp. 201–223.

Arghiros, Daniel, *Democracy, Development and Decentralization in Provincial Thailand*, Richmond, Curzon, 2001.

Athiwat Sappaitoon, *Kruapkhrua Shinawatra* [The Shinawatra Family], Bangkok, Wannasan Books, 2003

Baker, Chris, 'Pluto-populism: Thaksin and popular politics', in Peter Warr (ed.), *Thailand beyond the crisis*, London, Routledge, forthcoming.

Bancha Tingsangwal 'Mai chai fah likit' [Not determined in heaven], *Nation Weekend,* 19 August 2002.

Bresson, Jean Cartier, 'Corruption networks, transaction security and illegal social exchange', *Political Studies*, 45, 1997, pp. 463–476.

Brown, Andrew and Kevin Hewison, *Labour and Politics in Thaksin's Thailand*, Southeast Asia Research Centre Working Papers Series No. 62, Hong Kong, Southeast Asia Research Centre, City University of Hong Kong, 2004.

Cairns, Robert and Deunden Nikomborirak, 'An assessment of Thailand's new telecommunications plan', *Telecommunication Policy*, 22, 2, 1998, pp. 145–155.

Callahan, William A., 'The ideology of vote-buying and the democratic deferral of political reform', paper presented at Trading Political Rights: The Comparative Politics of Vote Buying, International Conference, 26–28 August 2002, Massachusetts Institute of Technology, Cambridge MA (forthcoming, *Pacific Affairs*).

Callahan, William A. and Duncan McCargo, 'Vote-buying in Thailand's Northeast: the case of the July 1995 general election', *Asian Survey*, 36, 4, 1996, pp. 376–392.

Chai-Anan Samudavanija, *The Thai Young Turks*, Singapore, Institute of Southeast Asian Studies, 1982.

——, 'Educating Thai democracy', *Journal of Democracy*, 1, 1, 1990.

——, 'Old soldiers never die, they are just bypassed: the military, bureaucracy and globalisation', in Kevin Hewison (ed.), *Political Change in Thailand: Democracy and Participation*, London, Routledge, 1997, pp. 42–57.

Chang Noi, 'One handful of leaves: a lesson', *The Nation*, 7 July 2003.

——, 'Thaksinomics is all the rage', *The Nation*, 5 January 2004.

Chermsak Pinthong (ed.), *Ru Tan Thaksin* [Staying One Step Ahead of Thaksin], Bangkok, Kho Khit Duay Ton, 2004.

—— (ed.), *Ru Tan Thaksin 2* [Staying One Step Ahead of Thaksin 2], Bangkok, Kho Khit Duay Ton, 2004.

Cochrane, Joe, 'Business: the Bold Coast', *Newsweek*, 12 January 2004.

Connors, Michael Kelly, 'Political reform and the state in Thailand', *Journal of Contemporary Asia*, 29, 2, pp. 202–226.

——, 'Framing the "People's Constitution"', in Duncan McCargo (ed.), *Reforming Thai Politics*, Copenhagen, Nordic Institute of Asian Studies, 2002, pp. 37–55.

——, 'Thaksin's Thailand – to have and to hold: Thai politics in 2003–2004'. Paper presented at the Thailand Update Conference, Macquarie University, 20–21 April 2004 (http://www.latrobe.edu.au/socsci/staff/connor-thaksin.rtf).

Constitution of the Kingdom of Thailand, BE 2540 (1997), Bangkok, Office of the Council of State, 1997.

Crispin, Shawn W., 'Bigger party, bigger risk', *Far Eastern Economic Review*, 30 August 2001.

——, 'Ideas man', *Far Eastern Economic Review*, 1 May 2003.

——, 'Battle stations', *Far Eastern Economic Review,* 8 July 2004.

Crispin, Shawn W., and Rodney Tasker, 'Thai defence chiefs march out of step', *Far Eastern Economic Review,* 13 September 2001.

De Soto, Hernando, *The Mystery of Capital,* New York, Basic Books, 2002.

Dixon, Chris, 'Post-crisis restructuring in Thailand: Foreign ownership, corporate resistance and economic nationalism in Thailand', *Contemporary Southeast Asia,* 26, 1 pp. 45–72.

Enriquez, Juan, *As the Future Catches You,* New York, Crown Publishing, 2001.

Fairclough, Norman, *New Labour, New Language,* London, Routledge, 2000.

Ganesan, N., 'Thaksin and the politics of domestic and regional consolidation', *Contemporary Southeast Asia,* 26, 1, 2004, pp. 26–44.

Gearing, Julian, 'All out in China', *Asiaweek,* 29 August 1997.

Girling, John L.S., *Thailand: Society and Politics,* Ithaca, NY, Cornell University Press, 1982.

——, 'Development and democracy in Southeast Asia', *The Pacific Review,* 1, 4, 1988.

——, *Interpreting Development: Capitalism, Democracy and the Middle Class in Thailand,* Ithaca, NY, Cornell University Southeast Asia Program, 1996.

Glassman, Jim, 'Economic "nationalism" in a post-nationalist era: the political economy of economic policy in post-crisis Thailand', *Critical Asian Studies,* 36, 1, 2004, pp. 37–64.

Hewison, Kevin, 'Of regimes, states and pluralities: Thai politics enters the 1990s', in Kevin Hewison, Richard Robison and Garry Rodan (eds), *Southeast Asia in the 1990s: Authoritarianism, Democracy and Capitalism,* Sydney, Allen & Unwin 1993.

——, 'Thailand's capitalism: development through boom and bust', in Garry Rodan et al. (eds), *The Political Economy of South-East Asia: Conflicts, Crises and Change,* Melbourne, Oxford University Press, 2001, pp.71–103.

Hicken, Allen D., 'From Phitsanulok to parliament: multiple parties in pre-1997 Thailand', in Michael H. Nelson (ed.), *Thailand's New Politics: KPI 2001 Yearbook,* Bangkok, White Lotus, 2002, pp. 157–64.

——, 'The market for votes in Thailand', paper presented at Trading Political Rights: The Comparative Politics of Vote Buying, International Conference, 26–28 August 2002, Massachusetts Institute of Technology, Cambridge MA.

Hoffman, Jariya, 'Reformist general departs', unpublished World Bank paper, 2 September 2002.

Horn, Robert, 'This time he's serious', *Time*, 6 March 2000.

Huntington, Samuel, *The Third Wave: Democratisation in the Late Twentieth Century*, Norman, University of Oklahoma Press, 1991.

Hutchcroft, Paul D., 'The political foundation of booty capitalism in the Philippines', paper delivered at the annual meeting of the American Political Science Association, Chicago, September 1992.

——, *Booty Capitalism: The Politics of Banking in the Philippines*, Ithaca, NY and London, Cornell University Press, 1998.

Jeerawat Na Thalang, 'PM bangs the war drums of TRT's triumph', *The Nation*, 2 August 2003.

Kasian Tejapira, 'Post-crisis economic impasse and political recovery in Thailand: the resurgence of economic nationalism', *Critical Asian Studies*, 34, 3, 2002, pp. 323–356.

Khomdueon Jaudjaratfah (pseudonym) *Khum kom khawi kit: Thaksin Shinawatra* [Sharp Words, Sharp Thoughts: Thaksin Shinawatra], Bangkok, Siang Dao.

Klein, Joe, *The Natural*, London, Hodder and Stoughton, 2002.

Kramol Tongdhamachart, *Towards a Political Party Theory in Thai Perspective*, Singapore, Maruzen Asia, 1982.

Lees-Marshment, Jennifer, *Political Marketing*, Manchester, Manchester University Press, 2001.

Lovering, Daniel, 'Thai prime minister's display of powers ring alarm bells among democracy proponents', Associated Press, 7 February 2003.

Manop Thip-Osod, 'Hello, hello, hello. Who's in charge then?' *Bangkok Post*, 10 September 2003.

Marwaan Macan-Markar, 'Thailand – government promotes village handicrafts scheme', Inter-Press Service, 22 May 2002.

——, 'Premier's anti-poverty drive is under fire', Inter-Press Service, 20 November 2003.

McCargo, Duncan, *Chamlong Srimuang and the New Thai Politics*, London, Hurst, 1997.

——, 'Thailand's political parties: real, authentic and actual', in Kevin Hewison (ed.), *Political Change in Thailand: Democracy and Participation*, London, Routledge, 1997.

——, 'Alternative meanings of political reform in Thailand', *The Copenhagen Journal of Asian Studies*, 13, 1998, pp. 5–30.

——, *Politics and the Press in Thailand: Media Machinations*, London, London, London, Routledge, 2000 [Bangkok, Garuda Press, 2002].

——, 'Populism and reformism in contemporary Thailand', *South East Asia Research*, 9, 1, 2001, pp. 89–107.

——, 'Democracy under stress in Thaksin's Thailand', *Journal of Democracy*, 13, 4, 2002, pp. 112–126.

——, 'Introduction: understanding political reform in Thailand', in Duncan McCargo (ed.), *Reforming Thai Politics*, Copenhagen, Nordic Institute of Asian Studies, 2002, pp. 1–18.

—— (ed.), *Reforming Thai Politics*, Copenhagen, Nordic Institute of Asian Studies, 2002.

——, 'Security, development and political participation in Thailand: alternative currencies of legitimacy', *Contemporary Southeast Asia*, 24, 1, 2002.

——, 'Thailand's January 2001 general elections: vindicating reform?' in Duncan McCargo (ed.), *Reforming Thai Politics*, Copenhagen, Nordic Institute of Asian Studies, 2002, pp. 247–59.

——, 'Balancing the checks: Thailand's paralyzed politics post-1997, *Journal of East Asian Studies*, 3, 2003.

——, *Media and Politics in Pacific Asia*, London, Routledge, 2003.

——, *Contemporary Japan*, Basingstoke, Palgrave 2004.

McCoy, Alfred W., 'An anarchy of families: the historiography of state and family in the Philippines', in Alfred W. McCoy (ed.), *An Anarchy of Families: State and Family in the Philippines*, Quezon City, Ateneo de Manila University Press, 1993.

Mesher, Gene and Thawatchai Jitrapanun, 'Early telecom reform under Thaksin: Can Thailand meet its WTO commitment to liberalize by 2006?', paper presented at the ITS Biennial Conference, Seoul, 14–18 August 2002, http://www.its2002.or.kr/pdffiles/papers/199-Gene.pdf

——, 'Thailand's long road to telecom reform', *ASEAN Economic Bulletin*, 21, 1, 2004.

Meyer, Christopher and Stan Davies, *It's Alive: The Coming Convergence of Information, Biology and Business*, London, Thomson Learning, 2003.

Mizutani, Yasuhiro, 'The Development of the Modern Police Institution in Thailand: From the 1930s to the 1950s', unpublished paper, Graduate School of Asian and African Studies, Kyoto University, 2004.

Natthapong Thongpakdi, *General Agreement on Trade in Services (GATS) and The Thai Telecommunication Industry*, Bangkok, Thailand Development Research Institute, 1996.

Nelson, Michael H., 'Thailand's house elections of 6 January 2001: Thaksin's landslide victory and lucky escape', in Michael H. Nelson (ed.), *Thailand's New Politics: KPI Yearbook 2001*, Bangkok, White Lotus 2002, pp. 283–441.

——, 'Politicizing local governments in Thailand: direct election of executives', *KPI Newsletter*, December 2003.

——, *Central Authority and Local Democratisation in Thailand: A Case Study from Chachoengsao Province*, Bangkok, White Lotus, 1998.

Nichapha Siriwat, *Branding Thairakthai*, Bangkok, Higher Press, 2003.

Nophakhun Limsamaraphan, 'What's in a name?' *The Nation*, 24 August 2003.

Nualnoi Treerat and Noppanan Wannathepsakul, *Setthasat kanmuang torakhomanakhom:kanpraesanan sampratan torakhomanakhom: phon prayot khong krai?* [The political economy of telecommunications: who benefits from the allocation of telecommunications concessions?], Bangkok, Political Economy Centre, Faculty of Economics, Chulalongkorn University, 2001.

Ocampo, Luis Moreno, 'Corruption and democracy: the Peruvian case of Montesinos', *ReVista*, Fall 2002. http://drclas.fas.harvard.edu/publications/revista/democracy/ocampo.html

Ockey, James, 'Political parties, factions and corruption in Thailand', *Modern Asian Studies*, 28, 2, 1994, pp. 251–277.

——, 'Thailand: the struggle to redefine civil-military relations', in Mutiah Alagappa (ed.), *Coercion and Governance: The Declining Political Role of the Military in Asia*, Stanford, Stanford University Press, 2001, pp. 187–208.

——, 'Change and continuity in the Thai party system', *Asian Survey*, 43, 4, 2003, pp. 663–680.

Panebianco, Angelo, *Political Parties: Organisation and Power*, Cambridge, Cambridge University Press, 1988.

Pasuk Phongpaichit, 'Civilising the state, civil society and politics in Thailand', *Watershed*, 5, 2, November 1999–February 2000.

Pasuk Phongpaichit and Chris Baker, *Thailand's Crisis*, Chiang Mai, Silkworm [also Copenhagen, Nordic Institute of Asian Studies], 2000.

——, *Thailand: Economy and Politics*, Singapore, Oxford University Press, 2002.

——, *'The Only Good Populist is a Rich Populist, Thaksin Shinawatra and Thailand's Democracy'*, Southeast Asia Research Centre Working Papers

Series No. 36, Hong Kong, Southeast Asia Research Centre, City University of Hong Kong, 2002.

——, *Thaksin: The Business of Politics in Thailand*, Chiang Mai, Silkworm [also Copenhagen, NIAS Press], 2004.

Pasuk Phongpaichit and Sungsidh Piriyarangsan, *Corruption and Democracy in Thailand*, Bangkok, Political Economy Centre, Chulalongkorn University, 1994.

Pitch Phongsawat 'Senthang prachatippatai lae kanpraptua khong rat thai nai rabop Thaksin' [Democracy and the adaptation of the Thai state under the Thaksin system], *Fa diao kan*, 2, 1, 2004.

Piyawant Prayuksilp and Saowaluk Karnjanasali, 'Shinawatra mai mi khrai ngo' [There are no stupid Shinawatras], *Nation Weekend*, 28 October 2002.

Plai-Or Chananon, *Pho kha kap phattanakan rabop thunniyom nai phak nua pho so 2464–2532* [Traders and the development of the capitalist system in the North, 1921–1980], Bangkok, CUSRI, 1987.

Prangthip Daoreung, 'Obstacles await next premier', Inter Press Service, 8 January 2001

Prasit Saengrungruang, 'Telecom business in Cambodia', *Bangkok Post*, 23 June 2003.

Preeda Patthanathabut, *Guru kanmuang* [Political Mentor], Bangkok, Amarin, 2003.

'The Prime Minister's Speech in 2001 Fortune Global Forum', Government House Press Release 05/09, 9 May 2001.

Putnam, Robert D., *Bowling Alone: the Collapse and Revival of American Community*, London, Simon & Schuster, 2001.

Putzel, James, *The Politics of 'Participation': Civil Society, the State and Development Assistance*, Discussion Paper 1, Crisis States Programme, London School of Economics, January 2004. http://www.crisisstates.com/Publications/dp/dp01.htm

Rangsan Thanapornpan, 'The Political Economy of the 1997 Constitution,' Research report submitted to the Thailand Research Fund, 2003.

'Right royal headache', *Far Eastern Economic Review*, 10 January 2002.

Robertson, Philip, 'The rise of the rural network politician', *Asian Survey*, 36, 1996, pp. 924–941.

Royal Gazette, general announcement edition, Issue 120, Special Segment 134, 20.

Savitri Gadavanij, 'Discursive strategies for political survival: a critical discourse analysis of Thai no-confidence debates', unpublished PhD thesis, University of Leeds, 2003.

Scott, James C., 'Corruption in Thailand', in Clark D. Neher (ed.), *Modern Thai Politics: From Village to Nation*, Cambridge, MA, Schenkman, 1979, pp. 294–316.

Sirivudh Hongpanich, 'The Police and Thai Politics', unpublished MA thesis, Faculty of Political Science, Chulalongkorn University, 1976.

——, 'Local godfathers in Thai politics', in Ruth McVey (ed.), *Money and Power in Provincial Thailand*, Copenhagen, Copenhagen, Nordic Institute of Asian Studies, 2000.

——, *Luektang wikrit: panha lae tang ok* [Elections in Crisis: Problems and Solutions], Bangkok, Kopfai, 1993.

Somkit Lerdpaithun, 'Rathaban Thaksin kap kan (mai) patibat tam jetana khong ratthathammanun' [The Thaksin government and its [not] acting in line with the intentions of the constitution] in Chermsak Pinthong (ed.), *Ru than Thaksin* [Staying One Step Ahead of Thaksin], Bangkok, Kho Khit Duay Ton Books.

Sophon Ongkara, 'Why is Thaksin hiding from the House?' *The Nation*, 3 March 2002.

Sorakon Adulyanon, *Thaksin Shinawatra: asawin khloen luk thi sam* [Thaksin Shinawatra, Knight of the Third Wave], Bangkok, Matichon, 1993.

Suchit Bunbongkarn, 'The Thai military in the 1990s: a declining political force?', in Wolfgang S. Heinz, Werner Pfennig and V. T. King (eds), *The Military in Politics: Southeast Asian Experiences*, Hull, Centre for South-East Asian Studies, University of Hull, 1990.

——, *Thailand: State of the Nation*, Singapore, Institute of Southeast Asian Studies, 1996.

Sungsidh Phiryarangsan and Pasuk Phongpaichit, *Jitsamnuk lae udomkan khong khabuankan prachatipatai ruam samai* [Consciousness and ideology of the contemporary democracy movement], Bangkok, Political Economy Centre, Chulalongkorn University, 1996.

Suparat Chuayaurachon, 'Ten technocrats accept Thai cabinet posts: officials', Agence France Press, 24 October 1997.

Surathian Jakataranund, *Nathi thi prian prawatisat* [A Minute that Changed History] Bangkok, Matichon.

Surin Maisrikrod and Duncan McCargo, 'Electoral politics: commercialization and exclusion', in Kevin Hewison (ed.), *Political Change in Thailand: Democracy and Participation*, London, Routledge, 1997, pp. 132–148.

Suthichai Yoon, 'Umno-isation of Thai politics has begun', *The Nation*, 12 February 2002.

Tasker, Rodney, 'General agreement', *Far Eastern Economic Review*, 1 October 1998.

Tasker, Rodney and Shawn W. Crispin, 'How to save Thailand', *Far Eastern Economic Review*, 6 November 2000.

Tasker, Rodney and Prangthip Daorueng, 'New-Age Leader', *Far Eastern Economic Review*, 17 June 1999.

Tasker, Rodney and Gordon Fairclough, 'Star turn', *Far Eastern Economic Review*, 20 May 1993.

Thailand Country Report, February, London, The Economist Intelligence Unit, 2003.

Thanawat Suppaiboon, *26 nakthurakit chin phu mi prasoprakan* [26 Experienced Chinese Businessmen], Bangkok, Pimkum, 2003.

Thepchai Yong, 'Media reform is looking increasingly remote', *The Nation*, 23 December 2003.

Thirayuth Boonmi, *Jut plian haeng yuk samai* [Turning Point of the Era], Bangkok, Vinyuchon Publishing, 1994.

Thitinan Pongsudhirak, 'Thailand: democratic authoritarianism', *Southeast Asian Affairs 2003*, Singapore, Institute of Southeast Asian Studies, 2003.

Ubonrat Siriyuvasak, 'Anokhot sua seri nai rabop Thaksin' [Future of the free media under the Thaksin system], in Chermsak Pinthong (ed.), *Ru Tan Thaksin* [Staying One Step Ahead of Thaksin], Bangkok, Kho Khit Duay Ton, 2004, pp. 169–83.

Ukrist Pathmanand, 'Phuprakopkan asungharimmasap khanat yai 1960–1990: Khlum Srivikorn', [Giant real estate entrepreneur 1960–1990: Srivikorn Group], *Social Science Review*, 18, 1, 1996, pp. 40–65.

——, 'The Thaksin Shinawatra group: a study of the relationship between money and politics in Thailand', *Copenhagen Journal of Asian Studies*, 13, 1998, pp. 60–81.

——, 'From Shinawatra group of companies to the Thaksin Shinawatra government: the politics of money and power merge', paper presented at International Conference on Crony Capitalism, Quezon City, Philippines, 17–18 January 2002.

——, 'Prathet thai kap kanprianplaeng yai nai phumiphak: kan topsanong khong rat lae ongkon mai chai rat' [Thailand and major changes in the region: the response of state and non-state actors'], *ASEAN in the New Millennium Project*, Bangkok, Institute of Asian Studies, Chulalongkorn University, 2003.

——, *Wikrit sethakit kap kanpraptua khong thanakan panit nai prateth thai* [Economic crisis and the adaptation of commercial banks in Thailand], Bangkok, Institute of Asian Studies, Chulalongkorn University, 2003.

———, 'Sethasat kanmuang khong khlum thun torakomanakhom rang wikrit sethakit thai' [Political economy of telecom capital groups in post-crisis Thailand], unpublished research report for Professor Pasuk Phongpaichit's Thailand Research Fund project 'Khongsang lae phonrawat khong khlum thun rang wikrit sethakit thai' [The structure and dynamics of capital in post-crisis Thailand], presented at Faculty of Economics, Chulalongkorn University, 29 January 2004.

Vatikiotis, Michael and Rodney Tasker, 'Prickly premier', *Far Eastern Economic Review*, 11 April 2002.

Walaya (Phumtham Vetchayachai), *Thaksin Shinawatra: ta du dao thao tit din* [Thaksin Shinawatra: Eyes on the Stars, Feet on the Ground] Bangkok, Matichon, 1999.

Wassana Nanuam, 'General has a point to prove', *Bangkok Post*, 24 October 2002.

———, 'Defence gets B 3bn after King's request', *Bangkok Post*, 20 July 2003.

Wassana Nanuam and Subin Khuenkaew, 'Armies join forces to curb trafficking, assist villages', *Bangkok Post*, 17 December 2003.

Wassana Nanuam and Yuwadee Tunyasiri, 'Army to toe government line on Rangoon', *Bangkok Post*, 6 August 2002.

Wichit Chaitrong, 'State lottery: top prize upped to Bt 100 m', *The Nation*, 23 March 2003.

Wingfield, Tom, 'Democratization and economic crisis in Thailand', in Edmund Terence Gomez (ed.), *Political Business in East Asia*, London, Routledge, 2002, pp. 250–300.

Yingyord Machevisith, 'Still on very firm ground. Thailand's tycoons: winners and losers', *The Nation Mid-Year Review*, July 1998.

Index

The Nordic Institute of Asian Studies (NIAS) is funded by the governments of Denmark, Finland, Iceland, Norway and Sweden via the Nordic Council of Ministers, and works to encourage and support Asian studies in the Nordic countries. In so doing, NIAS has been publishing books since 1969, with close on two hundred titles produced in the last ten years.

 norden